Islam in China

ISLAM IN ...

Series Editor: Malise Ruthven

The *'Islam in ...'* series explores the different cultural political and social manifestations of Islam in different contexts. Each volume represents both an investigation into Muslim life in that country, and a contribution to our understanding of the wider questions surrounding the relationships between Islam and politics, global and local influences, and minorities and the state.

Books in the series:

Islam in America, Jonathan Curiel
Islam in Saudi Arabia, David Commins
Islam in China, James Frankel

James D. Frankel, Ph.D. is an Associate Professor in the Department of Cultural and Religious Studies and Director of the Centre for the Study of Islamic Culture at The Chinese University of Hong Kong

Islam in China

James D. Frankel

I.B.TAURIS
LONDON • NEW YORK • OXFORD • NEW DELHI • SYDNEY

I.B. TAURIS
Bloomsbury Publishing Plc
50 Bedford Square, London, WC1B 3DP, UK
1385 Broadway, New York, NY 10018, USA
29 Earlsfort Terrace, Dublin 2, Ireland

BLOOMSBURY, I.B. TAURIS and the I.B. Tauris logo are trademarks
of Bloomsbury Publishing Plc

First published in Great Britain 2021

Copyright © James D. Frankel, 2021

James D. Frankel has asserted his right under the Copyright, Designs and
Patents Act, 1988, to be identified as Author of this work.

For legal purposes the Acknowledgements on p. vi constitute an
extension of this copyright page.

Series design by BRILL
Cover image: [top] © chriss73 / iStock; [bottom] Details of towers at the Great Mosque,
Hohhot, Inner Mongolia, China. (© RGB Ventures / SuperStock / Alamy Stock Photo)

All rights reserved. No part of this publication may be reproduced or
transmitted in any form or by any means, electronic or mechanical,
including photocopying, recording, or any information storage or
retrieval system, without prior permission in writing from the publishers.

Bloomsbury Publishing Plc does not have any control over, or responsibility for,
any third-party websites referred to or in this book. All internet addresses given
in this book were correct at the time of going to press. The author and publisher
regret any inconvenience caused if addresses have changed or sites have
ceased to exist, but can accept no responsibility for any such changes.

A catalogue record for this book is available from the British Library.

A catalog record for this book is available from the Library of Congress.

ISBN: HB: 978-1-7845-3980-1
PB: 978-1-7845-3981-8
ePDF: 978-0-7556-3883-3
eBook: 978-0-7556-3884-0

Series: Islam in Series

Typeset by Integra Software Solutions Pvt. Ltd.

To find out more about our authors and books visit www.bloomsbury.com
and sign up for our newsletters.

Contents

Acknowledgements vi
Preface ix

Introduction 1

1. Muslim origins in China 7
2. Muslim transplantation in early China 27
3. Muslim entrenchment in medieval China 47
4. Muslim renaissance and resistance in late imperial China 65
5. Muslim nation-building in post-imperial China 85
6. Muslims and the state in Communist China 103
7. Muslim diversity in contemporary China 123
8. Chinese Muslims, global Islam and the global power of China 145

Notes 163
Bibliography 178
Index 184

Acknowledgements

This work could not have been completed without the help and support of many people, and it would not be complete without acknowledging them.

I cannot forget those teachers who have their imparted knowledge and helped train me as a scholar. Among them the late Peter J. Awn stands out as incomparable advisor, mentor and role model. I owe my eternal gratitude to him for his guidance in the study of Islam. I will miss him as I fondly remember his tutelage and friendship. I am indebted to all of my Chinese language teachers over the years, including Helen Lau, Roger Yeu, Paul Rouzer and Ghopal Sukhu, and the late Wu Pei-yi. I must also thank my Arabic instructors, the late Maan Madina and Jeannette Wakin. In the field of Chinese studies, I am fortunate to have been taught by Robert Hymes, Myron Cohen and the late Wm. Theodore deBary while an undergraduate student at Columbia, and to have learned much from Roger Ames, my former colleague at the University of Hawaii.

Foremost among the scholars deserving recognition for their seminal role in advancing my knowledge and understanding of Islam in China is Jonathan Lipman, who has long been an invaluable source of learning and counsel and on whom I have relied for his practical help and unconditional support. I am also indebted to other esteemed colleagues, too many to mention in fact. Zvi Ben-Dor Benite, Dru Gladney, Kristian Petersen, Leila Chérif-Chebbi, Maria Jaschok, Jackie Armijo, Wlodzimierz Cieciura, Matthew Erie, Oded Abt, Roberta Tontini, Chai Shaojin, Wang Yuting, Mao Yufeng, Wang Jianping, Ding Hong, Yang Guiping, Masumi Matsumoto and Sachiko Murata are among my greatest influences and resources, both scholarly and personal, in this field.

I thank my professional colleagues at the institutions where I have worked, beginning with those in the Department of Religion at the University of Hawaii at Mānoa, where my former, department chair, Helen Baroni, gave me my first opportunity to teach a course dedicated to Islam in China. In my current position at the Chinese University of Hong Kong (CUHK), I must acknowledge the Faculty of Arts for their generous publication subvention support and personally thank Dean Max Tang for his counsel regarding the navigation of sensitive topics in the text. I am also lucky to have the support of colleagues in the Department of Cultural and Religious Studies, beginning with erstwhile chair, Tam Wai Lun, whose wise advice on career development helped to make this work possible. I must also thank Lai Chi Tim, Lai Pan-chiu and John Lai for helping me get settled in the department. Huang Weishan, who came to the university around the same time as I did, has been an indispensable comrade-in-arms. I would also like to acknowledge senior colleagues from other departments, including David Faure, Gordon Matthews and Maria Tam, for their kind support.

With the permission of CUHK in 2018, I was able to accept an invitation from the Oxford Centre for Islamic Studies, where I began researching and writing this book in residence as an Abdul Aziz al-Mutawa Visiting Fellow. This would not have been possible without the great generosity and hospitality of the Centre's director, Farhan Nizami. While there, the Centre's staff and colleagues made me feel most welcome and supported in my work, especially head librarian Dinah Manisty, Deputy Registrar Richard Yousif Weyers, and fellows Talal al-Azem, Michael Feener and George Malagaris.

Of course, no book could exist without its publisher. I am deeply grateful to I.B. Tauris, first for noticing my contribution to this field and then inviting me to write this volume in their 'Islam in … ' series. I would like to thank editors Alex Wright for making first contact and Sophie Rudland for seeing the project through to completion.

In Hong Kong, my home since 2015, I am graced with a circle of friends who have all contributed in one way or another to this work. I would not be where I am without the generosity of Imam Nureddin Yang, the benefactor of my Centre for the Study of Islamic Culture, and I could never have accomplished what I have at the Centre without the able assistance of Aida Wong and Asiah Yang. I must also acknowledge the Centre's talented and diligent postdoctoral fellows and research assistants: Ibrahim Bao, Gong Fang, Ruslan Yusupov and Elliot Lee. Hung Tak Wai, my first graduate assistant at CUHK and now a postdoctoral fellow and splendid colleague, has been particularly supportive ever since I arrived. Members of the local Muslim community of Hong Kong should also be mentioned for enriching my life and work here, including

Hei Honglu, Imam Uthman Yang, Basmah Lok, Mufti Arshad and so many others.

Family comes in two forms – inherited and chosen. I have been blessed with both, and they are as vital to me as my own limbs. I consecrate this work in loving memory of my parents, Edith and Joel Frankel, who were with me in spirit throughout the process. My sister, Risa Frankel Swersey, has always been there for me and was amazingly helpful while I was writing this book. Her husband, Kevin Swersey, may never know how much he has provided me the motivation necessary for me to succeed. Mark Gandolfi has made my burdens a little lighter through his lessons in perseverance and resilience. I send heartfelt thanks to my lifelong friend Blake Morgan for his unwavering belief in me, to Bishakh Som for so many years of friendship, to my close confidant and collaborator Mohammed Sudairi, to Amira He for sharing life's ups and downs, and to Maica Panek Knisely for listening, responding and heavy lifting (and to our mutual friend Klaus Märtens for helping me gain a firm footing during this project).

I ask forgiveness of those whose names I may have omitted but I am grateful to them all the same. Finally, I give thanks and praise to the Truth and take full responsibility for my errors in this endeavour.

Preface

The majority of foreign terms in this book are in Chinese or Arabic, which are rendered as follows. The transliteration of Chinese follows the Pinyin system, which is the official standard in the People's Republic of China and of most contemporary publications. However, like the American Library Association and the Library of Congress (ALA-LC) guidelines for the romanization of Chinese, I do not include tone marks, as they are quite cumbersome to both typesetter and reader. I deviate from the ALA-LC guidelines by linking syllables together to reflect the original polysyllabic Chinese compounds (e.g. *qingzhen*).

As for the romanization of Arabic words, I follow the 1997 edition of the *ALA-LC Romanization Tables: Transliteration Schemes for Non-Roman Scripts.* For the few instances of non-Arabic words from other Islamic languages that use the Arabic script (e.g. Persian), I also follow the ALA-LC guidelines for Arabic. For place names and proper nouns that have familiar English spellings (e.g. Mecca), I do use these rather than the ALA-LC transliteration (i.e. Makka).

Introduction

Islamophobia is not unique to Western societies. One finds many non-Muslims in China with comparable prejudices. Ignorance about Islam among Chinese citizens is rather incredible when one considers that Muslims have been living in China for well over a thousand years – almost since the beginning of Islam itself. Moreover, there is hardly a city in China where one cannot find a Muslim community and at least one mosque. Beijing alone has almost 200,000 Muslim residents, and over seventy mosques. Being a minority, Chinese Muslims are required to know about Chinese culture and history, but this obligation is not reciprocal.

As uninformed as many Chinese citizens are about Muslims in their own country, outsiders are even more ignorant. When told that there are Muslims in China and they have been there for so long, members of the general public around the world are often caught utterly unaware. Those who consider themselves well-informed about world affairs may have read about the Turkic Uyghur Muslims who live in China's westernmost Xinjiang region. Stories about government oppression of the Uyghurs in the People's Republic have grown increasingly common in the Western press. But even such readers are often surprised to learn that most of China's Muslims are Chinese speakers and like Han Chinese by all appearances. Those who wish to understand the socio-political situation in China today, and the geopolitical relations between China and the Muslim world, would be well-advised to learn more about the overlap, historical and contemporary, of these two great civilizations.

China is the world's most populous country poised to become its largest economy. Muslims are the world's fastest growing religious population and by the start of the next century, Islam may well have more followers than any other religion on earth. Chinese economic growth and industry still depend on fossil fuels coming from Muslim-majority states in Asia and Africa, which also constitute burgeoning markets for Chinese goods, technology and labour. In exchange, China offers military hardware and infrastructure logistics to Muslim countries. Chinese-Islamic collaboration is frequently also fuelled by a common interest in resisting Western (especially American) hegemony. As both China and its Muslim clients and partners continue to grow in power and prominence, their cooperation and interdependence will exert an even greater influence on international affairs in the foreseeable future.

As geopolitical focus shifts more and more towards Asia, the informed observer of world events ought to take note of relations between China and global Islam. Historical encounters between these civilizations have been crucial in shaping world history over centuries of economic, political and cultural exchange along the geographical continuum that connects western and eastern Asia. The 'Silk Roads' conveyed bidirectional transaction of goods and ideas, and China's current aspirations as a world power, and its quest for material resources, foreign markets and greater influence in globally strategic regions, recall a glorious past. These aspirations motivate outreach overland to Muslim countries in Central Asia and beyond. China and the Muslim world also engaged historically in maritime trade encompassing Southeast Asia and the Indian Ocean region, where they are interacting again today. These land and sea passages are the foundation of China's flagship 'Belt and Road Initiative' (BRI) whereby it seeks to link itself to half the world in commercial, political and cultural transactions.

Overland and sea commerce between China and the Muslim world brought Western and Central Asian merchants and mercenaries to China beginning in the Tang dynasty (618–906), who became the forebears of the sizeable Muslim population that now lives in China. According to official government estimates, between twenty and twenty-five million Muslims currently live in China. These Muslims belong to various minority communities, which are products of Chinese-Islamic relations, past and present, and continue to play a significant role in contemporary exchanges between China and the Muslim world.

Over the intervening 1,200 years since Muslims first set foot in China, their communities have undergone tremendous change, touched by the forces of Chinese history, the development of Islamic traditions outside China and geopolitics. Today, China's Muslims are an internally diverse population, comprising ten out of fifty-five recognized minority nationalities or ethnic groups, living alongside other minorities and amongst the great Han Chinese majority. Apart from the somewhat loose bonds of Islamic affiliation, these Muslim minorities are in many ways as different from each other as they are from non-Muslim ethnicities in a multicultural, multi-ethnic state. They are separated geographically, ethnically, linguistically, economically, educationally, and along sectarian and kinship lines, among other factors. Further complicating the matter, each group has its own internal diversity, with sub-groups distinguished by the degree of their religiosity as opposed to secularity, and their 'Chineseness' – the extent of their assimilation into mainstream Chinese society and culture. Unfortunately, dualities have often led policy makers, casual observers, and even some scholars to oversimplify China's relationship to its own Muslim population as one of either conflict or concord. In fact, Chinese culture, society and polity have exerted both centripetal and centrifugal forces on Muslim communities. Some have resisted loss of autonomy and distinctiveness while others have embraced inclusion and synthesis; both responses have contributed to the evolution of distinctly Chinese interpretations and expressions of Islam.

One of the central, recurring themes of this book is the layered and sometimes paradoxical situation in which Chinese Muslims have found and still find themselves as they negotiate a complex identity as both insider and outsider to Chinese society and state. Some might refer to Muslims in China as diasporic, or hybrid. This book uses the term 'simultaneity' to express the condition of being Chinese and Muslim at the same time. But even if Chinese Muslims themselves see no disjuncture in their dual heritage, the culture that surrounds them is not always so accepting. From the majority Han perspective, there is a sense of the perpetual foreignness of their Muslim compatriots and this has created in Chinese Muslim individuals and communities a constant and ongoing impulse to assimilate into the mainstream in order to belong or, in some more extreme cases, to survive. Historically and in an emergent Chinese nationalist point of view, there exists a strong sense of unequivocal Chinese cultural superiority, the inferiority of non-Chinese cultures and a mistrust of foreigners. Even after so many centuries of habitation and naturalization in China, Muslims are still stigmatized by their perceived alien origins. The divide between the historical trend of Chinese secularization and the tenacity of Islamic traditionalism may exacerbate an apparent incongruity. Yet, despite, perceptions and realities of separateness Muslims are inextricably part of China. The '*yin and yang*' of compatibility and difference is an undercurrent throughout the narrative that follows.

Despite having its own local flavours and accents, Islam in China is recognizable as the same religious tradition practised by approximately 1.8 billion Muslims worldwide.[1] Chinese Muslims believe in the one God, Allah, and affirm that Muhammad is His prophet and messenger. They turn their faces in prayer towards the holy city of Mecca five times a day. They practise the other pillars of Islam – payment of alms, fasting in the month of Ramadan and, if they are able, pilgrimage to Mecca. Although they eat Chinese or other regional cuisines, they observe the same dietary laws stipulated by the Qur'ān and the teachings of the Prophet. They take pride in their traditions of cleanliness and moderation, and place great emphasis on the values of marriage and family found throughout the Muslim world. Yet, they do all of these things using Chinese or other ethnic languages, under the social norms and legal framework of China.

The diversity among Muslims in China presents both challenges and opportunities. On the one hand, some Muslims are less than amiable to Chinese rule. Particularly among the Uyghur minority, independence, or 'separatist', movements have received much negative attention. Uyghur cultural politics, including maintenance of a distinct Islamic identity, is sometimes seen as a threat to China's national unity. On the other hand, other Muslims, especially among the Hui (Sinophone Muslims, or Sino-Muslims), feel inextricably tied to China, and thus, despite their affiliation with Islam, normally co-exist peacefully with their Han compatriots (with whom they share genetic, cultural and linguistic commonalties), and generally comply with government dictates. The government's relatively harmonious relationship with Hui Muslims projects a positive image for international audiences, which is used to persuade foreign Muslim nations of China's congeniality towards Islam, in an effort to offset the negative impressions caused by the Uyghur issue.

The chapters that follow delve into the past, examine the present, and speculate on the future of Muslims in China, as well as China's relations with global Islam. The volume follows various approaches and methodologies – historical, literary, anthropological and sociological – to tell its story. Its basic framework is a chronological narrative that takes us from the earliest period up to the present day. This narrative stops along the way to look in detail at specific cultural developments and analyse particular aspects of historical context. So many historical narratives rely on distant overviews of nameless masses, occasionally focusing on the deeds of prominent figures. To counterbalance this tendency, each chapter herein begins with a vignette, sometimes historicized fiction, that transports the reader into an image-filled story within the story, intended to breathe life and provide a human dimension to the broader historical survey.

Chapter 1
Muslim origins in China

The Tang emperor awoke with a start, terrified by the unnatural vision he had just seen. In his dream, the rafters and pillars of his palace shook, under attack by a monstrous entity, a demonic force that foreboded imminent death and destruction. Suddenly there appeared a strange man – a foreigner – dressed in green, his head wrapped in a turban, possessing the power to quell the monster and avert the impending doom. 'Who was this stranger? What was the meaning of this terrible nightmare?' were the emperor's first questions to the ministers and advisors he summoned immediately upon awakening. One of the ministers replied, 'A great evil threatens to destroy your realm. Yet a great sage has arisen in the West who can repel demons with his prayers. Only he can save the empire. You must find this man and bring him to China at once to assure the peace and safety of all.' The emperor thereupon dispatched a delegation to travel westward in search of the holy man. They travelled well past the boundaries of the empire, beyond the remote Kunlun Mountains, deep into the heart of the barbarian regions. They finally arrived at a desert oasis, where the great sage ruled over his people in simplicity and security. The sage received the Chinese delegation. They told him of the emperor's dream and desperately requested that he accompany them back to their country. But he told them he could not because he was occupied with affairs in his own land. Instead he appointed a delegation of his own, from among his followers, to go to China and bring glad tidings of peace. The emperor received the foreign emissaries, and in appreciation for restoring peace and stability to his realm he permitted them to remain in the empire, giving them land and permission to marry Chinese brides and establish their progeny in China.

This is a rendering of a story retold countless times, in spoken and written form, over centuries, by Chinese Muslims to account for the origin of Islam in China. The core elements – a mission sent by the Prophet Muhammad and received by the emperor, with some part of the Arab delegation remaining in China to become progenitors of today's Chinese Muslim population – are consistent even as other details seem to vary with each retelling. A narrative of special significance to a particular group of people, transmitted from one generation to the next, expressing some of their most deeply held beliefs, values and communal aspirations, is an apt definition of a myth. Factual historicity has never been key to the value of myth. As the historian of religion Mircea Eliade explained, the value of myth is in its ability to connect people to the sacred, allowing them to be other than they are in their profane existence. The question of whether the events recounted in a mythic narrative *actually* happened is immaterial: 'To tell a myth is to proclaim what happened *ab origine*. Once told, that is, revealed, the myth becomes apodictic truth; it establishes a truth that is absolute.'[1] An origin myth, as the one above, transports people beyond their history and permits them to conceive of themselves as part of a sacred reality, giving their existence ultimate meaning. Historical (or pseudo-historical) details in the narrative serve as reference points to the known world, tethering the sacred to the profane. Thus, myth and history are two separate, though sometimes linked, enterprises.

Living in a culture and society where genealogy is highly valued, where families trace their lineage back centuries, or millennia, Muslims in China quite naturally wished to promote a sense of belonging as well as communal legitimacy. They have tried to comprehend and make comprehensible their diverse, hybrid heritage. They do this mythically. By claiming a legacy traced back to the Prophet Muhammad they construct a powerful narrative and a noble identity. Chinese Muslims, in their profane existence, are embedded in China, a minority living amidst an overwhelmingly and enormous non-Muslim population. In their religious aspiration and collective cultural memory, however, they are linked to the roots of Islam in Mecca and Medina, and, spiritually, to the Prophet and his companions. We shall return to the mythic tradition later, after examining the historiographic record.

The arrival of Islam in China must be understood more as an historical process than an event. There is no identifiable singular moment, no discrete point of origin. The myth contains fragments that may be correlated to historical facts, but these too are part of a much more complex history. Gathering data about the history of Islam's arrival in China is partly an exercise in speculation and deduction. Scholars have pieced it together from various sources, including early archival references, later written accounts, as well as archaeological evidence. These sources indicate that there were certainly multiple points of entry for Muslims into China and numerous significant historical events that paved the way for increased Islamic influence over time. The multipolar nature of this historical process helps to account for the tremendous diversity we see within Islam as it is practised and embodied by Muslims in China today.

The earliest Muslim engagements with imperial China took place within the larger context of a much older history of contacts between peoples from the eastern and western ends of the Eurasian landmass. Long before the advent of Islam on the Arabian Peninsula in the seventh century CE, China had developed into one of the world's most sophisticated civilizations. The Yellow River valley, like the Nile in Egypt, the Tigris and Euphrates in Mesopotamia, and the Indus in the Asian Subcontinent, provided the fertility and richness of natural resources necessary to support widespread agriculture, economic surplus, the growth of large sedentary population centres at the dawn of recorded history, and later ancient cities and states. The peoples of these respective alluvial cradles gave rise to parallel bases of human civilization, which, when they had expanded sufficiently to outgrow their nascent geographic confines, continued to spread their cultures and territorial claims. Confirming that the contemporary phenomenon of globalization is but the latest phase of a process that began in prehistory, archaeological and written evidence proves that the movement of peoples and exchange of cultural ideas and products has been ongoing for millennia.

By the second century BCE, China, united under the Han dynasty (206 BCE–221 CE), had already expanded its political, military and economic interests westwards into Central Asia. The Han imperial envoy Zhang Qian 張騫 (d. 133 BCE) went to secure China's commercial and diplomatic relations in the region. Chinese goods travelled by caravan along routes established by semi-nomadic Central Asian peoples, across the Eurasian steppes and deserts, until they eventually reached the markets of the ancient Mediterranean. Among the commodities that were most coveted by consumers in those markets was Chinese silk (sericulture at the time was a monopoly of China), and thus the network of East–West trade routes came to be known in history as the 'Silk Road', though it was never as single 'road' (we might rather call it the 'Silk Roads') and countless wares of many varieties passed along it. Nor was the traffic of commerce unidirectional: China imported horses from Central Asia as well as luxury goods, such as the Roman glass discovered in a Chinese tomb dating to the early first century BCE.

The overland trade routes that connected the Han and Roman Empires at the height of their power continued to function even after these empires declined and eventually fell. The stage was thus set historically for commercial and cultural exchange across Eurasia and North Africa long before the advent of Islam. So too were the peoples of pre-Islamic Arabia connected to the existing trade networks, both overland and by sea. Damascus was one of the principal trading posts at the western end of the Silk Roads and it was from there that goods were brought to and from Arabia. Caravans from Syria to Yemen travelled along a trade route that passed directly through the settlements of western Arabia, among them the cities of Yathrib (Medina) and Mecca and made the return trip carrying spices and fragrances – henna, musk, frankincense and ambergris. Thus, the pre-Islamic Arabs were aware of the existence of China, albeit from an indirect vantage point, as Arabia was peripheral to the main network of the Silk Roads. Arab traders in the marketplaces of the Byzantine Empire (285–1453) in the Levant and the Sasanian Empire (224–651) in Persia might have enjoyed exotic tales of China's vast riches, though few if any of them would have made the great overland journey themselves.

To the south, Persian and Arab seafaring traders had ventured from the Gulf[2] into the Arabian Sea and Indian Ocean at least two centuries before the Islamic period. Ships from Persian ports in the Gulf had almost certainly reached China by the late sixth or early seventh century CE.[3] It is therefore conceivable that some pre-Islamic Arabs could have sailed to China around the same time. Trade routes in the Indian Ocean and South China Sea were connected via the narrow Strait of Malacca, comprising what has come to be known as the Maritime Silk Road, another means of conveying goods, people, and cultures between China and the vast Indian Ocean region unto the eastern coast of Africa. The ships brought with them a range of luxury goods from the Middle East and Africa, including spices and incense, pearls from the Gulf, and elephant ivory; they returned from China with such precious commodities as silk and ceramics. On the eve of the birth of Islam in Arabia, maritime trade between the Gulf and the southern coast of China was routine, and

Arab and Persian merchants had long since landed in port cities like Guangzhou 廣州, later known to the West as Canton and called Khānfū in Arabic sources.[4]

While it is impossible to pinpoint the time or place of the first arrival of Islam in China, and leaving aside the mythic narrative for the moment, it is almost certain that the first Muslims to come to China were merchants. Since the first Muslims were Arabs, and the Arabs first came to China with the maritime trade, an initial arrival via the sea route is likely. Since it is unlikely that many Arabs would have made the journey along the entire overland Silk Roads, the Muslims who eventually entered China via the caravan routes were probably mostly not Arabs, but rather Persians and other Central Asians. And since these peoples were only converted to Islam after it had spread beyond Arabia, the arrival of Muslims in China overland was probably secondary. In the year 605 CE, the government of the Sui dynasty (589–618) undertook the massive infrastructure project of building a network of canals, including the Grand Canal, to link the port cities of southern China to the rivers and waterways of central inland China, unto the imperial capital of Chang'an 長安 (present-day Xi'an 西安). This network effectively joined the overland and maritime Silk Roads, further facilitating the movement of goods and people within the empire.

Trade was doubtless the principal means by which Islam was carried to China, as it was for countless other cultures and religions, including Buddhism, Hinduism, Zoroastrianism, Manichaeism, Judaism and Nestorian Christianity, all of which similarly travelled along the Silk Roads. Whether Arab, Persian or of some other nationality, the first Muslims in China followed trade routes, both overland and maritime, established well before Islam emerged in seventh century CE Arabia. When they arrived, they would have found in the capital, and in trading centres and port cities around the country, enclaves of other foreign merchants, with whom they transacted and interacted. These encounters occurred in the cosmopolitan milieu of Tang dynasty (618–907) society, notwithstanding later Chinese Muslim traditions placing the arrival of Islam during the preceding Sui period.

The Tang dynasty oversaw a westward expansion into Central Asia and a revitalization of Silk Road trade, accompanied by increased appetite for foreign goods and interest in 'exotic' cultures among Chinese elites. Tang territorial expansion was both cause and effect of economic growth through foreign trade, and was thus enthusiastically pursued by the regime, despite objections by the official bureaucracy whose Confucian ideology disdained commerce as a profession and viewed foreigners with contempt and suspicion. Foreign cultures were seen by the scholar-officials as inherently inferior and as a potentially corruptive to Chinese Confucian civilization. These misgivings were, however, assuaged by the Confucian literati's confidence in the self-evident superiority of Confucian civilization, which fuelled their expectation that foreigners would naturally be attracted to the virtues of Chinese culture, abandoning their own 'barbarian' ways to become acculturated, or 'civilized' (laihua 來化).

Since as far back as the Han dynasty Chinese foreign relations and trade were regulated by a strict code based on this Confucian ideological worldview that posited China as the centre of the civilized world. Foreigners from nations and states on the empire's periphery were regarded as culturally inferior. In order for them to enter into diplomatic relations with China, they were required to acknowledge Chinese superiority and suzerainty, symbolized by ritual prostration, or kowtowing (ketou 磕頭) before the emperor. They would also honour the Chinese emperor with 'tribute' gifts of precious commodities, gold and silver. In return, the emperor would present gifts of equal or even greater value (depending on the importance of the relationship and exchange with the visitor). This tributary system governed diplomatic relations between China and other countries until the Qing dynasty (1644–1911). It served a dual function of upholding the Confucian notion of China's cultural supremacy while also circumventing, on an official level, the sullied appearance of trade. Although commerce was an economic reality in China since ancient times, Confucian doctrine, which elevated agriculture and craft as means of livelihood, viewed merchants with disdain as the lowest class of society – parasitic middlemen who produced nothing and simply extracted wealth from the labour and creativity of others. The dual Confucian prejudice against 'barbarian' cultures and trade would cast a shadow over sojourning foreigners, including Muslims, presenting a recurring challenge to their acceptance throughout the history of the introduction and development of Islam in China.

Trade was the principal means of conveyance of Muslims and Islam to China, but it was not the only one. As attested throughout history, trade often travels hand-in-hand with diplomacy. This is clearly enough illustrated by the tributary system of foreign relations in imperial China. Indeed, the very impetus of the expedition led by the Han dynasty official Zhang Qian, traditionally credited with establishing Chinese contact with Central Asian nations, was to open diplomatic relations in order to facilitate trade. Subsequent dynasties continued this policy and expanded upon it. The Tang Empire extended its reach further westwards than its predecessors, leading to a flourishing of overland Eurasian commercial, political and cultural exchange. The dynasty's official annals document the many tribute-bearing political missions that the regime welcomed to the imperial court in Chang'an.[5] Neighbouring kingdoms and khaganates regularly sent emissaries to the Tang court, including Korea and Japan to the east; Kashmir, Nepal, Tibet, Kucha, Kashgar, and Khotan to the west; Vietnam and Champa to the south. To the north, the Tang maintained a special alliance with the vast and powerful Uyghur Khaganate,[6] who provided a buffer between China and various nomadic Turkic, proto-Mongol and Khitan tribes. Principalities further abroad in the then-known world also sent missions, among them the Byzantine Patriarch of Antioch and the Sasanian Empire of Persia, whose emissaries visited the court of Emperor Taizong 太宗 (r. 626–49).

The early Islamic polity in Arabia and the Tang Empire of China were jointly involved in the geopolitics of the seventh century CE. The international affairs of early medieval Eurasia, as in any era, were complicated by shifting power dynamics. At opposite ends of the Asian continent, the first Islamic state and the Tang dynasty came into existence nearly contemporaneously. The first Tang ruler, Li Yuan 李淵 (566–635), later known as Emperor Gaozu 高祖 (r. 618–26), established his new dynasty in 618 CE on the foundations of the preceding Sui dynasty, following ancient Chinese imperial traditions. The Prophet Muhammad, on the other hand, established a new theocratic state upon his arrival with his followers from Mecca to Yathrib (thereafter known as Medina[7]) in 622 CE.[8] While the nascent Islamic state of Medina was still struggling against the non-believers of Mecca for its survival, one of Gaozu's sons, Li Shimin 李世民 (598–649) killed two of his rival brothers, then deposed and succeeded his father, consolidating his rule as Emperor Taizong 太宗 (r. 626–49). His reign ushered in the 'golden age' of the Tang dynasty, marked by territorial expansion, a strong economy and the flowering of a cosmopolitan culture based on foreign influences.

It was during this golden age that the Tang Empire cultivated the tributary system of suzerainty and maintained its position as a geopolitical power to which other empires felt the need to send their diplomatic missions. Thus, in the mid-seventh century CE, the rival Byzantine and Sasanian Empires continued their respective diplomacy and trade relations with China, even as a major power shift was taking place in southwestern Asia. These two dynastic powers, who had vied with one another for control over the Middle East throughout late antiquity, now faced an utterly new, common threat that had erupted to their south, on the Arabian Peninsula – the advent and subsequent spread of Islam.

According to Islamic tradition, between 628 and 632 CE the Prophet Muhammad sent emissaries to the nations surrounding Arabia, bearing messages inviting their rulers to accept Islam and submit to his authority. These invitations were summarily dismissed by the leaders of Byzantium, Egypt, Persia and Yemen and ultimately Muslim armies conquered all four states. While the Prophet was largely successful in bringing most of the tribes in Arabia to Islam, it was not until after his death in 632 CE that the religion and its polity really began to spread beyond Arabia. In the subsequent decades, under the leadership of Muhammad's first four successors, or Caliphs,[9] the Muslim state made enormous advances in spreading Islam and expanding its territory. After prevailing in the Ridda Wars (Wars of Apostasy, 632–3) against rebellious tribes in Arabia, the Caliph Abu Bakr (r. 632–4) began military campaigns against Sasanian forces in Iraq and Byzantine forces in the Levant. Under the Caliph ʿUmar (r. 634–44), the Muslim army scored a decisive victory against the Byzantines in the Battle of Yarmuk in 636 CE, effectively completing the conquest of Syria. In the same year, the Muslims defeated a Sasanian army in the Battle of Qadisiyyah, resulting in the conquest of Iraq. In 642 CE, a Muslim victory in the Battle of Nahawand dealt the death blow that led to the flight of the Shah Yazdegerd III (r. 632–51) and the Islamic conquest of Sasanian Persia.

Both the Byzantine and Sasanian Empires had maintained tributary diplomacy with Tang China, which was disrupted by the Islamic conquests. After Yazdegerd III, who had fled to Central Asia, was assassinated in 651 CE, his son, Peroz III (b. 636 CE), sought refuge at the Tang court and even appealed to Emperor Gaozong 高宗 (r. 649–83) to help him re-establish Sasanian rule. With assistance from the Tang Empire, Peroz III made several failed attempts to regain power in Persia, but in the end settled in China where he was given protection and a noble rank before dying of an unknown illness. His descendants remained in China and were absorbed into the Tang nobility.

Also in 651 CE, during the reign of Gaozong, ʿUthmān (r. 644–56), the third Caliph, reportedly also sent an ambassadorial delegation to China.[10] The Tang dynasty had been allied with the Sasanian Empire and maintained friendly relations with the Byzantine Empire, both of which waged war with the Muslim state. Yet, in a move of *realpolitik* pragmatism, recognizing the strength of the emergent Islamic Caliphate, the Tang regime hedged their bets by welcoming this first and multiple subsequent diplomatic missions from the country the Imperial Annals referred to as *Dashi* 大食,[11] a catchall term for the early Arab Muslim polity. This account of the Caliphate's delegation to Chang'an has sometimes been conflated with alternative versions of the Chinese Muslim origin myth, which we will revisit later.

The Muslim defeat of the Sasanian dynasty, which had presided over a vast empire that extended deep into Central Asia, also opened the way for Islamic conquest and expansion into the region. Within a decade after winning the Battle of Nahawand, in which the Caliphate took control over the central Persian lands, Muslims extended their campaigns into the regions of Sistan and Khurasan. With the conquest of the Khurasani city of Merv[12] in 651 CE, Islamic rule had reached the Oxus river (known today as the Amu Darya).[13] Crossing the Oxus, the Muslim armies swept through the fertile plains of Transoxiana, between the Amu Darya and Syr Darya rivers, within the next half century. The conquest of Central Asia continued after the establishment of the Umayyad Caliphate (661–751),[14] which incorporated the ancient Silk Road centres of Bukhara and Samarkand into its territory. Despite initial military success in the region, the Muslim pacification of Transoxiana was hindered by insurgencies among local Persian and Turkic inhabitants, some of whom remained loyal, nominally at least, to the former Sasanian rulers, and who appealed for support from the Tang Empire. It was one such appeal that led to the failed attempt to prop up the deposed Sasanian prince Peroz III. The newly established Ummayyad Caliphate was still occupied with the so-called 'Second Fitna',[15] consolidating its control and putting down rebellious challenges to its rule in Iraq and Arabia, which diverted it from imposing its full might along the eastern frontier. For a time, the Muslim forces even retreated from Khurasan. After the Ummayyads regained their footing in the early eighth century CE, however, the campaign to assume firm control over Central Asia began in earnest.

Heading this military effort was the renowned Umayyad General Qutayba ibn Muslim (669–*c*. 716). By 713 CE, Qutayba had led his armies through Central Asia to the borders of the Tang Empire. The Islamic scholar and historian al-Ṭabarī (829–923) wrote that Qutayba even crossed into Tang territory near Kashgar, though this claim is disputed by later historians. Traditional accounts, however, support the idea that Qutayba did indeed have his sights set on invading China; a famous legend tells of the general's oath to seize Chinese land, which was only fulfilled when the local Tang government representative presented him with 'a load of soil to trample on, a bag of Chinese money to symbolize tribute, and four royal youths on whom he imprinted his seal'.[16] The dubious historicity of this story notwithstanding, assuming Qutayba was killed before entering China proper, his conquests in neighbouring lands showed the Chinese that the Muslim armies were a force with which to be reckoned. This perception surely prompted the combination of diplomacy and military readiness pursued by the Tang dynasty with regard to the Caliphate. In two subsequent military encounters, Tang armies repelled Umayyad incursions east of Transoxiana: (1) the defeat of King Alutar of Ferghana, an ally and client of the Umayyads, at the Battle of Namangan in 715 CE; (2) the Battle of Aksu in 717 CE, where the combined forces of Tang soldiers and tribal Turkic Qarluq warriors defeated the Umayyad army led by al-Yashkurī.

Domestic politics in both the Islamic Caliphate and Tang Empire had a consequential impact on the greater geopolitical situation of the seventh and eighth centuries CE. As for the former, even as the Umayyad regime presided over the greatest expansion of the Islamic state's wealth and territory, it also faced relentless challenges to its authority, as various constituencies questioned the dynasty's religious and political legitimacy. No sooner had the Caliphate withstood the 'Second Fitna' and turned its attention to securing the eastern frontier in Central Asia than new political and military challenges to Umayyad rule began to stir. Historians[17] have theorized that the rapid territorial expansion of Islamic political and religious hegemony and the spread of Arab cultural dominance led to the 'Third Fitna', the fall of the Umayyad and rise of the 'Abbasid Caliphate (750–1258). Many of the challenges to Umayyad rule came from factions made up of newly converted non-Arab Muslims[18] treated as inferiors by Arab elites, Muslim religious minorities such as the Shi'a, and non-Muslim populations in conquered lands. The further the Caliphate expanded geographically, the greater the influx of these disenfranchised groups, and the more resentment grew against the Arab ruling elite. Consequently, and paradoxically, the Umayyad Caliphate's increase in wealth and geopolitical clout also contributed to its internal strife.

The Third Fitna was effected by a coalition of disgruntled Umayyad subjects that included: elements of the Shi'a community who still harboured resentment against the Umayyad dynasty for their treatment of the descendants of ʿAlī; members of rival Arab tribal lineages; pious Muslims who considered the Umayyads religious reprobates; and non-Arab Muslims with their own ethno-political grievances. In the 740s, this coalition supported a movement against the Umayyad dynasty led by a branch of the Hashimite clan[19] descended from al-ʿAbbās ibn ʿAbd al-Muṭṭalib (c. 568–c. 653), a paternal uncle and companion of the Prophet Muhammad. Receiving their name from this notable patriarch, several successive leaders of the ʿAbbasid movement opposed the latter Umayyad Caliphs. Finally, in 750 CE, the ʿAbbasid leader Abū'l-ʿAbbās al-Saffāḥ (721–54) defeated the Umayyads and was declared caliph, becoming progenitor of the ʿAbbasid dynasty.

In the words of Clausewitz, 'War is a continuation of policy with other means.'[20] The Tang court had welcomed Muslim embassies from the mid-seventh century CE onwards. Yet while the Islamic conquest of Central Asia progressed in fits and starts, China also sought to fill the power vacuum left by the fall of Sasanian Persia and secure its control over the overland trade routes. Islamic eastward and Chinese westward expansion placed the two great powers on a collision course in the mid-eighth century CE.

One of al-Saffāḥ's first actions as Caliph was to send troops, under the leadership of Ziyād ibn Ṣaliḥ, to defend the Caliphate's eastern frontier in Central Asia. Although the Tang dynasty had maintained diplomatic relations with the various Caliphs purportedly since the rule of ʿUthmān, and had continued so during the Umayyad period, perhaps the perception of political instability within the Caliphate, and the temporary retreat of its forces in Khurasan, lured the Chinese Empire to build up its forces in Central Asia to explore the possibility of expanding beyond its existing western borders. In the late seventh and early eighth centuries, Tang forces fought against the Tibetan Empire[21] and Turkic armies[22] as China re-established control over its western frontier region. By 728 CE, the Tang dynasty had reclaimed the oasis city of Kashgar. General Ziyād, appointed governor of Samarkand, was tasked with firming up ʿAbbasid control over Islamic Central Asia and preventing a Tang military incursion into the region of the Syr Darya river,[23] a gateway to Transoxiana. Thus, in 751 CE, exactly a century after the first reported Muslim diplomatic mission to China, the two powers collided in a military confrontation.

Tang troops led by the general Gao Xianzhi 高仙芝 (d. 756 CE)[24] had been on a prolonged expedition to control the empire's western frontier region. While engaging Tibetan forces in the Pamir mountains, Gao's army were drawn into a regional conflict on the side of the ruler of Ferghana, against the ruler of Tashkent, who was allied with an anti-Tang tribal confederation. The Tang army subdued Tashkent in 750 CE, but the son of its ruler managed to escape to Samarkand, beseeching the ʿAbbasid government for help. Ziyād likely saw in this circumstance a serendipitous opportunity to engage the Tang Empire. He mobilized his army, along with other ʿAbbasid divisions for reinforcement, and advanced towards China.

In July of 751 CE, the ʿAbbasid and Tang armies met in the valley of the Talas river.[25] The ʿAbbasid side was joined by Tibetan troops, while some two-thirds of the Tang forces were made up of mercenaries from the Qarluq tribal union, nomadic people from western Central Asia. Reported estimates of troop numbers vary widely, reaching the hundreds of thousands on either side. The battle was evenly fought for several days. This stalemate, however, did not last long as events took a sudden turn. The Qarluq mercenaries proved to be unreliable allies when, in the midst of the battle, they switched sides. The Tang army, besieged on one side by ʿAbbasid forces and Qarluq warriors on the other, were soon overwhelmed. General Gao escaped with his life and a few thousand troops. The Muslim army briefly gave chase before being repelled by Tang reinforcements to the east. In the end, while the ʿAbbasids could claim a victory over the Tang dynasty in the Battle of Talas (or Artlakh), the territorial status quo was essentially maintained. The Caliphate could not press any advantage as a result of the victory, and never advanced further eastwards. Perhaps this is the reason why the Battle of Talas does not figure prominently in Islamic historiography of the time, though it is mentioned in later Muslim sources as well as in the official Chinese histories of the Tang dynasty.

The immediate effects on the ground of the ʿAbbasid victory and Tang defeat may not have been obvious. Legend has it that the Muslim army captured some Chinese artisans, including a few who knew how to make paper (a Chinese invention). These artisans were brought to Samarkand where they transmitted their craft, thereby spreading papermaking technology to the Islamic lands. More importantly, Islamic influence over Central Asia up to the Amu Syr region was permanently established in the aftermath of Talas. But Chinese involvement in the region did not cease as a result of the defeat. The dynamic, if volatile, politics of Central Asia often meant that allegiances could change swiftly against the persistent background of ongoing trans-Eurasian trade and cultural exchange. Arabic sources hardly mention the victory at Talas, which was treated more as a border skirmish than a great military triumph. Official Chinese sources, on the other hand, likely exaggerate the size of the Muslim armies (by some accounts, upwards of 200,000 troops), perhaps to account for the defeat. Because the battle caused no significant territorial loss or gain, and the borders remained virtually unchanged, its geopolitical consequences were minor. Muslims continued to consolidate their hold on western Central Asia, while the Chinese maintained considerable influence (political, economic and cultural) in its eastern extremes. Consequently, in spite of the tensions that precipitated the Battle of Talas, the ʿAbbasid Caliphate and Tang dynasty would have to find a way to co-exist at the crossroads of their empires in the aftermath of their conflict.

An unusual turn of events helped to improve relations between the Chinese and Muslims empires. Beginning in 755 CE, only four years after Talas, the Tang Empire experienced internal strife, an existential threat to its survival. In what turned out to be the final year of the reign of Emperor Xuanzong 玄宗 (r. 713–56), a Tang general of Central Asian descent by the name of An Lushan 安祿山 (703–57) fomented rebellion against the regime. Having seized Luoyang 洛陽, the Tang dynasty's eastern capital, An Lushan declared himself Emperor of the Great Yan 大燕 dynasty in early 756 CE. From Luoyang he set his sights on the western capital of Chang'an. When the rebel forces were poised to invade, Emperor Xuanzong and his court fled the capital to seek refuge in present-day Sichuan province. It was there that Xuanzong abdicated in favour of his son, who ascended as Emperor Suzong 肅宗 (r. 756–62) in Lingwu 靈武, present-day Ningxia province.

Emperor Suzong, determined to retake Chang'an, supplemented his regular (loyalist) army with troops from the Uyghur Khaganate, Tang allies based in present-day Mongolia. In addition, desperate for any assistance he could receive, the emperor requested military aid from the ʿAbbasid Caliph al-Manṣūr (r. 754–75) in Baghdad.[26] Al-Manṣūr sent approximately 4,000 mercenary troops to fight alongside the Tang loyalists and the Uyghurs. Intrigue and treachery within the Great Yan court made the rebel dynasty increasingly vulnerable. An Lushan was assassinated by his son and two of his ministers in 757 CE. Soon thereafter the Tang coalition ousted the rebels from Chang'an, and recaptured Luoyang not long afterwards. The ʿAbbasid Caliphate, having helped to defeat the rebels, resumed friendly relations with the Tang Empire. An 'Abbasid diplomatic mission was welcomed by the Tang court in Chang'an in 758 CE.[27] Emperor Suzong also rewarded the Arab-Muslim soldiers who had fought for him, inviting them to remain in China where they were given plots of land and permitted to marry Chinese brides.

The remnants of the rebellion, now under the command of An Lushan's deputy, Shi Shiming 史思明 (703–61), tried to regroup and regain lost territory, including the capital, but were finally defeated in 763 CE, during the reign of the Tang emperor Daizong 代宗 (r. 762–79). However, the damage done to the dynasty began the slow decline of the empire over the next one and half centuries. Tang China would never regain the power, prestige and prosperity it had enjoyed during its golden age before the rebellion. The empire lost its footing in Central Asia, as other smaller regional frontier states filled the power gap. Nevertheless, the post-rebellion era ushered in a period of good political relations and robust maritime trade between the Tang and 'Abbasid spheres.

Generally speaking, Chinese-Islamic contacts during the Tang/'Abbasid period fell into three main categories: military (first confrontation and then collaboration), diplomatic and commercial. Cultural exchange occurred in the context of these categories. Muslim mercenary soldiers had helped the Tang regime retain power, and 'Abbasid emissaries endeavoured to smooth political relationships, thereby paving the way for favourable trade policies and conditions. Over time, the role of Muslim merchants in introducing Islamic influence in China became primary and indispensable. It is noteworthy that, unlike the introduction of Buddhism previously or Christianity later, Islam came to China principally via trade rather than proselytizing missions. Most of these Muslim travellers who arrived in China were not missionaries but merchants seeking commercial opportunities:

> Their number was small and had little impact on the Chinese community … Islam as a religion was confined to the Arabs only because it was brought to China by the Arabs without any intention of gaining proselytes.[28]

Of course, as we have already seen, it was not only Arab Muslims who came to China. Both Arab and Persian merchants from the Gulf sailed to China's southeast coast, while Persians and other Central Asians, perhaps recent converts to Islam, travelled the overland Silk Roads to arrive via the northwest. Since there are no records of any overtly religious missions of Muslims arriving in Tang China, what then are we to make of Chinese Muslim traditional accounts, like the one cited at the top of this chapter, which claim that the Prophet Muhammad dispatched some of his companions to bring good tidings and the message of Islam to the emperor himself? Is there any factual, historical basis for these stories? In this connection, we find ourselves at the crossroads of myth and history.

In an oft-repeated ḥadīth (of questionable authenticity) the Prophet urges his disciples to travel far and wide to 'seek knowledge even though it be in China'.[29] This tradition demonstrates that people of Arabia had a perception of China, probably gained via second-hand accounts circulating around the ports of the Gulf and/or trade routes to the north of the peninsula. Whether the Prophet actually spoke these words, or any of his companions ever made it to China, is dubious. But it is clear that around the advent of the Islamic era, people in the Middle East considered China the frontier of the known world and a place of riches and advanced culture and learning. China represented the ends of the earth because it was the farthest point of the Arabs' eastward expeditions, and someplace beyond the imagination of most people at the time.

According to some Chinese Muslim traditions, relations between the Islamic world and China began even before the Tang dynasty. One account puts the arrival of Islam in the Sui dynasty.[30] The Qing period Chinese Muslim scholar, Liu Zhi 劉智 (c. 1660–c. 1730) cites this story in his authoritative Chinese language biography of the Prophet, *Tianfang zhisheng shilu* 天方至聖實錄 (True Record of the Ultimate Sage of Islam):

> In the sixth year of Kai Huang of the Sui dynasty, which was the first year of the Prophethood of Muhammad, there was seen in the sky a strange star. The Chinese Emperor Wen Ti commanded the Chief astronomer to divine its meaning, and he said that an extraordinary person had appeared in the West. The Emperor sent an envoy to investigate if this was really so, and after about a year he arrived in Mecca. He desired the Prophet to accompany him back to the East, but he declined. The Prophet sent Sa'd Wakkas and three others to go with the envoy to China. Muslims first entered China in the seventh year of Kai Huang of the Sui dynasty.[31]

Several facts in this account are implausible, or impossible. First, the Sui dynasty was established in 581 CE. The Kaihuang 開皇 era of the reign of Emperor Wendi 文帝 (581–604) lasted from 581 to 600, making the sixth year 587 CE. Muhammad did not even receive his first revelation and call to prophethood until 610 CE. It is furthermore unlikely that he sent any such delegation before the fall of the Sui in 618 CE because, at this time, he was only eight years into his prophetic mission. He and his early followers were still in Mecca, victims of persecution as a religious minority. The Prophet and his community would have been in no position to send out a religious/diplomatic mission until their position as a theocratic city-state in Medina was secured years later. Moreover, records of the Prophet's life were written in such meticulous detail that it is improbable that an early delegation of such importance as a mission to the Chinese court would have been omitted from the Hadith collections and biographies.[32] The tradition of Islam's arrival in China, as documented by Liu Zhi, is clearly in error, which is surprising given the author's erudition and his own scholarly attention to detail. But he is not entirely to blame for he was merely adopting facts found in earlier sources he considered authoritative.

Numerous other traditions correctly document the arrival of Islam in China in the Tang dynasty. Many of these traditions also contain apparent mistakes and disagree with Liu Zhi's narrative chronology. Yet they do overlap with Liu Zhi's version in one notable detail: many mention the figure of Saʿd ibn Abī Waqqāṣ (c. 595–c. 674 CE). Apart from Liu Zhi's spurious narrative, numerous oral and written Chinese Muslim accounts identify Saʿd and a few fellow travellers as the delegation sent by the Prophet at the behest of the Tang emperor (putatively Gaozu). In an attempt to harmonize divergent dates of the various accounts, some versions of the narrative claim that Saʿd actually made two return journeys via different routes (maritime and overland) before his final voyage, which took him to the southeast port city of Guangzhou. There, he is reputed to have built the first mosque in China, identified as the still-extant Huaisheng ('embracing the Prophet') Mosque 懷聖寺. He also purportedly died in Guangzhou and is buried in the 'Old Tomb of the Ancient Worthy' (Xianxian Gumu 先賢古墓).

According to Arab tradition, Saʿd, a cousin of Muhammad's mother, was one of the closest and best-known Companions (sing. ṣaḥaba, pl. aṣḥāb) of the Prophet. In fact, he was one of the ten whom the Prophet guaranteed would enter Paradise after death and a veteran of the early battles of Islamic history, including Badr (623 CE) and Uḥud (625 CE). He was a general in the campaigns against the Sasanian Empire at Qādisiyya

(636 CE) and Nahāvand (642 CE), and later served as governor of Kufa and Najd. He stayed on as governor of Kufa under ʿUthmān. He died at his home in al-ʿAqīqa (near Medina), was carried to the Prophet's Mosque in Medina for his funeral and buried in Jannat al-Baqī graveyard alongside other Companions of the Prophet.

The fact that he wasn't born until around 595 CE would have made him only eight years old when Liu Zhi claims the Prophet first sent him to China. Indeed, his presence in Arabia during the life of the Prophet and the reign of the first three caliphs make it all the more difficult to believe he ever travelled to China. Finally, his death and burial in Medina preclude the possibility that he occupies the tomb in Guangzhou.

The Chinese Muslim versions of the narrative may be found in inscriptions at mosques and other Chinese Muslim monuments scattered throughout China. Most of these inscriptions date to the Ming (1368–1644) or Qing dynasties. Different inscriptions have alternative Chinese transliterations of Saʿd's name and also contain chronological discrepancies. Another interesting account of the coming of Islam to China is found in a book entitled *Huihui yuanlai* 回回原來 (The Origin of the Muslims), attributed to Liu Zhi's father, Liu Sanjie 劉三杰. In the preface of an edition from 1712, he clearly states his motivation for writing was that future generations of Chinese Muslims should not forget their heritage and the history of how their religion came to China.[33] The introduction summarizes the history of Chinese Islam:

> Formerly, Islam was found only beyond the western border,
> Who would know that Muslims were to dwell in China forever?
> It came about through the Tang Emperor's dream in the night,
> That three thousand men were brought to establish it by Imperial Command
> the seal of the Board of Astronomy was given to one of them.
> They dwelt peaceably in China tranquilizing the State.
> All thanks to the grace of the Emperor of Tang that today the State is firmer than ever.[34]

The closing line of this passage reveals an obvious compromise of the Islamic precept 'all praise is due to Allah'. We also see reference to the alleged ominous dream of Emperor Taizong. One of the many versions of the narrative of Islam's origins in China, when describing the mission sent by the Prophet, refers to an emissary named 'Ko' (possibly a distortion of one of the many transliterations of Saʿd ibn abi Waqqāṣ' name, e.g. Wan Kousi). This version states that the emperor was so impressed by Ko that he appointed him chief astronomer. Furthermore, he requested that 3,000 Arab horsemen be sent to live in China. It is hard to say whether the Chinese Muslim oral tradition is influenced by Liu Sanjie's version of events, or vice versa. As Broomhall points out, however, the theme of an emperor's dream prompting a visit by a foreign religious missionary is a recognizable literary trope indicating a supernatural premonition, probably inspired by a similar story about the Han emperor Mingdi 漢明帝 (r. 58–75 CE). In the year 64 CE, Mingdi is also said to have dreamt of a foreign sage in a turban, which precipitated the introduction of Buddhism to China.[35]

The trope is repeated in a variation of the story of the Tang emperor's dream found in another Chinese Muslim work called *Xilai zongpu* 西來宗譜 (Genealogy of the Arrival from the West).[36] In this account, three delegates were sent by the Prophet to China, one of whom was called Wan Kousi, who was said to have made three trips from Arabia to China. After the third voyage he settled in Guangzhou where he is supposedly buried. Because of Sa'd's well-known grave in Medina, this tradition leads to yet another historical dead-end.

In spite of the evidence in Arab sources to the contrary, many Chinese Muslims still accept these popular accounts. Therefore, in a metanarrative that blends the components of several traditions, a prevalent belief among Chinese Muslims about their origins maintains that the Prophet Muhammad dispatched his kinsman Sa'd ibn Abī Waqqāṣ to convey the message of Islam in China at the request of the Chinese emperor who had the premonition that a great sage had arisen in the west. The Huaisheng Mosque and Tomb of the Ancient Worthy in Guangzhou are still upheld as proof of the legends and have become sites of veneration and religious tourism. These dubious Chinese Muslim traditions are mythic in nature, a clear attempt to glorify a forgotten past. Anachronisms and errors notwithstanding, a religious myth that links China's Muslims to the genetic and spiritual lineage of Muhammad serves to give them a sense of legitimacy; if the Prophet planted the seeds of Islam in Chinese soil then the existence of Muslims in China is divinely ordained. Thus, we can understand the importance of perpetuating this narrative even when its historicity is in doubt.

The metanarrative, however, echoes actual events recorded in Chinese historiography. The delegation sent by the Prophet could be a mistaken reference to the diplomatic mission dispatched by the Caliph 'Uthmān in 651. Such early diplomatic overtures may have failed in part because the Muslim envoys refused to prostrate before the emperor. This act of religious piety to Muslims, who would not bow or prostrate themselves to any save God, was considered a gesture of obeisance to the 'Son of Heaven' in China; not kneeling would have been seen as a grave insult. It is also possible that the supposed journeys ascribed to Saʻd ibn Abī Waqqāṣ may be conflations of historiographic and geographical references from travelogues and histories written by later Arab-Muslim travellers to China.

Of note, Arabic texts of the ninth century CE referring to early Muslims in China make no mention at all of Saʻd in connection with the Muslim diaspora community of Guangzhou. Abū Zayd al-Sīrāfī (878–916) compiled a book entitled *Silsilat al-Tawārikh* (The Chain of Histories) around 886 CE.[37] This compilation includes an anonymous manuscript called *Akhbār al-Ṣīn w'al-Hind* (Accounts of China and India),[38] completed in 851, which provides the oldest surviving first-hand accounts based on testimony by Arab-Muslim travellers to China. Abū Zayd mentions an Iraqi-based traveller known as Ibn ʻAbd'al-Wahhāb, or simply 'Ibn Wahhāb', who was descended from the Quraysh tribe of Mecca. He departed from Basra and travelled the sea route to China, arriving first in Khanfu (Guangzhou) before travelling overland to Chang'an. In the capital, he was purportedly granted an audience with Emperor Xuanzong 宣宗 (r. 846–59). According to the story, Xuanzong was so impressed by Ibn Wahhāb that he bestowed upon him lavish gifts. In his conversation with the sovereign, Ibn Wahhāb referred to the Prophet Muhammad as his cousin, which may simply have meant both were of the Quraysh tribe. Is it perhaps possible that Ibn Wahhāb was misidentified with Saʻd ibn Abī Waqqāṣ, who is colloquially referred to as Ibn Waqqāṣ (a difference of just two letters different from Wahhāb in Arabic), and who was actually Muhammad's cousin? Could this be the basis of the entire mythic metanarrative that is so important to Chinese Muslims until today? Because the origins of Islam in China are shrouded in the fog of history, myths about the convergence of Tang China and the early Caliphates are impossible to prove or disprove, but they provide a quasi-historical backdrop to the Muslim settlements that are supposedly the roots of China's present-day Chinese-speaking Hui Muslim population.

Chapter 2
Muslim transplantation in early China

Nestled in the heart of the Pearl River Delta, the metropolis of Tang Guangzhou is bustling. The dockyard, amidst an archipelago of riverine islands, is a vibrant venue for the exchange of Chinese and foreign goods. Dinghies dart to and fro from one bank to the other, carrying merchants and, occasionally, local government officials inspecting practices at the port. The population is multi-lingual, multi-ethnic, multi-cultural, multi-religious – Chinese and non-Chinese, indigenous and alien at once. Precious commodities from far-away places with names like Basra, Sīrāf, and Muscat await transfer to cosmopolitan marketplaces of the empire. Chinese workers mingle with Middle Eastern traders. The fragrance of frankincense fills the air, wafting alongside the sound of crates being hoisted onto palettes, punctuated by shouts and barked instructions. Two different files form, one moving in either direction. Cargo is loaded and unloaded on and off the ships docked by the embankment. Crates full of ceramics and textiles move up the planks and those containing spices, incense, and pearls move downward. Amidst the commotion, from a slight distance, a view of ant-like precision emerges from the up-close chaos and cacophony. A trader dressed in the turban and tunic of his native land beholds the grandeur of Guangzhou, not knowing that within a century this well-oiled mercantile machine will be plundered and burned.

Muslims came to reside in China overland and by sea: mostly merchants; a few mercenaries; and apparently hardly any missionaries. Nevertheless, Chinese Muslim tradition remembers the first Muslim pioneers as emissaries of the Prophet Muhammad, who arrived at the Tang court extending peace to the empire. Later, the traditional accounts maintain, brave Arab warriors from the 'Abbasid Caliphate fought alongside the Tang armies against An Lushan's rebels to help restore peace to the realm. Some of these soldiers supposedly settled in China, establishing a permanent Muslim presence. Later Chinese Muslims have viewed their forebears as having played an essential role in the pacification and preservation of the great Tang dynasty.

This imagined origin deviates from the historical record significantly. In reality, relations between the Muslims and the Chinese were erratic during the Tang period, especially at the official level. On the one hand, Chinese and Islamic sources agree that some sort of formal diplomacy occurred even as early as the administration of the third Caliph after the Prophet's death. On the other hand, Chinese and Islamic historiographies also agree that a century later, Tang and 'Abbasid armies squared off at the Battle of Talas. Even such military conflict, however, did not result in any official deportation of those Muslims residing in China at the time,[1] and Muslims continued to arrive in China, mainly for trade. After the Caliphate came to the aid of the Tang, sending reinforcement troops during one of the dynasty's darkest hours, friendly relations between the two great powers resumed. More importantly, a steady flow of commerce between Chinese and Muslims proved mutually beneficial. The Tang government in particular drew tremendous benefit from the revenues that streamed from international trade. So, in a way not documented in traditional narratives, Muslims did in fact play a major role in boosting the Tang economy, and therefore contributing to the power, wealth and stability of China at least for a time.

The Tang court, realizing the value of trade, frequently showed its beneficence to the Muslims and other foreign merchant communities. The Confucian scholar-officials, however, were often mistrustful of these outsiders, and worried about their negative influence on the court and society at large. We do not know exactly how the common people in Tang China felt about Muslims and other foreigners in this period; the historical record shows no indication of untoward discrimination or hostility. As time went on, however, despite the fact that Muslims had found favour with the regime under multiple emperors, popular sentiment began to turn against the alien minorities. In fact, the wealth and influence of many foreign merchants almost certainly engendered resentment among the Chinese populace. A lack of direct contact with the foreigners living in their midst only served to heighten the sense of suspicion and prejudice.

Muslim merchants in the Tang period were mostly sojourners rather than permanent residents. They came to China, frequently travelling back and forth to the Middle East on import and export voyages, stayed for months or years at a time, but most probably intended finally to return to their homelands. The Tang Empire maintained trade relations with many countries, motivating Muslims and other foreign merchants to settle and establish businesses in multiple locales within China. The choice of location was usually determined by their entry point and, by extension, whether they had arrived by land or by sea. Generally, those who entered China via the overland Inner Asian trade routes came to their eastern terminus at Chang'an; from there they may have ventured to other inland urban centres, like Kaifeng 開封 in Henan province. Those who came via the maritime routes arrived usually arrived in Guangzhou but may have also followed the coastline northward to other ports like Quanzhou 泉州 and Xiamen 廈門 (Amoy) in Fujian province, Yangzhou 揚州 in Jiangsu, or Hangzhou 杭州 in Zhejiang. Of course, because different regions within the empire were well-connected by rivers, canals and roads, we cannot presume such a sharp distinction between inland and coastal foreign merchant communities. And while foreigners may have dispersed to various nodes in the commercial network, the vast majority of them were clustered in two places: Chang'an and Guangzhou.

Camel caravans from the West travelling along the fabled Silk Roads, brought goods from the Middle East and Central Asia into northwest China – their destination the capital. These merchants were predominantly Persians, Turks or other Central Asians; very few Arabs made the long overland trek (most coming by sea instead). They spoke different and/or multiple languages and represented various faith communities: Zoroastrians, Jews, Nestorian Christians and Muslims. The silk for horse trade was a mainstay of Chinese commerce with Central Asia since the Han dynasty, but goods from even farther away, including the Byzantine Empire, also made their way via the Silk Roads.

Tang dynasty Chang'an was perhaps the grandest city in the world, and one of the most populous; at its peak, it was home to around one million. Besides the imperial household, government officials and diplomats, the capital was inhabited by artisans, craftsmen, service providers, manual labourers, entertainers and merchants. The city plan was arranged as a grid on a north–south and east–west axis, based on ancient Chinese cosmological and geomantic principles, with the palace positioned to the north of the central node. So, the capital, enclosed within a square defensive wall, was divided into quadrants, each quadrant further subdivided into wards made up of a number of blocks. Each class of society had its own quarter or district for work and residence. These different quarters were tightly regulated such that each had its own guarded boundaries, some closed in by walls and accessible only through gates. Residents were kept under a nightly curfew and had to produce identification documents to enter or exit the quarter; those found in the wrong neighbourhood at the wrong time were subject to penalty.

The city was served by two enormous official marketplaces (each a square kilometre in area): the West Market (Xishi 西市) and the East Market (Dongshi 東市), located in the northwest and northeast quadrants, respectively. Both markets were located strategically at the intersections of major imperial thoroughfares and canals. Under strict government control, the markets were only allowed to operate from midday to sundown. Each market had its own specializations: West Market was reserved for foreign goods; East Market carried all sorts of local Chinese commodities, including tea, silk and textiles, precious metals, gems (and jewellery), salt, grain, lumber, slaves and animals. The West Market was host to a bazaar selling goods and comestibles popular in Persia. The district around the market contained all manner of establishments and services. Numerous taverns and tea houses lined the narrow lanes, interspersed with food stalls and street vendors selling porridges, soups and pastries. A depository held visitors' valuables while they roamed the quarter. Imperial government offices in the central block oversaw the conduct of business, administering the west side of the city.

Since the West Market housed purveyors of foreign goods, residential quarters designated for foreigners were in its vicinity, in the Northwest, West Central and East Central districts.[2] Chang'an played host to numerous foreign merchants (as many as one-third of the overall population). Tang period ceramic sculptures often depict various non-Chinese phenotypes with almost caricature-like features – camel riders with fierce or grim expressions, moustaches and/or beards, aquiline noses and thick brows. These depictions distinguished between Sogdians, Turks etc., but foreigners of different backgrounds and nationalities were frequently lumped together for administrative purposes. As a rule, foreigners were kept separate from the local Chinese population; they were only to mingle during daytime business hours. Official policies to prevent co-mixing were instituted. Some of the segregation laws affecting foreigners seemed intent on discouraging assimilation into Chinese society. A specific imperial edict of 779 CE required Uyghurs in Chang'an to wear their own distinctive customary dress, forbade them from assuming Chinese cultural habits in order to pass for locals and prohibited their intermarriage with Chinese women. In the centuries before the Uyghurs embraced Islam, especially during the Tang period, they had close political, military and commercial ties with China, but even so the Tang regime kept them apart from ordinary Chinese subjects. Not all foreign communities were treated equally, however. As we have seen, Muslims at different points in the Tang period were expressly granted permission to marry Chinese women.

Whereas sinicization by foreigners was discouraged, the government did not interfere with their cultural customs, including religious practices. Iranian traders, for example, performed their ritual duties at houses of worship devoted to different religions found in Persia: Zoroastrianism, Manichaeism, Nestorianism and, later, Islam. In Tang Chinese cities, churches, fire temples, synagogues and mosques sometimes stood nearby Chinese religious sites: Buddhist monasteries, Daoist abbeys, family shrines and Confucian temples.

The religious tolerance and peaceful co-existence that had characterized Tang society, especially in Chang'an, at the height of the dynasty's rule came under attack as the regime went into decline in the late eighth and ninth centuries CE. An Lushan, whose rebellion almost brought the dynasty to its knees, was Central Asian, of mixed Sogdian-Turkic heritage. Although he had been one of the empire's most respected and honoured generals before the rebellion, demonstrating how non-Chinese loyalists could be trusted and rise to high status in the Tang hierarchy, the memory of his treachery left a lingering anti-foreign bias in its wake. This bias was probably the impetus for increasing suspicion of resident aliens, and the fear of foreign sedition may be the reason behind such policies as the discriminatory statute against Uyghurs mentioned above. The Uyghur Khaganate (744–840), a tribal confederation based in present-day Mongolia, had served as a powerful ally of the Tang Empire, helping to put down the An-Shi rebellion. The khaganate increased in wealth and power in the mid-eighth century CE, largely due to their conquest of other Inner Asian tribes (much to the delight of the Tang regime), and as a result of tribute received from China (in order to secure this important alliance, the Tang court actually *paid* tribute *to* the Uyghur rulers). This arrangement helped secure Tang China's northern and northwest frontiers for almost a century.

Internal political conflict and a war with the neighbouring Kyrgyz tribes precipitated the decline of the khaganate towards the mid-ninth century CE. These conditions also weakened the Tang–Uyghur alliance, as the Tang court probably saw diminishing returns on their investment. Having lost swaths of territory, in a last-ditch effort to retain power, the faltering khaganate launched an ill-conceived invasion of Shaanxi province in 841 CE. The Tang Empire defeated the Uyghurs after a drawn-out conflict that lasted two years. The khaganate was dealt a death blow in 843 CE, but at great cost to the Tang dynasty.

His court nearly bankrupted by the war against the Uyghurs, Emperor Wuzong 武宗 (r. 840–6) saw an economic remedy in exploiting the growing anti-foreign sentiment of the times. He pursued nativist policies that targeted communities and institutions deemed un-Chinese and harmful to social cohesion. In particular, his edict of 845 CE launched a persecution of Buddhism throughout the empire. The new policy addressed multiple problems at once. First, by closing Buddhist monasteries, the court could seize the vast wealth they had accumulated over centuries. Then, forcing monks and nuns to return to the laity, the empire's labour force and tax base were multiplied. These measures produced an immediate benefit to the economy. The justification for the policies was, however, couched in social and religious terms.

Buddhism had flourished under the early Tang dynasty, as many within the imperial family supported its institutions with lavish gifts and donations and many common people flocked to monasteries to take the vows and don the robes of monks and nuns. The Confucian elite, whose own ideological supremacy was threatened by the rise of Buddhism, argued on social grounds that the practice of monasticism was a direct violation of Confucian norms, as it called upon followers to leave their families, neglecting their filial duties and the natural desire to produce progeny. Moreover, in leaving the workforce they no longer served society by promoting economic productivity and paying taxes; rather, by relying on donations for their sustenance, Buddhist clergy parasitically drew resources from society, while the tax exemption of monasteries deprived the government of essential revenue. Emperor Wuzong repeated these criticisms in his edict. He also criticized

Buddhism as a foreign heresy that compromised the 'unification of our manners' and culture.³ The emperor himself had converted to Daoism, which he regarded as a 'pure' Chinese religion and much more positive towards leading an active life within society. The xenophobic aspect of the edict was reinforced in a passage heaping Zoroastrianism and Nestorian Christianity together with Buddhism as harmful, anti-Chinese doctrines; the institutions and followers of these foreign faiths were similarly attacked under the policy.

This clear appeal to nativism in Wuzong's religious policy did not implicate Islam in China, despite its foreign origins. Muslims continued to live under the protection of the state. Perhaps one of the most convincing explanations for Islam being spared under the policy is that Muslims in the capital and throughout the empire did not actively proselytize their faith. They had no formal clergy that sought special benefits from the state. Indeed, the Muslim community, with its focus on commercial interests, actually brought economic benefit to the regime. The Tang court's attitude towards Muslims ranged from benign neglect to outright solicitousness. The court treated Muslim dignitaries especially well, viewing them as 'foreign guests', or *fanke* 番客:

> Thousands of Muslims live as guests in the capital. They are attired in foreign clothes and treat the Chinese gently. In the town of Chang-an, the number of Muslim traders is about double that of the Muslim guests. The emperor of China has built special inns for them. Words cannot describe the grandeur of the Guest-House. It is a magnificent building and lends glory to the city and prestige to the bazaar. Muslim guests live in this building and the whole of its expenditure comes from the royal treasury.⁴

Muslim merchants also seem to have benefitted from the court's magnanimity. According to a later Chinese Muslim tradition, the Muslim community was permitted to build its first mosque on the site of the Great Mosque (Qingzhen Dasi 清真大寺) in present-day Xi'an 西安, near the old West Market.⁵ So, it is clear that there was no imperial bias against Islam as a religion. Yet Confucian officials retained a level of disdain for all merchants and especially those of foreign origin. Because the foreign traders maintained direct contact with their homelands, officials always suspected their loyalties resided abroad and they were capable at any time of espionage and sedition. Government officers scrupulously observed the merchants' business transactions. Because they were legally only permitted to do business in the two regulated marketplaces and were restricted to certain residential quarters, police could also monitor their movements. This extended to their traffic between cities within the empire, as checkpoints were established for the scrutiny of travel documents.

The Muslim community of Chang'an became the hub for Muslim dispersion and settlement throughout the Yellow River region of central China. Silk Road merchants who opted to stay in China to set up businesses and trading posts tended to settle in Chang'an and other large cities such as Kaifeng. When subsequent waves of Muslim traders came to China, they followed a pattern of 'chain migration', settling in places that already had an established Muslim mercantile community. Thus, the Muslim districts in the foreign quarters of various cities, which were originally centred around the business of a handful of merchants, continued to grow as more merchants arrived, took up residence and started families.

In addition to the waves of Muslim immigration via western China, many thousands of Arab and Persian traders arrived by sea in Southeast China during the Tang period. According to *Akhbār al-Ṣīn w'al-Hind*, during the Tang dynasty a peak population of 100,000 to 200,000 foreign merchants – including Muslims, Jews and Christians – resided in Guangzhou.[6] The volume of maritime trade between China and the Islamic world actually increased precipitously from the mid-eighth century CE onwards, largely due to the disruption of overland trade through Central Asia in the wake of the An-Shi rebellion. Guangzhou therefore became the most important entrepôt of the late Tang period, eclipsing Chang'an as a destination for foreign merchants.

Located on the Pearl River Delta, Guangzhou sits at the eastern end of the oldest and most trafficked long-distance maritime trade route of pre-modern times. Arab and Persian merchants from the Gulf traversed the Indian Ocean to reach the port cities along China's southeast coast long before the advent of Islam. Once the peoples of these regions became Muslims, they continued their trade while bringing their new faith and religious values with them. Guangzhou has attracted a diverse gathering of people for centuries, most of them traders plying their wares, seeking riches and co-existing in a melting pot amidst an imperative ancient Chinese civilization. Once it had become the main commercial port, Guangzhou was designed as a hub for transport of goods to China's interior. The port's function and status increased during the reign of Emperor Xuanzong when the Dayuling 大庾嶺 roadway was opened, linking Guangzhou to the inland transportation network. As a gateway to the Chinese heartland from the rest of the known world, the city was a living paradox where trade thrived against the backdrop of Confucian anti-mercantilism, built on an almost insatiable appetite for foreign goods in an environment tinged with suspicion of outsiders that verged on xenophobia.

The desire for foreign luxury goods was greatest at the top of the social hierarchy; the most voracious consumers were among the imperial household. Confucian officials criticized the court for its extravagant tastes and expenditures, to the point that Emperor Xuanzong once addressed such criticism with a grand gesture of burning his pearls and other gems outside the palace. It was not long, however, before he heard news of a cache of jewels in the South China Sea and ordered his aides to obtain it. The addiction to exotic treasures from abroad was hard to break. A dynasty that reached its apogee in the mid-eighth century then declined from opulence to decadence within a century and a half.

The foreign traders who catered to the appetites of the Tang elite were often the bane of Confucian ministers, whose general disdain for merchants and mistrust of foreigners coalesced into a particular form of antipathy. But even these officials could not ignore or deny the great value maritime trade in Guangzhou brought to the imperial coffers and national economy in the form of tax revenue. The government officials were determined to squeeze every taxable drop from the city's foreign merchants, even if they had to hold their noses while doing so. For their part, while they may not have enjoyed being forced to part with as much as one-third of their gross intake, the net profit must have been so great that the merchants continued for generations to submit their goods and themselves to a demanding process.

Immediately upon arrival in Guangzhou, foreign ships were inspected by local government agents. The foreign merchants were then invited into the customs house for a 'welcoming reception',[7] which included the imposition of three exacting trading conditions. First was the tax for setting down anchor, which Arabic sources indicate cost as much as 30 per cent of the cargo's value.[8] The government could impound the cargo for up to six months, until the fee was paid. The second condition was the government's prerogative to declare its monopoly over precious and rare imports. Third, a small portion of the goods were sent to the emperor as tribute. Once they had paid and agreed to these terms, the foreigners were free to trade locally. However, in addition to these established costs of doing business, officials would sometimes capriciously impose additional charges such as a 'transaction tax' of 2 per cent in 750 CE, which increased to 5 per cent in 783 CE. In 834 CE, Emperor Wenzong 文宗 (r. 827–39) acknowledged that foreign trade had been taxed unfairly by government officials for too long and decreed that only the three original conditions and charges would continue going forward.[9] This solicitous measure was surely a welcome relief to foreign traders, but did it have the reverse effect of engendering resentment among the common people, perhaps provoked by spurned officials? We know that Chinese popular protests and anti-foreign riots occurred as early as 760 CE, and that these, in turn inspired a wave of Muslim piracy in the South China Sea in the years that followed. This back and forth antagonism between foreigners and local Chinese residents of Guangzhou always lay under the surface of the usually still waters of the city. Official interference into the lives and livelihood of foreign merchants did not end at the port. As the number of *fanke* in Guangzhou increased, raising the stakes of tax revenues as well as concerns about security in the city, the government implemented policies intended to control the alien population and segregate it from indigenous Chinese residents as a measure of 'mutual protection'. As in Chang'an, it proved expedient to group and gather all foreign settlers in a single residential area, ostensibly to make commerce more convenient, but also so that they could more easily be watched and controlled. In Guangzhou, this policy gave rise to the system of organization known as *fanfang* 番坊, literally a 'place for foreigners'. Meng provides a justification for the institution in the interest of safeguarding the cultural integrity of foreign communities:

> The *fanfang* ... provided the *fanke* with a favorable and convenient settlement, serving as a social constraint to sustain their society. A foreign religion or minority is inevitably faced with the acculturative pressure of the majority. Thus, a separate community with its geographic demarcation was necessary to serve as self-protective cultural borders for perpetuating its own cultural landscape and keeping its own traditions alive.[10]

This argument might be more persuasive if the foreign residents of the *fanfang* were not grouped together regardless of their unique national, linguistic or religious backgrounds. Confining members of different communities together would not help maintain their distinctiveness but segregating them from the general Chinese population would certainly prevent unwanted mingling.

The argument has sometimes been advanced that the Great Wall was constructed not so much to prevent foreign invasion as to prevent Chinese subjects from leaving the empire. In recent times, the requirement for citizens of the PRC to obtain exit permits before traveling abroad seems similarly motivated. The restrictions of the *fanfang* may have had the same purpose of controlling and curbing the degree of contact between alien and indigenous populations. While we have already observed that Muslim settlers in Tang China showed no apparent interest in spreading Islam among the local population, government officials nevertheless wanted to keep intercommunal relations to the minimum required for conducting business. Social or intimate connections were not welcome. An anti-intermarriage policy implemented by the minister Lu Jun 卢钧 in 836 CE sought to 'obviate the conflicts between *fan* and Han',[11] by requiring segregation and forbidding intermarriage. The exact nature of these 'conflicts' is not mentioned in the record. In fact, intermarriage must have been occurring for generations before this law was enacted, and perhaps became a source of alarm because officials suspected disloyalty among the Chinese partners and their progeny in such unions. The imposition of such an explicitly discriminatory regulation at a time when ethnic and religious affairs in the Tang Empire were already showing signs of trouble begs the questions: Was the *fanfang* intended to protect *fanke* from Han acculturation or shield Han from corruptive foreign influence? Was it a foreign quarter or a quarantine?

We may never know with certainty the inner motivations of individual players in the historical socio-political drama. But we can be sure that the government and merchants shared a common interest in maintaining the flow of trade and commerce, even if it meant tolerating scrutiny and indignity on the part of foreign residents. The predominance of commercial interests in the maintenance of the *fanfang* is clearly represented in the fact that affairs in Guangzhou's foreign quarter were the jurisdiction of the Overseas Trade Commissioner, or Shiboshi 市舶使, whose main purpose was to secure profits from international trade.[12]

One of the non-commercial yet essential functions of the Shiboshi was to maintain law and order within the *fanfang*. A means to this end was granting certain lifestyle concessions to the residents of the quarter. The tight restrictions imposed from outside the enclave also allowed a degree of leeway in its internal workings albeit under government supervision. Different cultural and faith communities within the *fanfang* were permitted to live according to their respective customs and traditions, as long as these did not contradict local laws. In order to help structure life within the *fanfang* and provide mediation between the foreign communities and the imperial authorities, Tang officials eventually created the position of *fanzhang* 蕃长, an internal leader within the foreign quarter, selected under the aegis of the emperor and answerable to the government. Generally, the *fanzhang* was a religious leader chosen by the state to serve the religious needs of the community alongside his municipal duties. The residents of the quarter had a role in nominating candidates from among the respected and qualified members of their community, but the final selection was made by the Tang court with the emperor giving ultimate approval. Though serving a clerical role within his community, the *fanzhang* was simultaneously a Tang government official, who was expected to dress as a Chinese official and honour official customs, including those that overlapped with Chinese cultural norms.

In the case of Guangzhou's Muslim community, the *Akhbār al-Ṣīn w'al-Hind* reports that a judge (Ar. *qāḍī*) was appointed by the Tang regime to rule in intra-Muslim legal cases according to the principles of Sharī'a, the Sacred Law of Islam.[13] This *fanzhang* served the largely Arab (primarily Iraqi) community, as described in the text:

> Due to the residency of many Muslim merchants in Khanfu, there is a Muslim entrusted by the ruler of China with arbitration over the Muslims who travel to and stay in this region. This is according to the instruction of the King of China. On festival days, he leads the Muslims in prayer; he delivers a sermon and prays for the Sultan. Indeed, the Iraqi merchants do not contest the authority of his judgment, his implementation of law, as well as what is found in the Book of God, the most High and Almighty, and the regulation of Islam.[14]

The Muslims of the Guangzhou *fanfang* shared a commitment to the Qur'ān, the Law, and meeting their collective religious obligations. Praying for the well-being of the Caliph in Baghdad shows that the diaspora community in China still felt very much a part of the greater Islamic community, the Umma. This likely confirmed suspicions among Confucian scholar-officials that foreign residents' allegiance lay elsewhere and they therefore could not be fully trusted by the Tang regime. But the same segregation policy that upheld foreigners' ability to maintain their religious and cultural distinctiveness also prevented them from fostering strong relationships with the local Chinese population. Islam as the religion and culture of this community remained a distinctly foreign entity in China, kept apart from the mainstream of Chinese society by differences of language and custom, and by official policy. On the one hand, this policy helped Muslims to adhere to their traditions in the face of acculturative pressures because the

> *fanfang* was a unique organization based on politics, economy and religion. The government facilitated the persistence of ethnic boundaries of the *fanfang* by actively establishing or passively permitting self-governing. The *fanfang*, in turn, perpetuated the umma's distinctive cultural landscape and maintained the Islamic way of life more or less intact.[15]

On the other hand, the relative autonomy enjoyed by the Muslim community served as both cause and effect of their alienation from the larger society. The privileges that permitted Muslims to prosper within their small communities in the Tang period may also have contributed to their isolation and thence, in turn, may have turned Chinese popular opinion against them. Official segregation guaranteed the insularity of the enclave community, which provided some sense of religious and cultural integrity. At the same time, however, the *fanzhang*, with his mixed allegiance, gave the government a device for maintaining control over the alien population. His leadership combined two sources of legal authority: 'Shari'a and Chinese statutes comprised a complex code regulating individual and communal life at different levels. They worked together to form for good order and discipline within the umma.'[16]

The 'hands-on/hands-off' approach of the Tang government to the foreigners under their jurisdiction had the short-term effect of giving the authorities significant control over the lives of the merchants, while allowing them the semblance of autonomy. In the long term, however, this policy created barriers, physical and perceptional, between the *fanke* and the Chinese population, which would make the *fanfang* population extremely vulnerable. Discouraging the kind of intercommunal contact that would breed greater mutual understanding between *fan* and Han was a miscalculation with devastating long-term effects.

Throughout the long decline of the Tang dynasty after the An-Shi rebellion, the regime found it difficult to rein in the power of provincial military governors (*jiedushi* 節度使), who operated semi-autonomously in various parts of the empire. Common people, who suffered directly at the hands of the *jiedushi*, blamed the regime and rose up in rebellion several times in the mid-ninth century. A criminal element linked to the illegal salt trade mixed in with the aggrieved peasants and labourers, leading the rebellions to increase in violence and scope. Towards the end of the century, a salt smuggler from Shandong province, Huang Chao 黃巢 (835–84), who had already cut his teeth as part of an earlier rebellion, became leader of an anti-government movement that swept across China in the 870s to 880s.

Huang Chao's rebellion was mainly targeted at toppling the Tang dynasty; indeed, he captured the twin capitals of Luoyang and Chang'an in 880 CE and ascended the throne as the self-styled Emperor of Qi. Before that, he marched his rebel forces from the north to Guangzhou. His movement attacked anyone associated with the regime. Fuelled by the growing resentment of foreigners, especially wealthy merchants perceived as cosy with the imperial court, the rebels sacked Guangzhou. According to *Silsilat al-Tawārikh*, in 878–9 Huang Chao's army entered the *fanfang* and massacred its residents, mostly Persians and Arabs – Zoroastrians, Christians, Jews and Muslims, reportedly around 120,000 victims in total. Abū Zayd's account was published around 886 CE and served as a warning to Muslim traders considering travel to Guangzhu. Chinese sources corroborate the attack on the city, but not the massacre of the *fanke*. Huang Chao's attack was primarily intended to harm Tang economic interests, as evidenced by his systematic destruction of silk-producing mulberry trees in south China. By killing the merchants of Guangzhou, the rebels spilled the lifeblood of maritime trade. But the movement also tapped into a resentment of foreigners that had been on the rise for at least a century. The catastrophe dealt yet another debilitating blow to the dynasty. International trade continued, but the grandeur of Tang China's most prosperous port was destroyed, never to be fully restored. After the fall of the Tang dynasty in 906 CE, the former empire was broken up into smaller rival states known as the Five Dynasties and Ten Kingdoms. This period of fragmentation lasted about sixty years before central rule was restored by the Song dynasty in north China in 960 CE. It took longer for Song hegemony to proliferate as far south as

Guangzhou by 971 CE. The Song regime helped to restore the city's maritime commerce, but not before many of the foreign merchants had left, either to return home, or to find friendlier ports along China's southeast coast. In fact, as the Song period progressed, the volume of sea trade between China and the Islamic world increased.

As in the Tang period, Song Guangzhou upheld the organization of the *fanfang*. According to Zhu Yu 朱彧, port superintendent of Merchant Shipping in Guagzhou from 1094 to 1099, in his work the *Pingzhou ketan* 萍洲可談, the office of *fanzhang* continued to play an important role in the early 1100s. In addition to the responsibilities of administering the daily affairs of the *fanke*, the *fanzhang* was also tasked by the government with trying to attract foreign merchants back to China to trade and offer tribute.[17] According to Zhu Yu, the *fanzhang* of the Guangzhou foreign quarters succeeded in bringing the Arab shipping magnate Abū Ḥamīd (Pu Ximi 蒲希密), to Guangzhou in 933.[18]

Once the dynasty managed to persuade foreign merchants to return, maritime trade became the principal source of revenue for the regime, but it was no longer concentrated in one port. Other port cities such as Quanzhou eventually eclipsed Guangzhou in importance. The construction of the Masjid al-Aṣḥāb, or 'Companion's Mosque' (Shengyou Qingzhensi 聖友清真寺, also known as the Qingjing Mosque 清淨寺) in 1009 indicates the establishment of a significant Muslim community in Quanzhou.

The Song dynasty faced an ongoing threat from foreign invaders coming from the north, making overland trade between China and Muslim territories in the west nearly impossible as maritime trade experienced a marked increase.[19] Muslim merchants were content to deal with whichever authorities were in power and could protect their commercial interests. So, when the Song dynasty ruled in northern China (960–1127), Muslim traders and ambassadors dealt with them. And when the Khitan Tartars from Manchuria invaded China and established the Liao dynasty (916–1125), Muslims in that region dealt directly with them. Other Muslims in southern China, however, remained loyal to the Song who moved their capital from Kaifeng to Hangzhou 杭州 in 1127 and ruled as the Southern Song dynasty until their eventual defeat by Mongol invaders in 1276. For this reason, during the Song–Liao period embassies from Arabia, numbering around twenty, visited the courts of both dynasties.[20]

The first Song emperor, Taizu 太祖 (r. 960–76), sent a mission to the court of the 'Abbasid Caliph al-Mutī (r. 946–74) in the year 966.[21] The 'Abbasids, like the Song, were a dynasty constantly under siege by foreign invaders so the Caliph welcomed the offer of economic cooperation and mutual non-aggression from the Chinese Empire. The friendly relations between these two great powers was of vital importance to both of them because each knew that if the other was defeated by invaders, a power vacuum would be created in Central Asia which would, in turn, threaten its own security. Therefore, Muslims were again welcomed in China, as they had been in the Tang period, by the emperor himself. Ties between the 'Abbasid and Song courts led to an increase in the migration of Arab, Persian and Central Asian Muslims.

Among the Muslims who came to China during the Song period were prominent individuals who rose to lofty positions in the official hierarchy. In particular, two Arab Muslims not only made names for themselves during their own lifetimes but also left important legacies and established families in China, which wielded significant influence in subsequent generations. In 1070, during the reign of Emperor Shenzong 神宗 (r. 1067–85), a group of 5,300 Arabs from the Central Asian city of Bukhara came to the imperial court at Kaifeng.[22] Their leader was the Bukharan nobleman Sayyid Safar (known in Chinese as Su Feier 蘇菲爾), a descendent of the Prophet Muhammad in the twenty-sixth generation.

At the time of Safar's arrival, the Song was in conflict with the Liao dynasty whose power was rapidly increasing in the North. In an act of political expediency, Shenzong welcomed the Arabs and invited them to settle near the Song-Liao border, north of Kaifeng, in order to create a pro-Song buffer zone between the two warring states. The emperor appointed Safar Marquis of Yining 伊寧 (in present-day Xinjiang).[23] This influx was followed ten years later by another 10,000 Arab men and women, led by Safar's military aides, whom the emperor permitted to settle throughout the northern provinces of the empire. Safar's family and his affiliates became deeply entrenched in the north leading to even greater Muslim influence and autonomy there. These settlers were no longer confined to strictly regulated *fanfang* in a few cities and became more widely dispersed. The new Muslim communities not only maintained good relations with the Song dynasty but also cooperated with Tibetans, Tanguts and, most importantly, the Liao Khitans. Safar's descendants rose to prominence in the twelfth century and continued to grow in power and prestige all the way through the nineteenth century.

One of Safar's sons was made governor of Shandong province.²⁴ His grandson, Shams Shāh, was given the title of 'Protector of the Tartars' while his great grandson, Kamāl al-Dīn, was appointed commander-in-chief of the Chinese army under the tenth Song emperor, Gaozong 高宗 (r. 1127–62).²⁵ Kamāl al-Dīn's son, Maḥmūd, served as governor of Yunnan and later Shaanxi province. His sons and grandsons were also honoured with influential positions in the Song state.²⁶

Besides Safar and his family, another prominent Muslim lineage was first established during the Song period by an ʿAbbasid ambassador named Abū ʿAlī (known in Chinese by the surname Pu 蒲, derived from the transliteration of the second syllable of Abū). Abū ʿAlī arrived in 1031 during the reign of Renzong 仁宗 (r. 1022–63), the first Southern Song emperor.²⁷ He came to the court in Hangzhou bearing tributary gifts and was well-received by the emperor, who awarded him 50,000 ounces of silver.²⁸ Soon after his arrival, Abū ʿAlī retired from his official duties to pursue commercial ventures in Guangzhou. Demonstrating the extent to which the strictures of the old *fanke-fanfang* system had been loosened, in 1137 Abū ʿAlī married the daughter of a high-ranking Chinese general and established his family. He was later commissioned by the emperor to act as a go-between in the trade between Guangzhou and Baghdad whereupon he made several return voyages, accumulating vast wealth along the way. The mainstay of this trade was Chinese silk in exchange for Arab perfume and incense.

Abū ʿAlī 's progeny includes important figures who played significant roles in the shaping of Chinese Muslim history, and the history of China in general. According to family tradition Abū ʿAlī was a descendant of the Caliph Abū Bakr and the purported progenitor of a line of Chinese Muslims that included Yuan dynasty officials including Sayyid Ajal Sham al-Dīn ʿUmar (Sai Dianchi 賽典赤, 1211–79) and Ibn Yaʿqūb (Bai Yan 白儼).²⁹ Whether Abū ʿAlī was actually the ancestor of such prominent figures is unverified. Official Chinese sources, however, attest that the Pu family, first established in Guangzhou, produced individuals who distinguished themselves in service to both the Song and Yuan governments. One of them was the scholar-statesman Pu Zongmeng 蒲宗孟 (1032–98), a descendant of Abū ʿAlī in the fourth generation. He moved his family from the Pu stronghold in Guangzhou to Langzhou 閬州 in Sichuan province. He was a civil degree holder, a fact that would have required his fluency in classical Chinese and deep knowledge of Confucian philosophy. He served Emperor Shenzong as palace editor, grand secretary and vice minister.³⁰ Though an accomplished Confucian scholar, he was also a devout Muslim throughout his life. Another descendant of Abū ʿAlī, in the tenth generation, was Pu Shipin 蒲實品 who, after passing the official examination, was made a magistrate in Jinjiang 晉江, Quanzhou, whereupon he moved his family from Sichuan in 1230.³¹ Pu Shipin had three sons, all of whom became high-ranking officials in the Song hierarchy. The most renowned of them was the youngest, Pu Shougeng 蒲寿庚 (c. 1230–c. 97).

Pu Shougeng followed in the family business, becoming involved in shipping and trade between China and the Middle East by the age of thirty.³² Between 1245 and 1276, he held an authoritative imperial commission, named superintendent of Maritime Trade in Quanzhou,³³ essentially filling the same role as the former overseas trade commissioner, or Shiboshi. Within a few generations of Muslims having been under the strict supervision of the Shiboshi of Guangzhou or Quanzhou, a Muslim was now in charge of the maritime trade. Pu Shougeng was later named military pacification commissioner in Fujian and Dongjian, effectively placing him in command of the bulk of the naval force along China's southeast coast. Pu Shougeng's rank, combined with his family wealth, made him one of the most powerful men in southern China in his day.

Pu Shougeng presided over the most important port city, in charge of the vast wealth that passed through Quanzhou. He was thus an eminently important player in late Song politics and economics at the most critical time in the dynasty's turbulent history. Mongol invaders had already subdued most of China north of the Yangzi river. They now threatened to conquer the south. Pu Shougeng was responsible for defending Quanzhou and was a stalwart loyalist of the Song regime. As circumstances unfolded, however, he found himself in a position that would make him an active agent in the dynasty's downfall. Naturally, the Song government expected him to help them defend against the Mongol invasion of south China in 1276. But as the Mongols set their sights on coastal Fujian, they also wished to attract Pu Shougeng to their side. In an attempt to persuade him, the Mongol commanders sent another prominent sinicized Muslim already in their service, Bai Yan (a descendent of Safar and possibly a relative of Pu), to convince him. Pu's decision was made easier for him in 1277 when the forces of the penultimate Song ruler, the child emperor Duanzong 端宗 (r. 1276–8), were defeated by the Mongols at Fuzhou. The imperial family was now on the run and fled to Quanzhou. The commander of the Song army, General Zhang Shijie 張世傑, believing Pu had already shifted allegiances, and trying to secure an escape route for the emperor and his family, captured some of Pu's ships in Quanzhou. Pu took this as a betrayal and in retaliation aligned himself with the Mongols and deployed his resources to help defeat the Song forces. When the Mongol armies arrived, Pu Shougeng surrendered Quanzhou to the invaders. Though branded a traitor by Song loyalists, and remembered as such in later imperial sources, Pu's actions probably helped avoid much more bloodshed by facilitating a peaceful transition of power in the city.[34] The decisive battle ending Song rule took place in Guangdong province shortly thereafter.

Pu Shougeng was richly rewarded by the Mongols and for the remainder of his life served the newly established Yuan dynasty; he was appointed military commissioner for Fujian and Guangdong, a position inherited by a number of his descendants. Muslims from the Safar and Pu lineages played a vital part in the growth of Chinese civilization as well as the establishment of a firmly entrenched Muslim community in China, not only in the Song period but, also, into the Yuan.

Chapter 3
Muslim entrenchment in medieval China

'The martyr Amīr Sayyid Toghan Shāh bin Sayyid Ajal ʿUmar bin Sayyid Ajal Amiran bin Amīr Isfahsalar of the Bakr family was from Bukhara. May God enlighten their houses in the hereafter and make paradise their permanent abode.' Amīr Sayyid died in Quanzhou on the 9th day of Safar, 702 AH (3 October 1302).[1] On the eastern outskirts of the city, at the foot of Mount Qingyuan, lie the Lingshan hills with their massive complex of cemeteries. Among them, gravestones with Arabic inscriptions, like this one, stand out. This is the burial site of Quanzhou's medieval Muslim community.

Marco Polo extolled it, and Ibn Battuta too, as perhaps the greatest port in the world. After Guangzhou had faded from glory at the end of the Tang dynasty, Quanzhou eclipsed it as the bustling site of international trade. The Song dynasty had lured Muslims and other foreign traders back to China, and the city became the new jewel at the eastern end of the Maritime Silk Road. This prize was captured by the Mongols when they conquered the South, and it continued to flourish during their rule. Muslims came by sea and by land in droves during the Yuan period to serve the new regime. Many made Quanzhou their home. No longer were they a segregated minority, sojourners in a trade diaspora waiting to return home after their brief business venture. Burying their dead and building several large mosques in Quanzhou signalled a shift as Muslims became a permanent fixture in the city and throughout the empire. They were there to stay, generation upon generation, even resting in Chinese soil until the final resurrection on the Day of Judgement. And yet, history was destined to repeat. Imperial beneficence and popular opinion again turned against the foreigners, followed by persecution and a counter rebellion by Muslim soldiers in the city. By the end of Mongol rule, the mosques were ruined; the once familiar aroma of incense no longer permeated the air. The graves too were neglected, heralding the fall of one dynasty and the rise *of another. All the while, Muslim fortunes ascended and declined with the vicissitudes of the Mandate of Heaven.*

The story of Islam in China at the advent of the Song period had been a tale of two cities: Guangzhou and Quanzhou. Although it continued to function as a maritime port, the former never regained its preeminent status after the social, political and economic upheaval at the end of the Tang dynasty. It was effectively supplanted by the latter when the Song government consolidated its position in southeast China and revived the seafaring trade from abroad. At this time, the maritime network not only connected the Gulf and Arabian Sea, via the Indian Ocean, to China, but also incorporated routes traversing the South China Sea to Southeast Asia as far as the Indonesian archipelago, where Muslims had also established mercantile outposts. Quanzhou became a major hub and it was effectively administered by Muslim subjects of the Song Empire right up until the superintendent of Maritime Trade, Pu Shougeng, surrendered the city to the invading Mongol army. His actions allowed Quanzhou to escape being sacked and destroyed in the conquest and continue seamlessly operating as the leading port of the newly established Yuan dynasty under Khubilai Khan (r. 1260–94).

Pu Shougeng remained in his influential position under the Mongols and was given even greater honours and responsibilities. Moreover, the Yuan government, in need of capable and loyal administrators, allowed Pu's position to be transferred hereditarily to his son and descendants in successive generations. As a conquest regime of nomads, the Yuan dynasty had no experience in governing a large, sophisticated empire built upon an ancient sedentary civilization like China or Persia. Consequently, they employed talented administrators and functionaries from among the peoples they conquered. As conquerors, they were also conscious of the resentment of subjugated local people and sought to deflect it while they consolidated their rule. Throughout their vast domains, the Mongols implemented an ingenious strategy of population transfer, forcing the migration of thousands of people from one region to another. The diaspora was intended to bring foreigners to administrate on their behalf, firstly to limit the power of indigenous officials whose loyalty could not be trusted, and secondly to create a buffer between themselves and the conquered population. In China, this meant the infusion of a new elite drawn from West and Central Asia to be inserted into the socio-political hierarchy; Chinese administrators were in turn transferred to places like

Bukhara or Samarkand. Thus, the period of Mongol rule witnessed the greatest ever influx of Muslims into China.

Under the Song dynasty, Quanzhou and other cities like Kaifeng and Hangzhou had seen a rise in the number of Muslims, mostly of Arab and Persian descent, along with other foreign merchants. Quanzhou became a particular magnet for Muslims. As the Muslim population grew, local institutions catering to their religious and cultural traditions were established. In 1009, the grand mosque of the city, known the Masjid al-Aṣḥāb (Shengyousi 聖友寺), was built; it was one of seven mosques serving the Muslims of Quanzhou. The mosque's name, meaning 'Companions' Mosque', reflects the Chinese Muslim tradition, linking back to the Saʻd ibn Abī Waqqāṣ narrative, that of the four emissaries sent to China by the Prophet Muhammad, two of them went to Quanzhou where they died and are supposedly buried in nearby Qingyuan. The mosque is dedicated to their memory and built in a medieval Middle Eastern architectural style. Today the mosque is in ruins, the original wooden structure long since destroyed. But its skeleton of stone pillars and the granite arched portal still stand as reminders of its grandeur. Stone steles with Arabic and Chinese inscriptions from the twelfth to fourteenth centuries are still extant and tell the traditional narrative behind the construction.

The Lingshan 靈山 cemetery, where the Prophet's Companions are said to be buried, also contains the graves of multiple generations of Muslim residents of Quanzhou, whose identities and stories are recorded in stone tomb inscriptions. Building mosques and consecrating burial grounds reveal a maturation of the diaspora community. The long-term investment in such institutions does not befit the itinerant. Clearly, the Muslims of Song Quanzhou saw themselves as a permanent community. The days of the walled-in *fanfang* were past:

> *Fanfang* in Quanzhou were not walled, as in Guangzhou and Yangzhou, but began to sprawl and disperse evenly into the city, encouraging intermingling of religion and language with it. In contrast to the *fanfang* in Guangzhou, Quanzhou seems to have had a more intermingled spreading of foreigners. Foreign merchants are recorded as being 'scattered among the people'.[2]

Muslims were completely at home in Quanzhou, so much so that by the end of the Song dynasty they literally ran the place. Islamic influence in the city was so pervasive that in Western sources (like Marco Polo and Ibn Battuta) Quanzhou was known only by its Arabic name, Zaytūn, the 'City of Olives'.[3]

The transition to Mongol rule in China was anything but smooth, characterized by extreme violence in places. But the Muslim population weathered the storm well. A feature that made Mongol rule remarkable was a general policy of religious tolerance, which stands in contrast to the common perception of the Mongols as ruthless conquerors. The Mongols were neither the demonic barbarian horde they are often portrayed to be, nor enlightened promoters of 'pure theism and perfect toleration' as Gibbon has labelled them.[4] The Mongols were at times quite ruthless in battles yet tolerant, even solicitous, in their dealings with foreigners and their religious traditions. Above all, the Mongols were pragmatists who consciously sought means to attain their goals: first conquest and then governance.

The empire was huge (the largest contiguous land empire ever) and internally diverse. Under Chinggis Khan (c. 1162–1227), the Mongol Empire stretched from Korea to the Caspian Sea, and after his death his successors expanded their territory to encompass all of China with western boundaries in Hungary and Syria. The *Pax Mongolica*, an unprecedented stability in which extensive trade and cultural exchange could take place, prevailed. It may be summarized as the ability of a subject or protected traveller to pass through the length and breadth of the empire in peace and safety because of the security guaranteed by Mongol rule.

Before this peace could take hold, however, the Mongols emerged as a distinct political body, which first had to overrun, destroy or absorb other peoples and their civilizations. Many accounts blame Mongol conquest for demolishing entire cities and exterminating their inhabitants; for example, the Arab historian Ibn al-Athīr (1160–1233), in the wake of Chinggis Khan's first Middle East campaign, described Mongol conquest as 'a tremendous disaster such as had never happened before … It may well be that the world from now until its end … will not experience the like of it again, apart perhaps from Gog and Magog.'[5] According to his estimation, the Mongols killed 700,000 people in the Persian city of Merv alone.[6]

The Mongols were efficient conquerors, to be sure, but many negative accounts are likely exaggerated. Such historiography promotes a stereotype of the Mongols as predisposed to brutality and acts of indiscriminate violence, but we must remember that these narratives were written by those who had recently suffered at their hands. Other sources, such as the Daoist cleric Chang Chun,[7] suggest that, insofar as cities like Samarkand and Bukhara flourished soon after they were conquered, the wholesale devastation reported by many Muslim writers must have been greatly exaggerated. Despite the commonly held demonization of Mongol terror, it was not

> a spontaneous barbarian rampage. Rather it was one of the coolly devised elements of the greater ... strategy for world conquest, a fiendishly efficient combination of military field tactics and psychological warfare designed to crush even the possibility of resistance to Mongol rule and to demoralize whole cities into surrendering without a fight. Once the armies had overrun Persia and set up garrison governments, wholesale carnage on the whole came to an end.[8]

Mongol religious tolerance likewise should be viewed as deriving not from high-minded ideals, but from a conscious pragmatism. Chinggis Khan's empire encompassed peoples who adhered to Buddhism, Islam, Zoroastrianism, Manicheaism, Judaism, Christianity (Catholic, Orthodox and Nestorian), Daoism and Confucianism, among others.[9] This complexity required a subtle policy to placate different groups with competing interests in order to maintain some measure of harmony within the empire. The situation became further complicated as Chinggis's unified empire broke up into distinct and virtually autonomous successor states. Each khanate was left to devise its own policies for dealing with religious, ethnic and cultural diversity. In general, later Mongol rulers followed the example of their revered progenitor and practised religious tolerance as far as it advanced their interests. Toleration of foreign religions was pragmatically based on the hope of gaining the approval of religious leaders, and thereby the loyalty of their followers among the conquered peoples. The general Mongol policy of religious toleration was most commonly manifested in one of three forms: (1) conversion by the Mongol rulers to one of the religions of their foreign subjects; (2) patronage of these religions, their clerics and their institutions; or (3) benign neglect of the religions within their domains.[10]

Chinggis Khan himself, however, was not always consistent in his application of religious tolerance nor were all religions equal in his view. As he grew older, he developed a growing concern for the future. When he heard that Daoists in China possessed the secrets of longevity, or even immortality, he summoned Chang Chun to accompany him on his campaigns. The Great Khan patronized Daoists, Buddhists, Muslims and others. But at times he would reverse his positions capriciously. For example, when he decided the Islamic ḥalāl method of slaughtering animals was distasteful he forbade it under penalty of death, requiring all subjects to slaughter using the traditional Mongolian method.[11] Chinggis ruled by decree, written down to create the law code known as the Yasa, followed throughout the Mongol Empire. Chinggis's successors upheld the Yasa, but added their own decrees, which varied from one region to another.

After the death of Chinggis in 1227, the unified empire he had established began to disintegrate. Conflict over succession ensued over the next two generations, even as Mongol expansion through conquest continued. Chinggis's heirs led campaigns in Russia, the Middle East, Central Asia and China. Some of these descendants focused their attention on consolidating practically autonomous power in the territories they had conquered. Chinggis's successors paid lip-service to the centralized authority of a universal khanate, but increasingly their domains developed into distinct states: the Ilkhanate in Persia and the Middle East, the Chagatai Khanate in Central Asia and the Golden Horde in Russia.

China had always been the primary target of Mongol conquest. Chinggis never realized this goal, but his descendants eventually did. In 1234, the Mongol Empire under the rule of Ögedei Khan (r. 1229–41) conquered the Jurchen Jin dynasty (1115–1234) of northern China; it would take his successors more than two decades to complete their conquest of the Southern Song dynasty. After another protracted conflict over succession, Khubilai emerged as the fifth Great Khan. In theory, he was sovereign over the entire Mongol Empire, but in practice his main focus was consolidating rule over China and East Asia, leaving his cousins to control their successor khanates to the West. In 1266, Khubilai began to build his Chinese capital in Dadu 大都 (present-day Beijing 北京), known to Turks and Mongols as Khanbaliq. Khubilai's consultation with Confucian scholars and the naming of his dynasty 'Yuan' (元) exemplify the profound influence of Chinese tradition on the new regime.[12] But Khubilai's imperium was never purely Chinese, a fact that many Chinese subjects, especially the Confucian elite, would never forget. Khubilai's policies for ruling

China were an amalgam of diverse ideals and practices, reflecting the cultural diversity of his domain. While many of his policies were indeed based on Chinese precedent, others were derived from the Mongol Yasa and other foreign traditions.

Khubilai's policies of religious tolerance continued the tradition established by his forebears. His most direct influence came from his mother, Sorghaghtani Beki. Even before the ascensions of her sons Möngke and Khubilai, she groomed them for leadership. While building alliances and fostering unity among diverse factions, 'her political genius is perhaps best demonstrated by her religious toleration'.[13] A devout Nestorian Christian, Sorghaghtani saw the political value of befriending other religious groups, in much the same way as Chinggis and other Mongol rulers had done. She 'patronized Buddhism and Taoism to win favor with her Chinese subjects' as well as Islam, whose adherents were spread throughout the Mongol lands in great numbers.[14] Khubilai pursued similar policies in Yuan China.

Among Khubilai's more radical departure from Chinese tradition was the establishment of a four-tiered social hierarchy based primarily on ethnic distinction. The top class comprised the Mongols, followed by the Semuren 色目人 (mostly Western and Central Asians, trusted servants of the Mongols),[15] the Hanren 漢人 (Northern Chinese and Jurchens) and finally the Nanren 南人 (Southern Chinese).[16] The hierarchy may be viewed in descending order of those groups Khubilai regarded as most trustworthy and useful.[17] It so happens that the Semu class, due to their geographical and ethnic origins, consisted largely of Muslims. Muslims along with other foreigners occupied a relatively favoured position in a diverse, stratified society.

Semuren, or 'miscellaneous categories' of foreigners, also included various peoples living along China's Central Asian frontier. The Mongol policy of bringing in soldiers and bureaucrats from abroad meant that Muslims, including recently Islamized Uyghurs and other Turks, were incorporated into the empire. This, therefore, led to a further diversification of the Muslim population in China. The gradual Islamization of the Uyghurs, who had historically adhered to many different religions,[18] overlapped with the Mongol conquests, resulting in markers of Uyghur identity imprinting on Islam and Muslims in Yuan China. To wit, in official Yuan writings, the terms 'Hui' or 'Huihui' began to appear in reference to Muslims. At the time, Uyghurs were known in Chinese by the ethnonym Huihe 回紇.[19] Philologists believe that 'Hui' as a common name for

Muslims was derived from Huihe, which originally applied to Western foreigners in general.[20]

This generalization of Islam under Mongol rule notwithstanding, individual Muslims played an essential role in the building of the Yuan dynasty, with numerous examples of administrators and trusted servants of the court among them. Based on the events of the Mongol conquest, it may even be said that without the assistance of a Muslim, Pu Shougeng, the Yuan dynasty might never have come into existence. Muslims also played a major role in the Mongol victory at the pivotal Battle of Xiangyang 襄陽 (1267–73); Persian engineers Ismāʻīl and ʻAlà al-Dīn designed new and improved weapons, introducing trebuchet catapults, which were instrumental.[21]

Muslims served in some of the most important military positions in the newly established Yuan state, which had twelve provinces, each presided over by a military governor. During Khubilai's reign, eight out of those twelve governors were Muslims as were the deputy governors in the other four provinces. The commanders-in-chief of the three Mongol war zones in China (Central, Southwest and Southeast) were Muslims who had been in the service of the Mongols since before 1279.[22] Bai Yan, Sayyid Ajal Shams al-Dīn ʻUmar and Pu Shougeng were all putative descendants of Abū ʻAlī. Together, they helped the Mongols to overthrow the Song dynasty and were rewarded by Khubilai Khan with influential positions.

Sayyid Ajal, who served as governor general in the Shaanxi–Gansu–Sichuan region,[23] was particularly instrumental in spreading Yuan rule and Chinese culture in Yunnan, which was inhabited by numerous tribes and small kingdoms.[24] He helped the residents of the region establish a way of life based on Confucian principles and an agrarian economy, encouraging irrigation projects and trade with the rest of China.[25] The army under his command consisted of a Muslim majority. Many of these soldiers settled in Yunnan and took Chinese brides, establishing sinicized Muslim families. Sayyid Ajal's service to Islam also included building Yunnan's first two mosques.[26] He was succeeded as governor by his son Naṣr al-Dīn, who held the office until 1291, while his grandson Bayān served as finance minister for the second Yuan emperor, Temür Öljeitü (r. 1294–1307).[27]

Unlike all of the other successor khanates of the united Mongol Empire, whose subjects were mostly Muslims, the Yuan dynasty never converted to Islam; the Yuan ruling class mostly identified as Buddhists. Yet, their patronage allowed many Muslims to distinguish themselves in the Yuan Empire. Persian physicians introduced medical techniques and medicines; in 1284, the directors of the Imperial Dispensary were Muslims.[28] A Muslim architect, Amīr al-Dīn (Ch. Yeheidie'erding 也黑迭兒丁, d. 1312), designed and oversaw the construction of Dadu (completed in 1293), combining Chinese and Islamic styles and techniques.[29] Muslims were also responsible for great advancements in the field of astronomy in China. A Persian, Jamāl al-Dīn, built the observatory in Dadu,[30] and presented Khubilai with new astronomical devices in 1267.[31] Jamāl al-Dīn also introduced the 'Ten Thousand Years Chronology' for use by Chinese historians. Due to these achievements, the Khan established an Imperial Institute of Muslim Astronomy that thrived throughout the Yuan period, keeping China at the forefront of this science. Muslims were also appointed as officials within the newly established Institute of History.[32] In 1314, an official Institute of Islamic Studies was established and placed under the charge of prominent Muslims from around the empire. Many Muslim arts and sciences 'flourished more vigorously in China under the Mongols than in Baghdad itself'.[33]

Their privileged status in Yuan society afforded Muslims an opportunity for intellectual expression in addition to the commercial success Muslim traders had already enjoyed. Muslim craftsmen, artisans and merchants injected life into the Mongol economy by means of trade and were rewarded by Khubilai with benefits like tax exemption.[34] Muslims were firmly entrenched in all aspects of life in Yuan China, but they played a particularly significant role in the administration of the empire's finances. Khubilai's finance minister from 1262 to 1282 was Aḥmad Fanakātī. Khubilai frequently employed Muslim merchants as financial administrators, governors and tax collectors.[35] This policy had a twofold purpose. First, Muslims were regarded as shrewd businessmen who could raise revenues to finance Khubilai's grandiose projects including the building of Dadu, the extension of the Grand Canal, and military campaigns in Central Asia, Japan and Southeast Asia.[36] Using Muslims as tax collectors also deflected popular resentment of the heavy tax burden away from the Mongols and onto more immediate culprits. The unfortunate irony of collecting taxes while being tax exempt themselves further vilified Muslims in the eyes of the indigenous Chinese populace.[37]

The religious toleration Muslims enjoyed seems to have been a direct result of their special relationship with the Mongol court. Due to the contributions of certain notable Muslim figures, the community prospered as a whole. Khubilai rewarded the individuals with prestigious appointments and privileges, allowing many of them to amass large fortunes. At the same time, perhaps concomitantly, he rewarded the Muslim community with religious freedoms. As in the Song period, Muslim communities had their own leaders, including the Shaykh al-Islām in Quanzhou, who served as the direct intermediary between the community and the government.[38] Quanzhou also had a qāḍī who served as the local judge and interpreter of Islamic law. Overturning the decree of his grandfather, Khubilai permitted Islamic ritual slaughter of animals and circumcision of boys. A number of mosques were built with imperial sponsorship, among them in the capitals of Dadu and Shangdu.

Yet, these boons were only as enduring as the Khan's personal fiat. Just as the loyal service of certain individual Muslims translated into benefits for the Muslim community at large, so too did Khubilai's suspicion of treason on the part of his finance minister lead to persecutory policies. The employment of individuals of diverse ethnic, religious and ideological backgrounds had the negative effect of inspiring conflict among various factions within the government, each vying to gain favour with the Khan and promote their own interests at court. Aḥmad despised and was despised by other government officials.[39] Muslims had generally received a bad reputation for corruption and abuse of power among the Chinese. Aḥmad was eventually accused of nepotism and other crimes by his Confucian antagonists who seized the opportunity to blame him for the faltering economy of the 1280s. In fact, apart from his indiscretions, economic woes were the result of overall poor administration, Khubilai's extravagant expenditures, and an excessive tax burden on the masses. In 1282, Aḥmad was assassinated by a group of Chinese conspirators. No longer alive to defend himself, his rivals posthumously accused him of treachery, specifically the theft of a precious stone belonging to the Khan.[40] Khubilai believed the allegations and publicly disgraced the corpse of Aḥmad, killed several of his sons and punished officials whom he had appointed.

Nor was Khubilai satisfied simply to punish the house of Aḥmad and his associates. He implemented several policies that severely curtailed Muslim religious rights until 1287. Edicts were issued once again forbidding the ritual slaughter of animals and circumcision. Khubilai's punishment of the Muslim community was intended to curb their growing power, hence the argument that the 'repressive edicts … were inspired more by political considerations than by hatred of Islam'.[41]

The fortunes of Muslims in Yuan China certainly fluctuated as a result of being tied so closely to the Mongol elites and vulnerable to the caprice of the Khan. On the one hand, as members of a privileged social class, the Muslim population grew both in size and prosperity; by the fourteenth century approximately four million Muslims lived in China.[42] On the other hand, as loyalists to a foreign conquest regime with strong ties to non-Chinese cultures and societies, even after centuries of residence in China, Muslims still retained the stigma of being outsiders. The spread of Muslims throughout the country was greater in the Yuan than in any other period of Chinese history. Muslims played a disproportionately large role in the building and administration of the Yuan state. This may have put them in good standing with the Mongol court, but it also engendered increasing disdain from Chinese officials and commoners alike. Mongol favour was fragile and ephemeral, but Chinese contempt would endure long after the fall of the Yuan dynasty. In the late Yuan period, Muslims fell out of favour with the court, supplanted by Buddhists and Confucians in many top government posts. And the influx of Muslims to the empire slowed almost to a halt. The inscriptions on the gravestones at the Muslim cemetery of Lingshan all predate 1353, indicating a diaspora community in steep decline.

Around the same time, infighting among Muslims in Quanzhou led to greater devastation. Throughout the Song-Yuan period, the overwhelming majority of Muslims entering China were followers of the Sunni branch of Islam, but there was also a small proportion of Shiʻa followers.[43] Friction between the two groups became a growing concern of the Yuan government, who attempted to offset the population imbalance by stationing an additional 3,000 Shiʻa troops in Quanzhou, but this only exacerbated problems and militarized the situation. In 1357, as numerous anti-Yuan rebellions were erupting around China, the Shiʻa forces under the command of Persian generals Sayf al-Dīn and Amīr al-Dīn rose up against the Sunni residents of Quanzhou, who were still loyal to the regime. The Shiʻa army, known in annals as the 'Ispah' (or Sepoy), took over the entire city, followed by Putian 莆田 and part of the provincial capital of Fuzhou 福州.

Government forces came to put down the Ispah Rebellion, which they were finally able to do by 1366. In Quanzhou, the Yuan army under the command of the Chinese general Chen Youding 陈友定, seeking out the rebels but unable to differentiate non-Muslim from Muslims, let alone Shiʻa from Sunni, carried out an indiscriminate massacre of most of the city's foreign population. Mosques and other foreign religious sites were decimated. Moreover, the local Chinese population joined the soldiers in their rampage, venting their long-held resentment of Muslims who had collaborated with the Mongols. They sought out descendants of Pu Shougeng and his family for special retribution, murdering them and mutilating the corpses. Among the Muslims who survived the massacre, many chose thereafter to hide their ethno-religious identity, assimilating completely into the Chinese population to avoid persecution.

During the 1350s–1360s, a rash of natural disasters – drought and flooding, compounded by famine and a plague epidemic – coincided to create the circumstances for several peasant revolts to arise against the already-hated Mongol regime. This cataclysmic environment spawned a number of millenarian religious movements that combined a hope for spiritual renewal with political aspirations. The Red Turbans (Hongjin 紅巾), an offshoot of the White Lotus Society (Bailianshe 白蓮社), were a militant sect that regarded violent upheaval of the status quo as the necessary agent of social–political–spiritual change. A peasant from Anhui province by the name of Zhu Yuanzhang 朱元璋 (1328–98), rose up through the ranks of the Red Turban Army to become its leader. From 1356 to 1366, Zhu led his army in a series of campaigns to defeat rival rebel groups throughout eastern and central China, consolidating his power base by establishing a state called Ming 明 in the city of Nanjing 南京. In 1368, his forces conquered the Yuan capital of Dadu, ending Mongol rule over China. With his victory, he claimed the Mandate of Heaven and founded the Ming dynasty, ascending the throne as the Hongwu emperor (r. 1368–98).

The new dynasty was self-conscious as a regime that had overthrown nearly a century of 'barbarian' rule, thereby restoring indigenous Chinese supremacy. As heirs to the Yuan ethnically based social structure, the Ming re-shaped Chinese identity politics by replacing the Mongols with themselves atop the hierarchy as leaders of the 'Han' 漢 people. In this new system of ethnic politics, Chinese proto-nationalism would define other groups as minorities subordinate to the Han majority. Among the first actions taken by the new regime was to exile members of the Mongol ruling elite back across the Great Wall into Mongolia. From its outset the Ming dynasty manifested a heightened paranoia with regard to foreigners. The empire ceased engagement beyond China's natural borders and receded into an isolationist state. By this general policy, Ming rulers sought to defend against what they perceived as an ever-present threat of another Mongol invasion.

Contrary, perhaps, to logical expectation, the Hongwu emperor did not extend his punitive measures of deportation or persecution to other ethnic groups who had served the Yuan state. In fact, many of the non-Chinese who had served the Mongols were retained to continue serving the new regime. Muslims in particular were spared any severe backlash by the court. Muslims continued to serve as high-ranking officials under the new regime and made significant contributions to political, economic and intellectual life in Ming China. Muslim military officers, architects, astronomers and engineers, among others, even played an important role in helping build the Ming Empire. Imperial tolerance and patronage, however, could not shield the Muslim population from popular resentment, which had only grown more bitter as Muslims were regarded as avaricious collaborators with the Mongols, who enriched themselves at the expense of Chinese commoners. Therefore, at the same time that the early Ming government implemented an isolationist and protectionist foreign policy, its domestic policy sought to mitigate inter-communal conflict among its diverse constituents by homogenizing Ming society, encouraging acculturation and assimilation of heterogeneous groups, including Muslims in China.

According to Chinese Muslim tradition, the Hongwu emperor reserved special treatment for Muslims because he was secretly a Muslim.[44] Verifying this claim is impossible, and most Western scholars reject it outright. Yet, the emperor was notably solicitous of Muslims. He and subsequent Ming rulers continued to employ Muslims at court, as astronomers, calendar makers, diviners in the Directorate of Astronomy, envoys, translators and interpreters, explorers, philosophers and military leaders. During his conquest campaigns, Zhu Yuanzhang's army contained numerous Muslim troops and commanders, some of whom later became high-ranking officers in the Ming army. One of these was Chang Yuchun 常遇春 (1330–69), who fought alongside Zhu as a member of the Red Turbans, helped overthrow the Mongols, and after the establishment of the Ming was promoted to the rank of Yuanshuai 元帥 (Marshall), appointed State Counsellor, and named Duke of Hubei (湖北公); he died a year after the establishment of the new dynasty. Another was Mu Ying 沐英 (1345–92), who was raised as the adopted son of Zhu Yuanzhang, was named Marquis of Xiping (西平侯) and awarded the governorship of Yunnan.⁴⁵ Then there was Lan Yu 藍玉 (d. 1393), brother-in-law of Chang Yuchun and a war hero who was named Marquis of Yongchang (永昌侯), but met an ignoble end, executed for plotting to assassinate the emperor. Many of these post-war honours were titular, but their conferment demonstrates the Hongwu emperor's appreciation of those officers who had served him loyally.

Perhaps the emperor had no special sentiment towards his Muslim servants or subjects, but his willingness to employ them shows that he harboured no ill will against them either. Hongwu's court attempted to revive native Chinese traditions and institutions, but subjects of foreign heritage were allowed to remain in the country, to practice their religion and to participate in the political life of the Ming state. The Hongwu emperor ordered and sponsored the construction of mosques in several provinces and cities, including the Jingjue Mosque 净觉寺 in the capital of Nanjing. He is said to have written the 'Hundred-Word Elegy' (Baizizan 百字讚) praising Islam, the Prophet Muhammad, and Allah, which is inscribed on tablets displayed in numerous Ming mosques.⁴⁶ That said, besides the Hongwu emperor's beneficence towards his Muslim subjects, a series of policies were also implemented during his reign attempting to legislate and accelerate a process of assimilation that had been proceeding gradually over the previous centuries.

In its efforts to champion Chinese culture over foreign influence, the early Ming government was 'determined to compel the foreigners residing in China to adopt some Chinese ways'.⁴⁷ The regime 'hoping to defuse the potential for ethnic strife, therefore enacted policies intended to accelerate the "civilization" of "barbarian" minorities, including laws to help accelerate the natural process of acculturation of various ethnic and cultural communities.'⁴⁸ These policies clearly played a significant role in, and likely accelerated, this process, (but) they were not the only reason behind the social and cultural transformation of Muslims. Multiple and nuanced internal factors and pressures within the multifaceted Muslim community must also be acknowledged as a major impetus for this transformation.⁴⁹

Two major policy initiatives reveal a twofold – cultural and genetic – approach to the goal of sinicization. One of the practical measures intended to facilitate Muslims' integration into mainstream Han society was the requirement that they adopt Chinese surnames.⁵⁰ This custom had already been practised by some Muslim settlers in China as far back as the late Tang–early Song period, for example, in the cases of Abū ʿAlī, whose family adopted the surname Pu. However, the Ming government required all Muslims to follow this practice in order to mitigate cultural differences between Han Chinese and subjects of foreign descent. Before this period, most Muslims retained either Arabic patronyms (e.g. Ibn Husayn), or toponyms, known as *nisba* in Arabic, which identify them with a place (e.g. al-Bagdhdādī). Their given names also tended to be of traditional Arabic, Qur'ānic or Persian origin. The new Chinese surnames were monosyllabic and written as a single character. Usually, the syllable was chosen to resemble the sound of one of the syllables in the original Islamic name: for example, in the case of the Pu family, '*pu*' is derived from the second syllable in the name of their patriarch, Abū.

The second policy approached assimilation at the level of family planning, or possibly genetic engineering. The *Da Minglü* (Great Ming Law) decreed that non-Chinese people of foreign descent living in the Ming Empire must marry a Han Chinese spouse. Obviously, the purpose of this law was to eliminate existing ethnic and cultural differences through hybridization. If successful, this intermarriage and interbreeding could have eliminated such boundaries within several generations. However, simply decreeing intermarriage compulsory does not mean people will surmount centuries-old customs and prejudices. Thus, the Ming Law includes a stipulation that while Mongols and Semu are forbidden to marry within their own ethnicities, a dispensation is necessary: since most Chinese were reviled by the foreigners and would refuse to marry them, 'in sympathy for their extinction' should they not be allowed to do so, they were conditionally permitted to marry within their own groups.[51] So, ultimately, the goal of the intermarriage law was never realized. Muslim communities throughout China continued to grow, through both voluntary intermarriage and adoption. In the Ming period, it became a common practice for wealthy Muslims to adopt or, more precisely, purchase children who were then raised as Muslims.[52] Muslim men did marry Chinese women, as the law advised, but these spouses, frequently, converted to Islam.

Other sinicization-promoting laws included the requirement to attend Chinese schools, and erect tablets honouring and swearing allegiance to the emperor in or near mosques.[53] But while Muslims in Ming China did partially adopt Chinese culture, they also clung stubbornly to their own beliefs and practices. Muslims had already adopted many aspects of Chinese material culture: wearing Chinese clothing, speaking Chinese in public and eating Chinese food prepared according to ḥalāl standards. But many Muslims retained their religious identity and customs revealing their assimilation in the early Ming period to be largely superficial.

In many ways, Muslims still remained distinct from their non-Muslim compatriots. Rather than participating fully in Chinese culture, Muslims 'formed a new sub-culture, that of the Huihui or Sino-Muslims'.[54] In most areas with a sizeable Muslim population, locals held fast to traditions of following their religious authorities and attending their mosques and mosque-run schools,[55] where some students still learned Arabic and/or Persian. Despite the government's attempt to weaken their ties with other Muslims beyond the borders of China, many Chinese Muslims (particularly those living near the western frontier) continued to associate with co-religionists in Central Asia.[56]

After the Hongwu era, subsequent Ming emperors varied in their treatment of Muslims. Some were less solicitous than others – while they rarely persecuted Muslims actively, they did little to deter local Chinese officials and civilians from harassing them. Others followed Hongwu's example by treating their Muslim subjects well and involving certain Muslim individuals in court affairs and matters of state.[57] The Yongle 永樂 emperor (r. 1403–24), was one such ruler, though it took him some time to achieve consistency in his Muslim policies. Localized persecution of Muslims, as in Quanzhou, occurred during the early years of his reign.[58] In 1407, however, the emperor issued a decree protecting the Muslims of Quanzhou, threatening those who would 'maltreat, insult, cheat or bully' them with severe punishment.[59] It is thought that the emperor was persuaded to take this course of action because of his close relationship with his Muslim advisor, Zheng He 鄭和 (1371–1433 or 1435), who pleaded on behalf of the Quanzhou community.

Zheng He was an enigmatic figure who played a significant role in the fortunes of the Ming Empire and the Chinese Muslim community. Born Ma He 馬和, in the city of Kunyang 昆陽, Yunnan, he was the second son of a pious Muslim family.[60] During a campaign to pacify Sichuan and Yunnan, under the reign of the Hongwu emperor, Ma He, only twelve at the time, was captured and brought to the capital, Nanjing. There he was castrated and assigned as a eunuch attendant to the emperor's fourth son, Prince Yan (later the Yongle emperor). As a young man, Ma He became one of the prince's favourite companions, and was schooled by scholar-officials in the Confucian classics. He proved his military prowess, accompanying Prince Yan and his army to Beijing in 1391.[61]

Ma He became a trusted advisor to Prince Yan when the latter ascended the throne in 1403. He was appointed 'eunuch overseer of the imperial palace', one of the most influential positions in the empire.[62] In 1405 he was given the surname Zheng by the Yongle emperor.

1405 was also the year in which the emperor chose Zheng He to command a massive naval fleet dedicated to exploration, trade and diplomacy. In commissioning the undertaking, the emperor reversed the isolationist policies of his predecessors. For a brief period, China was re-opened to foreign trade and diplomatic relations, a tremendous boost to the Ming economy. Zheng He was sent on a total of seven voyages. One of the most successful navigators of his time, he travelled the Indonesian archipelago, through the Malacca straits, into the Indian Ocean to Sri Lanka, the Arabian Sea and Gulf, the Red Sea and the East African coast. Wherever he went, he made a lasting impression among the local people, and won prestige for the Ming Empire as a world power. The trade his voyages promoted also brought great riches to China.[63]

Zheng He's religious orientation was eclectic. Born into a Muslim family but stripped from his family at an early age, he was indoctrinated in orthodox Confucianism by court officials. He also underwent Buddhist initiation, receiving the precept name Fu Shan 福善.[64] Yet, he never ceased to be a Muslim. In his travels, he would stop to perform prayers at local mosques, both in China and overseas. It is during one such visit to the Aṣḥāb mosque that he witnessed the plight of the Quanzhou Muslim community and interceded on their behalf. Although half of his fleet reached Mecca on their seventh and final voyage in 1433 (or 1435), poor health prevented him from following in his father and grandfather's footsteps in making the pilgrimage (Ḥajj). Later that year he died near Calcutta (Kolkata). His body was prepared for burial according to Muslim practice, but he was buried at sea, his head pointing towards Mecca. Upon his request his 'shoes and a braid of his hair … were thought to have been brought back to Nanjing and buried near Buddhist caves outside the city', with a Muslim grave marking the spot today.[65]

The privileges enjoyed by the Chinese Muslims who were attached to the Ming court did not necessarily translate into prosperity for many ordinary Muslim subjects. While it is true that esteemed Muslim officials like Zheng He may have been able to secure certain favours for the Muslim community at large, Muslim commoners across China increasingly became targets of persecution by Chinese civilians and local officials. In fact, the prosperity enjoyed by individual Muslims, either because of their military and civil service positions, or their successful commercial pursuits, may have been the primary cause of Chinese resentment and hostility. These bitter sentiments were fuelled by the Chinese view of Muslims as Mongol collaborators with foreign ancestry. From the perspective of ordinary Chinese, Muslims were never adequately punished for conspiring with the invaders; they were rewarded with continued privilege by the Ming court and as wealthy merchants. While their outward appearance was Chinese, they were often thought to carry a sense of their moral superiority over non-Muslims, an attitude not always artfully concealed. Muslims during the Yuan–Ming period experienced many advancements, but also some setbacks. They became much more integrated in Chinese culture and society, but had they assimilated enough to be accepted?

Chapter 4
Muslim renaissance and resistance in late imperial China

Hu Dengzhou, scion of a wealthy Muslim merchant family, grew up in Xinyang prefecture, just upstream from Xi'an along the Yellow River. The Hu family was pious, but in no way extraordinary in its devotion. They attended the local mosque and the young Dengzhou studied in the adjoining school, where he learned basic liturgical Arabic and some Persian. Seated at the foot of the presiding imam, he spent long hours reciting prayers and memorising by rote passages of the Qur'ān in a rhythmic cadence. Even so, Chinese was the first-language of his community and he studied the classical Confucian curriculum in order to prepare him for life as a member of the upwardly-mobile Muslim bourgeoisie, to interact and transact with his Han Chinese peers. Yet, in this mainstream Chinese milieu, he and his community were hybrid, simultaneously with one foot in each world of their Chinese-Muslim dual heritage. Hu yearned for knowledge of the traditions and faith of his ancestors. He craved a deeper understanding of Islam than was available from the small mosque school he attended as a child. On the road to Beijing for business, he met an Arab traveller with whom he practiced Arabic. The man became Hu's mentor, answering questions about the finer points of Islamic doctrine, theology, law, and philosophy, and introducing him to secrets of Sufi mysticism. Such knowledge was inaccessible to most Chinese Muslims of his time. His mind and heart set afire, Hu wanted more – access to books, teachings, and masters – and he was willing to go to great lengths to attain it. The social norms and state policy of his day did not favour travel abroad. Realising that the learning he desired was impossible to find in China, and with the flow of ideas and people from the Islamic world curtailed by Ming foreign policy, he inverted the oft-repeated exhortation of the Prophet by 'seeking knowledge even beyond China'. Hu did what few others in his time dared, travelling for years through Central Asia, and eventually to Mecca, in search of instruction and texts he could bring back with him to China. Upon returning, he undertook the reform of existing mosque-based education and instituted a new system, combining traditional Islamic and local Chinese elements, rooted in Chinese soil, but fertilized by a fresh infusion of knowledge from the Muslim heartlands. To his disciples, he is remembered as the Great Master, Hu Baba.

The 'Ming period has been interpreted by some as providing a period of peace for the Muslims of China.'[1] Because 'assimilation proceeded rapidly during the Ming, historians have said that discrimination must have been rather low key.'[2] It was, however, also a time in which anti-Muslim sentiment brewed among the mainstream Chinese populace. On the level of the imperium, Ming rule was generally favourable to Muslim subjects. Officials, especially at the local level, were less conciliatory and sometimes abused their authority to discriminate against Muslims. And common people in the Ming period, as in previous times, harboured prejudices against their Muslim neighbours for reasons that were not entirely rational.

After the Yongle reign, during which the Ming Empire reached its zenith of engagement with the rest of the world both diplomatically and commercially, subsequent emperors withdrew extensively from international affairs. Through much of the remainder of the Ming period, a more inward-looking, isolationist foreign policy greatly reduced Chinese contact with the outside world, including Muslim Central Asia and the Middle East. One unintended effect of this policy was effectively to cut Chinese Muslims off from meaningful contact with their co-religionists abroad. The regime did not deliberately follow this course in order to do harm to Muslims, in the same way that 'benefiting its Muslim subjects was not a priority nor a direct objective of the dynasty. It was instead the result of a domestic policy based primarily on foreign policy concerns.'[3]

Ming China still engaged in international trade at a more limited rate. And Muslims continued to play an outsized role in the Ming court under various emperors. The Xuande (r. 1426–35) and Zhengde (r. 1506–21) emperors were known to have employed Muslim eunuchs and advisors,[4] much to the chagrin of Han Confucian ministers and officials. Zhengde was notorious for his unconventional, even bizarre, tastes and personal habits. By all accounts, his hedonistic pursuits took priority over affairs of state. Among his idiosyncratic hobbies, he maintained a menagerie of exotic animals, promiscuously indulged sexual experimentation and enjoyed dressing up in foreign costumes. His disinterest in the politics of the court frustrated the Confucian officials, who found him difficult to control. In order to distance himself from them, he surrounded himself with handpicked counsellors, including Muslim eunuchs. Castration is explicitly forbidden by Islamic law, yet it became a path to empowerment and enrichment for Muslims in the Ming court.

The Zhengde emperor was fascinated by foreign objects and sensual delights. He was especially enthralled by things from the Islamic world, what might be called *exotica Islamica*. This included dressing in Arab-style clothing and preferring Muslim concubines; there is even conjecture that he may have secretly converted to Islam.[5] This spurious claim is supported by the fact that in 1519 the emperor issued an edict banning the slaughter of pigs throughout the empire; the ban was soon overturned after three months. The actual reason for the ban, or whether it had anything to do with the emperor's relationship to Islam or his Muslim inner circle, is a mystery.

Clear evidence of the strong influence of Muslims in the Zhengde court, however, is found in its material culture. A large amount of art, including bronzes and blue-white porcelains bearing inscriptions in Arabic and Persian, was produced by the imperial workshops during the period. Such items could only have been manufactured in the imperial foundries and kilns with high-level authorization. Presumably, many of the works were commissioned by Muslim court eunuchs or other high-ranking advisors. Others were also exported as part of what remained of Chinese-Islamic international trade or given as gifts to Muslim regimes such as the Ottoman and Safavid Empires. Some of the eunuchs and officials were devout Muslims, who donated objects to Chinese mosques. Given his personal preferences, the emperor probably also collected some of these items. This burst of Chinese-Islamic artistic creativity and productivity was short-lived. Confucian officials reclaimed their power at court after the Zhengde reign, severely limiting Muslim influence thereafter. The dynasty's isolationist approach to foreign relations and international trade also restricted the import of cobalt from Persian and Central Asia, the so-called 'Muslim blue' (*Huihuiqing* 回回青) that gave the porcelains their vibrant underglaze colour. Nevertheless, this brief flourishing of a uniquely hybrid aesthetic bears witness to continuing evolution of a highly sinicized Muslim culture in China and the sometimes up, sometimes down conditions of Chinese Muslims in the Ming dynasty.

Not coincidentally, anti-Muslim sentiment among officials and commoners began to rise around the same time that Muslim influence at court declined. The prosperity enjoyed by some Muslims, either because of their civil service positions or successful commercial pursuits, was a primary cause of Han resentment. Muslims were still remembered for their collaboration with the Mongols and were stigmatized by their foreign ancestry, no matter how much they had acculturated since their ancestors had arrived in China.

As the Ming dynasty began to decline in the sixteenth century, imperial protection and patronage of Muslims waned. Muslim minority communities were left vulnerable to the whims of local government officials, who frequently shared the anti-Muslim bigotry of the Han majority. As Muslim communities were widely dispersed throughout the Ming Empire, they never developed a unified leadership, apart from their own local religious authorities – the imams, or *ahong* 阿訇 – of their independent mosque communities. These mosque-based communities became the standard solidarities of Chinese Muslim life in the Ming–Qing period, and would be referred to retrospectively as Gedimu 格迪目, from the Arabic *qadīm*, meaning 'ancient'.[6] Muslims in Central China also began to lose contact with their non-Chinese co-religionists, Turks and other ethnic Muslim peoples residing in China's western frontier regions and Central Asia. Isolated, yet dispersed, distinct from the Han Chinese majority by custom and belief but linked to Chinese society by economic interdependence and state policy, the position of Muslims in late Ming China became increasingly vulnerable. In the period of instability that characterizes the fall of any dynasty or government, the Muslim population became a scapegoat, and were regarded by their Han neighbours of a source of corruption.

Isolated from their brethren abroad and alienated from their non-Muslim neighbours at home, Chinese Muslims found themselves in a dilemma faced by diaspora communities throughout history: whether to succumb to pressures to assimilate into or differentiate themselves from the mainstream. On the one hand, assimilation offers the possibility of easing tensions with the majority culture and society, a sense of belonging in an otherwise hostile environment. But, on the other hand, it brings the risk of a community losing its distinct identity and its connection to ancestral traditions and cultural values. Differentiation facilitates the preservation of those traditions and communal traits, but also threatens to isolate the diaspora to a point of self-imposed ghettoization, leaving the community even more vulnerable. Of course, Muslims in China had already accommodated acculturative pressures for centuries. Even without the Ming dynasty's policies promoting accelerated assimilation by ethno-religious minorities, the Muslim adoption of Chinese language and material culture was inevitable; transplantation and entrenchment lead to naturalization. The crucial question is: How much assimilation is enough, and how much is too much?

The Muslim communities of Ming China faced a looming crisis. Without doubt, at extreme levels acculturation leads to attrition. There were Muslim individuals and families who lost, or let go, their Islamic identity. There are many well-known family lineages, especially in southeast China, whose ancestors were Muslims but eventually lapsed in their practice. The first things to go are often external markers of religiosity, such as traditional dress or facial hair, by which a minority is easily identifiable and may be stigmatized. Public expressions, including sharing Islamic greetings, going to the mosque or following dietary rules outside the home, follow. When these practices are abandoned publicly, it is usually not long before some individuals give them up in private as well. The wish not to stand out as being different from non-Muslim neighbours and associates often gives way to a lapse in devotion that is not easy to reinstate. Interestingly, the pork taboo is typically the last thing to go. Of course, it is not only a desire to blend in that motivates individuals to lapse in religiosity. Sometimes people have a genuine conversion of conscience. Living amongst followers of multiple traditions and faiths, such exposure may have attracted some to other religions. It is possible that so many Muslims, having been deeply immersed in Confucian thought through their early education, may have re-shaped their beliefs:

> As is true of any culturally hybrid community, Chinese Muslims did not merely use the language of the mainstream society without the values

and categories of that culture utterly penetrating their self-identity and worldview.⁷

In the case of Chinese Muslims, another major cause of attrition was the gradual loss of the ability to speak the languages of their ancestors. By the sixteenth century, many Muslim families would send their children to receive a classical Confucian education in order to prepare them to sit for the official examination, one of the surest means of advancing socially in Ming China. Most sinicized Muslims spoke Chinese as their mother tongue, and the better educated were proficient in literary Chinese. By contrast, proficiency in Arabic and Persian declined to the point where very few Muslims in China still used them apart from the modicum of Arabic necessary for daily prayers and other rituals. Children from more devout households would also attend schools at their local community mosques to learn enough Arabic to meet their personal and communal religious obligations. Some Muslims grew worried that the assimilation allowing their communities to survive might lead to the dissipation, possibly the complete loss, of Islamic knowledge and identity in China. Hu Dengzhou 胡登洲 (1522–97) of Xianyang 咸陽, Shaanxi, was one of these concerned Muslims who took active measures to turn back this alarming trend.

Hu came from an affluent family of merchants. He was schooled in Chinese, based on the Confucian classics, like his Han peers. Although he was groomed to follow in the family business, his parents tried to give him every advantage to succeed in mainstream Chinese society. Coming from a pious Muslim family, he was also expected to study in the school connected to his local mosque. There, the *ahong* would instruct him in the basics of Islamic doctrine and ritual practice and drill him to learn the Qur'ān and some Ḥadīth. In addition to rudimentary Arabic for reading and reciting, he probably learned some colloquial Persian. Having grown up in this way, Hu was typical of urban, middle-class Muslims in late Ming China. What was not typical, however, was his strong desire to go beyond the basic religious education he had received at the mosque school, and to delve deeper into the study of Islam, Arabic and Persian. A chance encounter on the road from Xi'an to Beijing with an Arab traveller, increasingly rare in those days, introduced him to more advanced topics in the traditional Islamic sciences – theology, law, philosophy – and a touch of the mystical teachings of Sufism. Having had a taste of the nectar, Hu was driven to seek out its source. He knew that he could not find what he was seeking in China anymore; that knowledge was mostly lost and access to it was blocked by the social and political climate of the times. If Muslim texts and teachers could not be found in his country, he would have to go directly to where they were. Foreign travel was not encouraged for ordinary subjects of the Ming Empire, nor was it an easy undertaking. Hu intrepidly retraced the steps of his early Muslim forebears in reverse, departing via the western frontier into Central Asia, stopping for a time in centres of learning like Bukhara and Samarkand. Along the way he received tutelage from scholars and Sufi masters and acquired oral teachings and books. He ultimately arrived in Mecca for the Hajj and stayed on for some years to study more. At last, he made his return voyage with his books in tow. Back home, aware more than ever of the paucity of Islamic learning in China, he decided to make the knowledge he had obtained available to others. To do so, however, would necessitate a radical overhaul of the existing mosque-based education system. Gathering some local students with similar academic interests, Hu began teaching locally. His methodology was adapted to provide a firm foundation in traditional Islamic studies in a way that was accessible to Chinese-speaking students.

This method came to be known as *jingtang jiaoyu* 經堂教育, literally 'scripture hall education', because it maintained the basic form of the old mosque school, but with a far more comprehensive curriculum based on that found in the religious schools, or *madāris* (sing. *madrasa*), of the Muslim world. Hu expanded the older curriculum to include newly introduced Arabic and Persian texts, the study of which would require intensive language training far beyond the level previously taught in the mosque schools. What was unique about Hu's innovative pedagogy was that the language of instruction was Chinese, since this was the common tongue of his students. Before they could master the Islamic languages, he assisted them by translating texts into Chinese. The more advanced students helped him in translating the large body of texts. These Chinese translations of Islamic books became the foundation of a literary canon of Chinese books about Islam that would come to be known by the hybrid name 'Han Kitab' (Han 漢 meaning Chinese, and *kitāb* the Arabic word for book).[8] The translation enterprise and curriculum production initiated a process of training teachers who could then go forth to other communities and train others in the new curriculum and pedagogy. Thus, Hu Dengzhou and his disciples created a network of schools, teachers, and students which proliferated at the end of the Ming period and flourished into the Qing dynasty.

In the seventeenth century, the declining Ming dynasty was invaded by Manchurians from the north. Despite decades of military and civilian resistance, the empire was eventually overrun and conquered. In 1644, the Manchus declared the new Qing dynasty. The invasion brought the social, political, economic and cultural upheaval associated with any military conquest. The Manchu invasion was a source of humiliation for the conquered populace, and the transition between the Ming and Qing dynasties created a period of grave uncertainty for them. These attendant issues of conquest were compounded by an ethnic element because the conquerors were foreigners. The Han population, especially the Confucian establishment, were left to ask themselves how such a debacle could have happened yet again:

> Their world turned upside down by foreign conquest, the Chinese majority also had major questions of identity to deal with, seeking a way to make sense of how they had become the servants of putatively culturally inferior invaders.[9]

And like the Mongols, the Manchus were alien conquerors hoping to establish hegemony and a sense of their own legitimacy as rulers over an ancient civilization and an internally diverse empire. The Manchu conquest occasioned a further development of ethnic and national identities, a process that had emerged in the Yuan dynasty, continued when the Ming dynasty attempted to restore and promote a distinctly Han Chinese national identity after ousting the Mongols, and now acquired new momentum under the Qing dynasty. Originating as a conquest regime, the new dynasty faced the obstacle of being accepted by a conquered population consisting of Han Chinese and others.

It is hardly a coincidence that during this period of re-examining and re-constructing group identities, Chinese Muslims, who had already undergone some dramatic transformations during the Ming period, also encountered a challenge *cum* opportunity to re-invent and project an identity that might create for themselves a secure place and air of acceptability in early Qing society. At the forefront of this effort were Chinese Muslim scholars, products of the Jingtang Jiaoyu educational system. Through their writings, the growing corpus of the Han Kitab, these scholars emerged as a powerful voice within the Muslim community, eloquently promoting arguments why Muslims belonged in China and why Islam was compatible with the dominant Confucian ideology and culture.

During this period, the Chinese Muslim scholars came to be referred to, by themselves and others, as Huiru 回儒. 'Hui' is of course the general term for Muslims that came into use in the Yuan dynasty. Because of how it was used in the Yuan–Ming period, Hui carried a somewhat pejorative connotation. *Ru* 儒 is a term of respect used to address and refer to Confucian literati, an elite class in imperial China. That the Jiangtang Jiaoyu/Han Kitab scholars had embraced, or reclaimed from ignominy, the term 'Hui' reflects a newfound confidence – the ability to take an insult and reform it into a badge of pride; the adoption of the honorific Ru reinforces that confidence. The Huiru thus became, on their own terms, the arbiters of a Chinese Muslim identity that was simultaneously Chinese and Muslim. Through their scholarship, their profound knowledge of both the Confucian and Islamic traditions, the Huiru helped bridge the gap between the polar assimilating and differentiating pressures faced by their community. In the middle space they occupied they found, or created, a state of 'simultaneity' to reconcile the duality of their hybrid identity and the stigma associated with it. Both the Qing regime and the Chinese Muslim community were involved in a parallel quest for legitimacy within the established socio-cultural categories of Chinese civilization. Thus, simultaneity represented a negotiation of identity among ethnic and religious minorities (Manchu, Hui, Mongolian, Tibetan etc.) throughout the empire.

With Jingtang Jiaoyu schools opening around central and eastern China, in cities as widespread as Xi'an, Ji'nan 濟南, Beijing, Yangzhou, Kaifeng and Nanjing, the number of students impacted by its teachings grew exponentially. The Han Kitab corpus, which had begun modestly as wholesale translations of Arabic and Persian texts into Chinese, later came to include Chinese commentaries on these translations and finally original Chinese treatises on Islamic topics among subsequent generations of Huiru. This new interpretation of Islam in a Confucian context reached its apogee in the writings of late Ming–early Qing Muslim literati, especially its most notable representatives, Wang Daiyu 王袋與 (c. 1570–c. 1660), Ma Zhu 馬注 (1640–1711), and Liu Zhi.

Wang Daiyu boasted that his ancestors were from Arabia[10] before arriving in China in the Yuan period. If Wang's autobiographical details can be trusted, he was descended from an appointee to the Directorate of Astronomy during the Hongwu reign, who resided in Jinlu 金錄 (present-day Nanjing). Wang's family had thus been established in Nanjing, where he was born and spent his youth, for approximately 200 years. He belonged to the sixth generation of the Jingtang school of Nanjing, where he received his early Islamic education.[11] Unlike many of his Muslim peers, he did not receive a classical Chinese education as a child. His Chinese was sufficient only for basic conversation and correspondence into his early twenties, when he resolved to improve his literary proficiency. Of his knowledge around the age of thirty, he lamented, 'I was so ashamed of my stupidity and smallness that I started to read books on metaphysics and history'.[12] Thus, Wang undertook the study of Confucianism, Buddhism and Daoism on his own.[13]

Wang's exposure to these other teachings began in earnest when he left Nanjing around the time of the Manchu invasion. He travelled to Beijing where he was sponsored by a wealthy Muslim who gave him a position as teacher in a local Jingtang school. In Beijing, Wang met and debated with representatives of various religious and philosophical schools of thought and continued this practice when he returned to Nanjing. The content of these conversations later informed his writings. As a resident of China's most cosmopolitan city inhabited by intellectuals of different persuasions, Wang's environment was abuzz with ideas and home to countless libraries and bookshops.

Wang did not publish until his forties. His first book, *Zhengjiao zhenquan* 正教真詮 (True Explanation of the Orthodox Teaching), dates to 1642. In the final twenty or so years of his life, Wang also produced two other major works, the *Qingzhen daxue* 清真大學 (Great Learning of Islam) and the *Xizhen zhengda* 希真正答 (Correct Answers of the Uncommon Truth). All of the titles of Wang's books contain the common character *zhen* 真, meaning 'true', or 'Truth'. By Wang's time, Chinese Muslims had already taken up the practice of translating Islam into Chinese as *Qingzhenjiao* 清真教, the 'Pure and True Religion'. His penname, Zhenhui Laoren 真回老人, 'True Muslim Old Man', incorporates *zhen* and *hui* as emblems of honour.

Throughout Wang's writings, he makes painstaking effort to discuss Islamic theological principles in familiar Confucian terms. One concept to which he devotes particular attention is that of the *Sanyi* 三一, or 'Three Unities'. According to Wang, Islam teaches three dimensions of oneness: *Zhenyi* 真一, the 'Unity of the Truth'; *Shuyi* 數一, the 'Unity of Multiplicity'; and *Tiyi* 體一, 'Embodied Unity'. In Islamic terms, this is none other than a discussion of the topic of *tawḥīd*, or *waḥdat*. *Zhenyi* corresponds to the theological notion of the absolute Oneness of Allah, the Ultimate Reality. *Shuyi* evokes the notion of *waḥdat al-wujūd*, the concept of the essential unity of all being, expounded by the Sufi philosophical school of Ibn al-'Arabī (1165–1240). *Tiyi* suggests the unity of humanity. Thus, Wang wrote about essential Islamic doctrines drawn from both the orthodox tradition of theology, called *'ilm al-tawḥīd* (Science of Oneness), and more mystical teachings.

These discourses were easily recognizable within the medieval Islamic context, but the language in which they were expressed is unmistakably Confucian. For example, Wang's discussion of *Shuyi* clearly demonstrates the long-standing Confucian comprehension of the essential unity of the macrocosm and microcosm. The Confucian tradition understood the origin of diverse beings (*wanwu* 萬物, lit. 'ten thousand things') to lie first in the dual principles of creation, *yin-yang* 陰陽, and ultimately in the Taiji 太極, the Supreme Ultimate, the source of all being. Confucianism also acknowledges *Tiyi*, the embodied oneness of humanity. This, Wang explains, is reflected in the Confucian social code and in the values of personal virtue, brotherly love, filial piety and loyalty to authority, all of which are shared with Islam.[14] What the Confucian view is missing, according to Wang, is the indispensable *Zhenyi*, faith in an absolutely monotheistic God. Thus, while he finds numerous parallels between the two traditions, Wang asserts the superiority of Islam, positing Confucianism as a tradition of incomplete truth.

Following in the footsteps of Wang Daiyu, Ma Zhu was the luminary of the next generation of Han Kitab authors. Ma was born in Baoshan 保山, Yunnan, to a devout Muslim family, descended from the Yuan dynasty military governor Sayyid Ajal. His father was a teacher of Confucian classics, who groomed his son to succeed in the civil examination, which he did by earning the degree of *Xiucai* 秀才. Ma never served as a government official, becoming a teacher like his father instead. In the 1660s he moved to Beijing, only then pursuing an education in Islamic studies in a Jingtang school at the capital. Like other Huiru, Ma was deeply worried about the state of Islamic knowledge among the Muslims of his day, and also feared that ignorance about Islam among non-Muslim Chinese would perpetuate and possibly worsen anti-Muslim bias. He therefore undertook to write a definitive text on Islam in Chinese to address both audiences. The product was the monumental tome, *Qingzhen zhinan* 清真指南 (Guide to Islam).

The work attempts to provide a comprehensive presentation and explanation of Islamic orthodoxy and orthopraxy in the literary Chinese idiom of Confucian scholarship. Ma expressed his motivation for writing as a fear that Chinese Muslims, under the influence of heterodox teachings and practices, and the impulse to assimilate, might become 'neither Confucian nor Muslim'.[15] Like any orthodox Confucian, Ma considered Buddhism and Daoism to be dangerous heresies, but as an orthodox Muslim he also objected strongly to some Sufi practices and teachings he considered to be innovations and corruptions of Islam. Even though his own writing was suffused with metaphysical principles coming from Sufi philosophical teachings, he could not abide what he considered the excesses of the Qadiriyya Sufi order, which had recently been established in Yunnan. Ma believed them to be a threat to both Confucian and Islamic norms and brought charges of heresy against them before a Qing civil court. As such, it is clear that he saw himself and those of his ilk as being simultaneously committed to the dual orthodoxies of Confucianism and Islam, which he regarded as completely congruous.

Although he was a defender of Confucian principles and values, like Wang Daiyu, Ma considered Confucianism to express only partial truth. He upheld the social teachings of its ideology, and even its metaphysical foundations, but believed that ultimate truth could only be found in Islam, because only faith in the one God could accurately account for the existence of phenomenal reality. Ma could agree with the idea that creation unfolded in a gradual, hierarchical process as explained by Neo-Confucian cosmogony, but before and presiding over that process is a wilful, conscious and personal creator – Allah.[16] By placing the Abrahamic monotheistic God atop and beyond the Confucian cosmic order, Ma honoured the dominant belief system of his native culture while affirming the supremacy of his ancestral religion.

The next generation produced the most prolific, and perhaps most prodigious, of the Han Kitab writers, Liu Zhi. Liu was from a literati family in Nanjing. His father, Liu Sanjie, was also a noted author and Jingtang Jiaoyu student and teacher. Liu Zhi's early education began under his father's tutelage. He next studied under Yuan Ruqi 袁汝契 – Qur'ān, Arabic and Persian. He learned to read and write classical Chinese and at age fifteen autodidactically began reading the Confucian canon for eight years. Systematically, he next turned his attention to reading Arabic and Persian texts for six years. He spent the next four years reading Buddhist and Daoist scriptures, and also read what he called 'Western books' (*xiyang shu* 西洋書) – probably Jesuit texts in Chinese. Liu's linguistic abilities and well-rounded knowledge were unmatched among the Huiru and other (non-Muslim) literati of his generation.

In his early thirties, Liu travelled around eastern and central China before returning to Nanjing where he spent the remainder of his life writing. Like previous Han Kitab writers, he invoked the classical Confucian tradition in order to explain Islamic teachings. But his works place Islam and Confucianism on an almost equal footing, treating both as originating from the same universal source of truth. Liu's writing, influenced by the *kaozheng* 考證 (evidentiary studies) movement within Qing Confucianism, was quite rigorous and meticulous in its citation of authentic sources. He therefore left behind detailed bibliographies of the texts he used, so we know that he was a keen student of Sufi philosophy besides more conventional Islamic books. Like Wang Daiyu, Liu frequently invoked mystical notions echoing Ibn alʿArabī's 'oneness of being' theory, at times even implying the metaphysical union of God and humanity, expressed in Neo-Confucian terms as the 'complete union of Heaven and man'. He justified this harmonization of Islamic and Chinese concepts by demonstrating how the Islamic prophets and ancient Chinese sages, and thus Muhammad and Confucius, taught the same fundamental truth.

Over three decades, Liu Zhi wrote dozens of books on a vast array of subjects: Arabic grammar and philology, history, geography, Islamic law, theology and philosophy. His most famous titles constitute a trilogy: *Tianfang xingli* (Metaphysics of Islam); *Tianfang dianli* (Norms and Rituals of Islam); and *Tianfang zhisheng shilu* (True Record of the Ultimate Sage of Islam), a biography of the Prophet Muhammad. He intended these three books to form an exposition of Islam in its totality. While his biography of the Prophet was the most popular title among Muslim readers of the Qing period and afterwards, *Tianfang dianli* has a unique status among all the Han Kitab for its inclusion in the *Siku quanshu* 四庫全書 (Compendium of the Four Treasuries), a compilation of the most important books in China commissioned by the Qianlong emperor (r. 1736–96). Liu Zhi became a cultural icon in the Chinese Muslim community and was recognized for his genteelness, erudition and eloquence by a number of non-Muslim Confucian contemporaries, thereby gaining a modicum of respect for Islam among the elite of Qing China.

The Han Kitab represent a Chinese Muslim intellectual flourishing in the seventeenth and eighteenth centuries, and the Huiru were its 'renaissance men'. They made great strides in projecting a positive image of Islam, both within their own highly assimilated community and among some Confucian elites. They even made a positive impression on the Qing court, as some of their works were presented and received by various emperors. Yet, in spite of these successes, there were still those in various regions of China, including local officials, who harboured hostility against Muslims. Consequently, 'the Qing period also gave rise to various other expressions of Islam and Muslim identity that were markedly less congenial to the prevailing Chinese social and political order'[17] than the harmonizing and conciliatory articulation of the Han Kitab. The dynasty witnessed not only concord with Muslims, but also conflict in the form of armed resistance.

The first such instance occurred from 1646 to 1648, during the reign of the first Qing emperor, Shunzhi 順治 (r. 1644–61). A rebellion in Gansu province, led by a Muslim Ming loyalist named Milayin 米喇印, threatened the empire's territorial integrity. In this case, Muslim rebels were joined by Han Chinese, Tibetans and Uyghurs in their resistance to the new dynasty. Nevertheless, the next Qing ruler, the Kangxi emperor (r. 1662–1722), understood that the majority of Chinese Muslims were loyal subjects; he resisted the urge to punish all Muslims because of the actions of a few. Rather, he took a more nuanced approach, making a distinction between 'obedient' and 'disobedient' Muslims. He expressed the same attitude towards all potential dissidents: 'They are our children – but they had better obey the law!'[18] Overall, Kangxi's policies towards the disparate Muslims in his realm alternated between paternalistic solicitude and cautious circumspection.

For their part, Chinese Muslims in eastern and central China for the most part exhibited model obedience. They knew well the risks of antagonizing the government and toed the political line appropriately. Moreover, they had no scruples about showing loyalty to the non-Muslim regime, provided the ruler dealt with them justly and permitted them to fulfil their religious duties. The Han Kitab writers, as the collective voice of a conservative, stable Chinese Muslim population, were also politically sensitive. They not only shied away from controversies that could offend the throne but actively sought to gain imperial favour for themselves and the community they represented. Their intent was to promote the legitimacy and acceptability of Islam. Simultaneously committed to the principles of Confucianism and Islam, the Huiru and their constituency affirmed that an integral part of one's religious duties is obedience to the ruler.

As if to respond to this communal submission to imperial authority, the Kangxi emperor issued an edict concerning Muslims that is prominently displayed at the Niujie (Ox Street) mosque (Niujie Qingzhensi 牛街清真寺) in Beijing. In it he proclaimed:

> The Han are not as good as the Hui. Let this be known in every province: If any officials or common people, due to a petty grudge, use some pretext falsely to accuse the Muslim religion of plotting a rebellion, the official in charge will execute them first and report to me afterwards. Throughout the realm, the Hui people abide by the principles of Purity and Truth, nor would they disobey a command or betray our kind intentions and appreciation of the significance of the Way. Respect this and comply.[19]

In 1781, Kangxi's grandson, the Qianlong emperor (r. 1736–96), issued a similar edict but drew a sharp distinction between Muslims of eastern and central China and those in the west and northwest, describing the former as 'being really no different from the native [Han] inhabitants. There are good and bad among them.'[20] A year later, another edict warned, 'If there is excessive inquisition and interference, then law abiding Hui people will be deprived of peace of mind [leading to] immense trouble.'[21]

The Qing regime's worries about Muslim instability in the northwest were exacerbated by its territorial expansion. The Kangxi emperor had initiated the invasion of present-day Xinjiang and Tibet. The conquest of Xinjiang (lit. 'new frontier') was completed under the Qianlong emperor in the mid-eighteenth century.[22] In annexing Central Asian territory, the empire encompassed large Muslim populations, particularly the Uyghurs, most of whom had been converted to Islam between the tenth and fifteenth centuries. Qing conquest of the region created the conditions for ethnic, religious, social, economic and political strife, leading to conflict amongst local peoples and against the state. By the mid-eighteenth century, much of Xinjiang was embroiled in rebellions by various Uyghur groups, leaving the Qing state no option 'but to impose an ongoing military occupation, which left the regime ill-prepared to deal with a rash of rebellions across China, throughout the late 18th and 19th centuries'.[23] The Uyghurs, however, were not the only Muslims to rise up against the Qing government. Chinese-speaking (Hui) Muslims in northwest China also rebelled, for example, in Gansu in the 1780s. Like many rebellions, this one started as a regional dispute between rival Sufi communities.

Sufi orders had begun entering the northwest in the late seventeenth to early eighteenth century from Central Asia, and targeted local Chinese-speaking Muslim communities for proselytization. The first pioneer of the Naqshbandi Sufi order was a saint called Afāq Khoja, who came to Xining 西寧 (present-day Qinghai province), where he taught and gained a reputation for working miracles. As a spiritual guide (Ar. *murshid*), he initiated two local Muslims who became his disciples (Ar. *murīd*), Ma Shouzhen 馬守貞 (b. 1633) and Ma Tai Baba 馬太爸爸 (dates unknown). The latter became a teacher, establishing a school in Hezhou 河州 (present-day Linxia 臨夏), where he became *murshid* to his own *murīd*, Ma Laichi (1673–1753), who in turn became a teacher.

Ma Laichi travelled to Mecca in 1728 to perform the pilgrimage. After returning to Hezhou, he opened his own mosque and madrasa for the transmission of Naqshbandi teachings: 'He emphasized veneration of saints, visitation and prayer at their tombs (Ch. *gongbei* 拱北, Ar. *qubba*), and, most notably, a silent form of *dhikr*, the ritual remembrance and invocation of the names of Allah.'[24] He attracted many followers and established a community based on the Naqshbandi order. His *menhuan* 門宦 (lineage, Ar. *silsila*) was passed through his descendants and became wealthy off of donations by the faithful.

In the next generation, another Muslim from Gansu named Ma Mingxin 馬明心 (1719–81), also went to Mecca for the Hajj in 1745, remaining in Arabia for sixteen years under the tutelage of the Naqshbandi *murshid* ʿAbd al-Khāliq. This master taught a more ecstatic, vocalized form of *dhikr*. When Ma Mingxin returned to China, he began to teach mystical practices that 'downplayed saint veneration, and opposed the construction of elaborate mosques or tombs, as well as the accumulation of wealth by religious teacher from donations'.[25] Because they practised a form of *dhikr* chanted out loud, Ma Mingxin's Naqshbandi sub-order came to be known as the Jahriyya ('aloud').

Ma Mingxin's group soon began to clash with the older *menhuan* established by Ma Laichi, which was known as the Khafiyya ('silent'). The two sub-orders vied for followers and territory. The Khafiyya proclaimed themselves the 'Old Teaching' (*Laojiao* 老教) and belittled the Jahriyya as the 'New Teaching' (*Xinjiao* 新教), whom they portrayed as a heretical sect. Relations between the rival communities became increasingly hostile, prompting local government to intervene. Khafiyya accusations of heresy proved influential on the local officials who took sides against the Jahriyya. Facing government suppression, the Jahriyya community erupted in violence against the Khafiyya and rebelled against the imperial authorities in 1781 and 1783 leading to yet another Qing military crackdown in Gansu.

The nineteenth century saw a wave of anti-Qing rebellions across China. Most of these were led by Han Chinese commoners with an array of grievances against the regime. During the first half of the century, the country was hit hard by a natural disaster, a failing economy and the encroachment of Western imperialism. Law and order broke down as peasants fled the countryside due to onerous taxation, crime plagued towns and cities and petty warlords took control of entire areas of the empire. Numerous secret societies, criminal organizations and revolutionary movements arose, blaming the Manchu regime for the woeful situation and turning to violence in order to advance their combined economic, nationalist and religious causes. Perhaps the most famous of the mid-century rebellions was that of the Taiping Heavenly Kingdom Movement (Taiping Tianguo Yundong 太平天國運動), a syncretic millenarian sect, whose leader, Hong Xiuquan 洪秀全 (1814–64), claimed to be the brother of Jesus Christ and promised a complete renewal of the world order after the overthrow of the Qing dynasty. The bloody conflict lasted fourteen years (1850–64), with battles waged in nearly every corner of China, and took tens of millions of lives.

Oddly, the one province untouched by Taiping-related warfare was Gansu but this did not mean the northwest was spared from rebellion. At the tail-end of the Taiping era in 1862, Gansu once again erupted in Muslim sectarian conflict. The ongoing feud between the Jahriyya and Khafiyya Naqshbandi sub-orders once again escalated into violence that spilled over beyond the Sufi communities. As before, the Jahriyya, led by their fifth-generation *shaykh* (master of the Sufi order) Ma Hualong 馬化龍 (d. 1871), initiated violence against the Khafiyya. Fighting went on for fifteen years (1862–77) drawing in various Muslim and non-Muslim factions and destabilizing the region. When the situation reached a crisis-point, Qing troops under the command of the famous general Zuo Zongtang 左宗棠 (1812–85), who had also helped defeat the Taiping, came to Gansu. With the assistance of Khafiyya fighters, the army put down the First Dungan[26] Revolt (Donggan Bian 東干變), so called because a Second Dungan Revolt occurred from 1895 to 1896, also sparked by Sufi infighting that drew in other Muslim groups and was eventually defeated by pro-Qing Muslim forces.

Around the same time as the First Dungan Revolt, the so-called Panthay[27] Rebellion (1856–73) in far-off Yunnan destabilized the empire's southwest frontier region. The revolt was originally triggered by Hui residents aggrieved over discriminatory practices by local Qing officials in Yunnan. After rebel forces attacked the provincial capital of Kunming 昆明 in 1856, the Manchu official charged with suppressing the uprising responded by massacring the local Muslim community. Outrage over the massacre incited riots across Yunnan. A rebel leader (from a Han family that had converted to Islam) named Du Wenxiu 杜文秀 (1823–72) captured Dali 大理 and declared himself 'Qā'id Jami' al-Muslimīn' ('Commander of the Muslim Collective'), establishing an independent sultanate opposed to Qing rule. Though the rebel leadership was Muslim, fighters of other ethnic groups, including Han and various tribal minorities, joined Du in his struggle against the regime. The conflict persisted for seventeen years before imperial forces finally vanquished the rebels.

During the early years of the revolt, a Yunnanese Muslim scholar called Ma Dexin 馬德新 (1794–1874), a twenty-fifth-generation descendant of Sayyid Ajal, had recently returned from the Hajj and a journey through the Muslim heartlands. When conflict broke out, Ma's first reaction was to come to the aid of the rebels in a show of Muslim unity. He fought against the Qing forces for a few years but became increasingly disillusioned by Du Wenxiu and his tactics. In time, Ma lost the heart to fight and resolved to try to broker peace between the rebels and the government. Ma was a student of the Han Kitab, and like the earlier Huiru he bore a simultaneous allegiance to Confucianism and Islam. He invoked the notion that Islam is fundamentally compatible with Confucianism, and therefore Muslims should be able to live harmoniously with their non-Muslim compatriots under the Qing state. But his argument fell on deaf ears, as the government still considered him a traitor. He was executed in 1874.

Ma embodied the duality of conflict concord with the Qing social order, and his story demonstrates an underlying precariousness of Chinese Muslim simultaneity. His valiant attempt to restore peace after years of conflict was overwhelmed by the prevalent anti-Muslim bias among many in the Qing government. This, of course, was nothing new in imperial Chinese history. Despite the best efforts of Chinese Muslim literati to make an intellectual case for peaceful co-existence of Muslims and non-Muslims, centuries-old prejudice endured. In fact, most Muslims in Qing China were law-abiding, loyal subjects of the regime. Those living in the eastern and central provinces took no part in the revolts that plagued the empire's peripheral regions. They were largely unaffected by the tumult and suffered no reprisals from the central government.

The various Muslim uprisings of the eighteenth and nineteenth centuries were by no means a concerted Muslim insurgency against the Qing dynasty. Most of the disputes at the heart of the rebellions were relatively minor local affairs. Moreover, Muslims frequently sided with the authorities against other Muslims, or fought alongside non-Muslims against the government. We must not imagine a unified Islamic front against the regime. Nor were the rebellions in any real sense religious wars, as most were based on economic and civil issues. The rebels had no 'plan to seize territory or set up an antistate or proclaim a *jihad*'.[28] Such ideas exceed the purview of a minority that knows its survival depends on maintaining good relations and a peaceful, positive image. And this image was not difficult to conjure for 'virtually all of the … Sino-Muslims … shared a strong sense of *belonging* in China and of the Qing state's legitimacy'.[29] Thus, while it is true that the Muslim revolts in the late Qing period weakened the regime and played a significant role in the fall of China's last imperial dynasty (alongside myriad factors including other rebellions, corruption, bankruptcy and incursions by foreign powers), Muslims would also play a major role in building a new China in its aftermath.

Chapter 5
Muslim nation-building in post-imperial China

As a child in Gansu, Ma Fuxiang studied the Qur'ān and Confucian classics, and had a love of calligraphy. But as an adolescent he traded his ink brush for a sword, attending military academy. He joined the Qing army and quickly rose up the ranks. By age twenty, he was given his first command: a Muslim unit sent to fight Muslim rebels. Notorious for his ruthlessness, he gifted the heads of his enemies to his officers. When the Qing fell, he pledged his allegiance to the new Republic. But during the chaos of the 1910s, he became a warlord, ruling the Muslims of the Northwest. He was a reformer and moderniser and when the Nationalist Party came to power, he served in several important government posts. He was a patron of education, a scholar-soldier, who strongly encouraged Muslim assimilation within the new nation.

Coming from a lineage of imams in Tianjin, Wang Jingzhai was groomed by his father for religious scholarship. He too studied Islam and Confucianism. By his mid-twenties he was recognised as a promising young imam and served congregations in several north-eastern mosques. Enthralled by the current of pan-Islamic revivalism flowing into China, he devoted himself to global Muslim unity and the success of Chinese Muslims through educational reform. As China opened to the world, Wang began to travel. He performed the pilgrimage to Mecca and then, amidst the domes and minarets of Cairo, he perfected his Arabic as he attended the revered university, Al-Azhar. When he returned home, he produced the first Muslim translation of the Qur'ān into Chinese. He also established several Islamic periodicals advocating Muslims' full participation in building the nation. For Wang there was no contradiction between nationalism and religious devotion, a sentiment echoed in the slogan: 'Love the country, love the religion'.

Ma and Wang were born within three years of each other early in the reign of Guangxu (1875–1908), at opposite ends of China. One a soldier, the other an imam, the two men lived parallel lives of disparate experience. Yet, the end of the empire and the dawning of a new national destiny brought them to a common purpose – ushering China's Muslims into a new chapter of history.

In the consistent pattern of cataclysm at the end of any imperial dynasty in China, each of these historical transitions has brought social, political and cultural upheaval. Yet, perhaps none caused the uncertainty accompanying the fall of the Qing dynasty because with it collapsed the entire imperial order. Those who lived through it could not rely upon the ancient guarantee that someone worthy would receive the Mandate of Heaven to rule, for the very mode of transmitting the mantle was eradicated. We have also seen how Muslim individuals and communities have suffered in the lead-up to dynastic collapse, while some seized the opportunity embedded in the crisis. The end of the last imperial dynasty and the founding of a new nation state upon its ashes provided a unique opportunity for all Chinese people, including the country's Muslims, to write history and take upon themselves significant roles in an entirely new scenario.

In the latter years of the Qing dynasty, the opening of China to Western influence and the devastation of many Muslim communities due to violent unrest created a window of opportunity for some Chinese Muslims to leave their homeland in search of knowledge and security. The ideas that they brought back with them from visits to the Muslim world had a profound impact on the re-shaping of Muslim identity at the dawn of the new century. At the same time, on the home front, many Muslims battled, literally and figuratively, to preserve the integrity of their territories and communities. Through their service, and with the power they gained, they also did their share to secure a place for Muslims in a rapidly changing China.

Two categories of Muslims of the late nineteenth to early twentieth century stand out for their achievements: scholars and soldiers. In the first half of the Qing dynasty, the Huiru emerged as eloquent expressors of Chinese Muslim simultaneity. Their intellectual and literary harmonization of Islam and Confucianism helped make Muslims acceptable in late imperial China. Their movement reached its heyday in the eighteenth century, however. Afterwards, like so many other institutions in Qing China, their educational and scholarly network showed signs of decline. The educated Muslim community did not produce luminaries like Wang Daiyu, Ma Zhu or Liu Zhi in the nineteenth century, with the possible exception of Ma Dexin. But even the talented Ma did not live up to his potential; he took part in the Panthay Rebellion, which cost him his life. In his dual role as Muslim fighter and would-be peacemaker, Ma could have been a transformative figure of nineteenth-century Chinese Islamic culture and politics, but instead he was branded a traitor by the Qing government. Before his untimely execution, however, Ma Dexin's journey to the West 'set the pattern for the next few decades for early connections with the Middle Eastern centers of learning – most notably Al-Azhar'.[1] In the years after the fall of the Qing, this precedent would be imitated by a number of young Chinese Muslim students whose experience overseas would have a tremendous impact on the position of Muslims in the new, post-1911 Chinese Republic, and the nation-building enterprise as a whole.

The other area in which Muslims excelled in both the late Qing and early Republican eras was military service. Although some historians focus on Muslims' part in the rebellions that plagued the northwest and southwest of the empire, this perspective fails to acknowledge that far more Muslims fought *for* the Qing regime than against it. And to infer from the uprisings that Muslims were more prone to revolt than other groups is to ignore the fact that many other, larger rebellions set China ablaze in the nineteenth century, and most of their participants were Han Chinese. Moreover, we will recall that in the Panthay and the two Dungan revolts Muslims were found fighting on both sides of the conflict. Some prominent Muslim leaders even defected from the rebel side to become Qing loyalists. For example, as mentioned above, Ma Dexin broke away from Du Wenxiu's rebellion in an (ultimately unsuccessful) attempt to broker a peace with the government.

In Gansu, the rebel general Ma Qianling 馬千齡 (1826–1910) defected from the rebels to the Qing army and was instrumental in quashing the rebellion. His son, Ma Fuxiang 馬福祥 (1876–1932), followed directly in his footsteps. Born during the First Dungan Revolt in Gansu, Ma Fuxiang was schooled in Islamic scriptures and Confucian classics. At age thirteen, however, he moved on to martial arts training. Fresh out of military school, in his teenage years he joined the imperial armed forces. A veteran of the First Sino-Japanese War (1894–5), he was soon given command of an all-Muslim unit known as the Gansu Braves (Ganjun 甘軍).

His first mission was to suppress the Muslim rebels of the Second Dungan Revolt, which he did with cold-blooded efficiency. After going back to school to pursue an advanced military degree, upon successfully passing the exam, he was quickly promoted to Brigadier General. In 1900, the Gansu Braves were dispatched to Beijing in the heat of the Boxer Rebellion (1899–1901), charged with holding the Eight-Nation Alliance forces at bay while the imperial family escaped the capital. In 1911, as rebellions swept across much of the empire, Ma led more than twenty Muslim battalions to Shaanxi province, where Muslim rebels had joined a larger anti-Qing uprising. Proving his loyalty to the regime, he once again showed no compunction about killing his co-religionists to accomplish his objectives in a decisive victory. Ma served the dynasty to the bitter end, but as soon as Qing rule officially ended, he and many Muslim officers were quick to ally themselves with the newly installed provisional government of the Zhonghua Minguo 中華民國, or Republic of China (ROC), under the leadership of the Nationalist Party, the Guomindang 國民黨 (GMD).[2]

While history records the establishment of the ROC on a precise date, 1 January 1912, the fall of the Qing dynasty was actually a painfully protracted process culminating in an abrupt end. With so many regional and nationwide rebellions, as well as ongoing incursions by multinational imperialist forces, the collapse was inevitable. As these factors aggregated and reached a critical mass in the year 1911 (called *xinhai* 辛亥 according to the traditional sixty-year cyclical Chinese calendar), the cluster of events leading to the demise of the Qing has come to be known as the Xinhai Revolution. It is difficult to find a single unifying purpose among the many factions involved in the various revolts around the country, apart from the wish to bring down the dynasty. Almost all agreed that the sociopolitical and economic condition of China was dire and sought some means of improving it, but there was hardly widespread agreement as to how. Some were driven by anti-Manchu sentiment. Others, fuelled by a rising sense of Han nationalism, sought to restore indigenous Chinese rule while maintaining the imperium. Some wished to do away with autocratic monarchy altogether and replace it with a more 'modern' form of constitutional government. Conflating the causes of nationalism, unifying a fragmented China, modernization, improving the economic life of the masses and introducing some democratic elements to the Chinese state, the faction in favour of establishing a republic came to dominate the political arena.

In 1911, as the many rebellions and disturbances of the Xinhai Revolution were raging across the country, the imperial family and others in the Qing court could clearly see that the days of the regime were numbered. Rather than wait for rebel mobs to storm the Forbidden City, they negotiated a settlement with the well-organized Republican faction based in south China to allow for the peaceful transfer of power. The sides agreed that in exchange for the abdication of the six-year-old Xuantong emperor (r. 1908–16), Pu Yi 溥儀 (1904–67), the Qing loyalist general, Yuan Shikai 袁世凱 (1859–1916), would in due course become president of the provisional government of the Republic, replacing the revolutionary leader Sun Yat-sen 孫逸仙 (1866–1925), who was serving de facto as the Provisional President in Nanjing since the beginning of 1912. The imperial family and Sun agreed to these terms. The abdication became official on 12 February 1912, without the child-emperor's knowledge that it had even happened.

As soon as the reins of government were turned over by the Qing authorities to the new republic, most Qing military officers, loyal to the end, accepted the new political order and swore allegiance to the ROC. Among them, many Chinese Muslims officers, favouring a quick restoration of law and order, immediately became defenders of the new government. But the relatively peaceful situation that accompanied the establishment of the provisional government was short-lived. The terms of agreement between the Qing court and the Republicans to have Yuan Shikai become president soon became a point of contention. While Sun Yat-sen had agreed to step down in favour of Yuan, he was concerned about Yuan's ambitions. As commander-in-chief of his own army in and around Beijing, Yuan controlled a staggering number of forces and heavy firepower. Sun feared that if he wanted to, Yuan could easily use this advantage to become a dictator. Therefore, Sun and his circle in the south demanded that Nanjing be made the capital of the ROC, so that Yuan would have to leave Beijing without his army. Yuan refused and the forces loyal to him, the Beiyang Army (Beiyangjun 北洋軍), supported his claim to Beijing as the capital. Eventually, a schism developed between the two rival factions of the ROC – Yuan's de facto Beiyang government 北洋政府 (1912–28) of the ROC in the north and Sun's shadow government movement in the south.

The country was split between opposing ruling philosophies and strategies. Sun harboured ideals of Western-style liberalism, nationalism, socialism and modernism. Aspiring to the maximum inclusion and participation of all the country's citizens, Sun's republic would be multi-ethnic, secular and founded on religious tolerance. Sun recognized maintaining the unity of a diverse populace and integrity of the territory bequeathed by the Qing Empire as crucial to the survival of the Republic. Separatist motives or thoughts of independence among non-Han Chinese groups threatened this fragile unity. Therefore, Sun conceived an innovative new identity for China's population. Rather than subjects of a multicultural empire, he urged them to see themselves as diverse members of a single nation, Zhonghua Minzu 中華民族, the 'Chinese Nation'.[3] According to Sun's theory, Zhonghua Minzu was one body with five constituent parts: Han, Manchurian, Mongolian, Tibetan and Muslim. Of course, China is home to many other ethnic groups, but these five represented the majority of the population and, more importantly, statistical majorities in large territories (Mongolia, Tibet, the northeast, the northwest and Xinjiang), which the Republic could not afford to let go. So, the ideal of the Chinese Nation was also a strategic reality. Sun's vision depended on all ethnicities to buy into it, but he specifically highlighted the place of China's Muslims because they were not only concentrated in key regions (e.g. the northwest, the southwest and Xinjiang) but also because they were dispersed throughout the rest of the country. Interestingly, Sun did not distinguish between Chinese-speaking Muslims (Hui) and other Muslim peoples such as the Uyghurs. Apparently, he wished all Muslims to be unified as part of the nation and probably hoped the more assimilated Hui could help bring the Uyghurs and others on board. Thus, in a speech at the beginning of the Republic he stated:

> In all, without the participation of the Muslim nationality (*huizu*), the Chinese national movement will not achieve its final success; without the union of all the world's Muslims (*huizu zhi zhengge jiehe*), the work of eliminating [global] imperialism cannot be completed.[4]

He clearly recognized the unique religio-cultural interests of Muslims as part of a global Ummah but wished that this loyalty could be harmonized with and harnessed for the sake of Chinese national interests.

Whereas Sun's ideology was conciliatory, Yuan Shikai's rule was autocratic and militant; he had no patience for opposing points of view. He conspired with old enemies, Japan and the West, in order to consolidate his hold on north China. Ideologically, he promoted Han chauvinism, seeking to eliminate all traces of Manchu culture and ignoring the interests of other ethnic groups. The GMD's worst fears about Yuan's narcissistic ambition were realized in 1915 when he shed the title of President and declared himself Hongxian Emperor 洪憲 (r. 1915–16) of the new Empire of China. This self-aggrandizement had devastating consequences when not only Republicans opposed him, but many of the ROC's high-ranking military officers also withdrew their support. In an era when national unity was most tenuous, Yuan's imperial aspirations wrecked what little cohesion existed. Regional generals and military governors who no longer held themselves answerable to any centralized authority began to exercise localized autocratic power, ushering in what has come to be known as the Warlord Era (Junfa Shidai 軍閥時代, 1916–28). Various Beiyang generals and their forces broke away from the government to form military cliques based on family bonds and professional alliances. Other regional factions similarly formed their own cliques across China. The strongmen heading these cliques were the warlords, who wielded real power in the fractured Republic.

Most warlords were Han Chinese, reflecting the ethnic majority of the entire country. In regions of high minority populations, warlords of other ethnicities arose. The traditional Chinese Muslim strongholds of the northwest – Gansu, Ningxia and Qinghai – were controlled by Muslim warlords of the so-called 'Ma Clique' (Majia Junfa 馬家軍閥). The clique was made up of several families with the surname Ma (the most common family name among Chinese-speaking Muslims), who were interconnected by history and related by kinship and marriage. Their roots were in the Qing military, under the command of the (non-Muslim) general Dong Fuxiang 董福祥 (1839–1908) in the Muslim unit called the Gansu Braves. Among this group were such prominent officers as Ma Haiyan 馬海晏 (1837–1900), Ma Qianling (the father of Ma Fuxiang),[5] and Ma Zhan'ao 馬占鰲 (1830–86), all born into the Khafiyya Naqshbandi Sufi sub-order and all anti-Qing rebels before defecting during the First Dungan Revolt. After switching sides, they helped to suppress the revolt and became Qing loyalists, as were their descendants.

Ma Zhan'ao's son, Ma Anliang 馬安良 (1855–1918), made a name for himself serving under the command of General Zuo Zongtang in the defeat of the Turkic Muslim rebel leader Yaʿqūb Beg (1820–77) in Xinjiang. Later he was part of the Gansu Brave unit who fought in the First Sino-Japanese War, before being called to quash the First Dungan Revolt. During the Boxer Rebellion, he was, along with Ma Fuxiang, among the unit that fought foreign coalition forces in Beijing. In 1903, he was promoted to Brigadier General. Ma Anliang never showed any scruples about fighting against Muslim factions who rebelled against the Qing regime or disrupted law and order in the territory under his charge. Thus, in 1905 he opposed the Yihewani 伊赫瓦尼 (Ar. Ikhwān, 'Brotherhood')[6] sect and attempted to capture its founder, Ma Wanfu 馬萬福 (1849–1934).

Although Ma Anliang had been one of the Muslim generals who quickly pledged his allegiance to the Republic upon the abdication of the last Qing emperor, he sided with Yuan Shikai's Beiyang government and their pro-monarchist ideology. Politically, he has been characterized as conservative, or even reactionary. For this reason, he opposed another new Islamic sect, the Xidaotang 西道堂 ('Hall of the Western Way'), founded in Gansu by Ma Qixi 馬啟西 (1857–1914) in 1901. The Xidaotang's ideology was one of Chinese Muslim simultaneity and Islamic-Confucian harmonization, highly influenced by the Huiru and Han Kitab.[7] He mistrusted the sect's leader and its lack of support of the Beiyang government in favour of the GMD Republicans. Already the de facto leader of Muslims in northwest China, in 1912 Ma Anliang was rewarded by Yuan Shikai for his loyalty, being recognized as Commander-in-Chief of Gansu province until his death in 1918, after which his subordinate Ma Fuxiang succeeded him as Muslim leader of the northwest.

After joining the GMD, Ma Fuxiang became increasingly powerful as a regional warlord. He was named governor of Ningxia by Yuan Shikai and during the late 1910s–early 1920s he achieved numerous victories over bandits and rebels to consolidate and extend his power. He also increased his reputation as a strongman, sometimes employing brutal methods. He invested in several local industries, amassing considerable wealth in the process. But he used his wealth and power to bring development to his territory, building infrastructure and educational facilities.

Sun Yat-sen recognized Ma Fuxiang's efficient management of affairs in his jurisdiction and Ma reciprocated by supporting Sun's leadership push in the mid-1920s. He joined the National Revolutionary Army (NRA) in its Northern Expedition (1926–8), led by General Chiang Kai-shek 蔣介石 (1887–1975) to oust the Beiyang government and re-unify the country under GMD rule. Thereafter, he pledged his allegiance to Chiang, becoming the first Muslim warlord to look beyond mere regional interests and become deeply involved in politics on a national level. As a result, Ma Fuxiang advanced within the GMD. He was appointed governor of Anhui province in 1930, far from his home base in the northwest. In time, he was appointed to the GMD's Central Executive Committee.

Throughout his military and political career, however, he never forgot his ethno-religious roots. He used his influence to benefit Chinese Muslims so that they would reach a more even socio-economic footing with their Han Chinese compatriots. He knew that education was key to improving their condition, so he sponsored schools and patronized students and teachers, and paid for the publication of books.[8] He wished Chinese Muslim education to combine the best of modern, Western science and technology, the social ideals of Confucianism and the moral tenets of Islam. By integrating these elements into the curriculum, he hoped to produce a highly assimilated, progressive Chinese Muslim community.

Ma Qi 馬麒 (1869–1931), son of Ma Haiyan, was a contemporary and comrade of Ma Anliang and Ma Fuxiang. The three of them served side by side as part of the Gansu Braves against the Second Dungan Revolt and during the Boxer Rebellion. Like Ma Anliang and Ma Fuxiang, Ma Qi was also a Qing loyalist who quickly submitted to the Republic upon its establishment, thereupon supporting Yuan Shikai even when he declared himself emperor. Despite their close relationship, when his superior Ma Anliang tried to arrest the Yihewani leader Ma Wanfu in 1905, Ma Qi disobeyed a direct order and helped Ma Wanfu escape to Qinghai. He was already the de facto leader of Muslims in Qinghai, which he ruled with a heavy hand. His base of power was in Xining, and he commanded his own militia, the Ninghai Army (Ninghaijun 寧海軍). As the regional warlord of Qinghai, he stamped out Tibetan rioting there in 1918, but this only exacerbated local tensions between Tibetans and Chinese Muslims, which continued for another decade. In recognition of his service to the Republic, the Beiyang government officially made him governor of Qinghai, whereupon his Ninghai forces were subsumed under the NRA.

Ma Fuxiang's son Ma Hongkui 馬鴻逵 (1892–1970) inherited his father's army, his position and his leadership style. Following in the family tradition, he attended military academy and soon after graduating in 1909 became a commander in the Ningxia Army. In the mid-1920s he folded his forces into the Guominjun 國民軍, or 'National People's Army', commanded by General Feng Yuxiang 馮玉祥 (1882–1948), a Chinese convert to Christianity.

After the death of Sun Yat-sen, when Chiang Kai-shek assumed control of the GMD, Feng Yuxiang and Ma Fuxiang supported his Northern Expedition to consolidate power and attempt to re-unify the country. Ma became a devoted ally of Chiang and was rewarded by being appointed governor of Ningxia in 1932. Reminiscent of, or perhaps surpassing, his father's brutality, Ma Hongkui was known for his ill temper towards those who crossed him. He was merciless to his enemies, and his reputation discouraged corruption within his jurisdiction. But he could be quite solicitous of the common people of his province. He used his position to enrich himself, but also used his wealth to support education and cultural institutions.

The Northern Expedition had revealed a growing rift within the GMD between the left and right wings of the party. The Nationalists backing Chiang grew increasingly suspicious of the communist faction, who seceded from the GMD. The subsequent growth of the fledgling Chinese Communist Party (CCP)[9] precipitated the outbreak of the Chinese Civil War (1927–37, 1945–9). Loyal to Chiang and staunchly anti-Communist, Ma Hongkui fully backed the Nationalist cause, rooting out and killing Communists in Ningxia during the Civil War. The Communists retaliated by spreading propaganda that Ma was dealing secretly with Japanese agents against Chinese interests. One rumour claimed that the Japanese government offered Ma his own Muslim state in northwest China in exchange for his defection to their side, which he summarily refused. In fact, after Japanese invasion sparked the Second Sino-Japanese War (1937–45), Ma Hongkui became a prolific transmitter of anti-Japanese propaganda, especially among his fellow Muslims. Ma's army successfully fought off the Japanese during the Winter Offensive of 1939, saving Gansu from invasion.

After Japan's defeat in the Second World War, the Nationalists and Communists, who had put their differences aside in order to present a united front for the resistance, immediately resumed their civil war. Ma Hongkui was a steadfast Nationalist supporter and was successful in several campaigns against the Communist People's Liberation Army (PLA), or Jiefangjun 解放軍, in the northwest. However, the PLA was steadily scoring victories all across the country. Ma Fuxiang met with Chiang Kai-shek to attempt to strategize a Nationalist counter-offensive, but the plan never took flight. His own cousins, Ma Hongbin 馬鴻賓 (1884–1960) and Ma Dunjing 馬惇靖 (1906–72), having been given assurances of protection by the PLA, defected to the Communist side. Reading the proverbial writing on the wall, Ma decided to flee China. In 1949, he left for Taiwan but he was not well-received by the GMD officials in exile on the island, who blamed him for not resisting the PLA strongly enough in the northwest. He therefore left Taiwan and emigrated to the United States. He settled in California, where he spent the remainder of his life. Despite his fall from grace, Ma Hongkui remained loyal to the GMD and Chiang Kai-shek and advocated for the Nationalist cause in the United States.

Ma Qi's son, Ma Bufang 馬步芳 (1903–75), was schooled in Islamic studies in his youth, whereas his elder brother Ma Buqing 馬步青 (1901–77) received a classical Chinese education. This is because Ma Qi groomed his older son for a military career but wished Ma Bufang to become an imam. Despite these well-laid plans, no doubt due to the exigencies of the age, both brothers grew up to be soldiers.

Ma Bufang first made his reputation as a commander of the GMD forces that fought against Tibetan tribal factions in Qinghai during the protracted Golok Rebellion (1917–49). Ma Qi was at the forefront of that conflict, and when Ma Bufang came of age, he played a significant role in the violent suppression of the Goloks in an effort to force them, and by extension all of Tibet, to submit to Chinese control. Ma Bufang waged several 'successful' campaigns in the 1920s–1930s in which many Tibetans were killed, but this fuelled ongoing hostilities between local Tibetans and Muslims in Qinghai. The rebellion did not fully end until after the establishment of the PRC, with the entry of the PLA into the region. Nevertheless, Ma Bufang had sufficiently proved his loyalty and his military prowess for Chiang Kai-shek to make him a general. In the 1930s, Chiang unleashed Ma and his army against the Communist forces in the northwest. Ma's troops defeated the Red Army in its retreat through Gansu during the Long March (1934–5). In 1936, joining forces with Ma Hongkui's and Ma Hongbin's Ningxia-based army, Ma Bufang and Ma Buqing helped obliterate the Communist army that had marched across the Yellow River into Qinghai. In 1937, at the start of the Second Sino-Japanese War, Ma Buqing and Ma Bufang formulated and presented a battle plan, approved by Chiang Kai-shek, to send Ma Bufang's elite cavalry division to fight the Japanese in the east. Throughout the War of Resistance, Ma Bufang proved to be a persistent and effective thorn in the side of the Japanese. He collaborated with Ma Hongkui in the defence of Gansu, preventing any Japanese incursion. While virtually the whole of eastern China was devastated during the war with Japan, Qinghai was mostly spared.

In recognition of his strong anti-Japanese fervour and excellent management skills, Ma Bufang was appointed governor of Qinghai and supreme commander-in-chief of the entire northwest. When Chiang Kai-shek made an inspection of the northwest in 1942, he saw for himself the efficiency of Ma Bufang's and Ma Buqing's administration. By then, Ma Bufang commanded an army of 50,000 well-trained, professional soldiers. He parlayed his military might into a role as a civilian politician and was elected to the Sixth Central Committee of the GMD in 1945. Also in 1945, Ma Bufang was ordered to enter Xinjiang with his troops in order to impose GMD control over Soviet-backed Uyghur separatists who had established the Second East Turkestan Republic (1944–6).[10] The GMD hoped this occupation would help assure the safety of Han Chinese settlers who had been encouraged to re-locate to Xinjiang.

During his tenure as governor of Qinghai Ma Bufang's administration was a model of efficiency and productivity. After the defeat of the Japanese and the resumption of fighting between the Communists and Nationalists, Qinghai enjoyed a period of development and prosperity while most of China was in the throes of war. Ma implemented numerous modernizing reforms, including a state-run industrialization project, and medical, agricultural and sanitation initiatives supported by the provincial government. He invested heavily in infrastructure, and especially in education. He built schools and the state paid for student's meals, books and supplies. His Ninghai School in Xining taught religious texts alongside general education.[11] He built a school in Linxia specifically for Muslim girls, stipulating that it provide a modern, secular education.

But Ma's reforms and development initiatives came at the cost of personal freedom for his constituents. His rule was autocratic and tolerated no dissent or criticism; there was no independent press. His ethnic policy was inconsistent: on the one hand, he employed draconian methods to control Tibetan and Mongolian populations, including efforts to sinicize them; but on the other hand, he exhorted all communities to mutual respect and tolerance. In recruiting troops to his forces, Ma gave equal opportunity to Muslims, Mongolians, Tibetans and Han, and promoted officers from all ethnicities.

Ma Bufang's religious views were less tolerant, especially within his own Muslim community. Politically, Ma was a staunch Nationalist and anti-Communist. As a modernist reformer, he tended towards secular policies, and maintained a clear boundary between religious institutions and matters of state and civil society. He did, however, grant Muslim clerics a say on education, morality and other non-administrative issues. While the Ma Clique were all Sunni Muslims, they represented a wide array of sectarian leanings, from traditional Gedimu, to hereditary membership in Sufi menhuan, to influence from modern Islamic revival movements. Ma Bufang came to embrace the teachers and teachings of the Yihewani, which had recently been reformed by the religious scholar Hu Songshan 虎嵩山 (1880–1955) to make it less 'fundamentalist' and more progressive. Ma Bufang supported the Yihewani movement because he believed it to be the most supportive of social, educational, religious and cultural modernization. He not only boosted the Yihewani, but also repressed other non-Yihewani Muslim solidarities. He did not at all tolerate the more 'puritanical' Salafi followers who had broken away from the Yihewani. Ma branded them as heretics who were indoctrinated under foreign influence and forbade them to worship publicly. For other Muslim groups, like the Gedimu and Sufis, he installed Yihewani imams in their mosques to teach them Islam 'correctly'. So, while he never realized his father's hopes for him to become an imam, Ma Bufang used his wealth and political clout to influence religious affairs in his domain by sponsoring some of the leading imams of his time.

The relative security and prosperity of Ma's rule would not last, however. While he managed to shield the northwest from the ravages of the Civil War for nearly a decade, by 1949 the momentum of the Communists was inexorable. The PLA entered Gansu where they defeated Ma's forces and occupied Lanzhou. With an invasion of Qinghai imminent, Ma Bufang, his family and inner circle fled Xining and made their way to Hong Kong. Fearing the loss of the Northwest, Chiang Kai-shek ordered Ma Bufang to return to fight the PLA. Ma defied the order and, under the pretext of going on the Hajj, brought his entire entourage with him to Mecca.

Once he was settled, he began to promote the Nationalist cause in the Middle East. In 1950, while in Cairo, Ma promised a pro-GMD Islamic Insurgency in China to resist Communism. While many of his former troops did wage a guerrilla war against the PLA through much of the decade, an organized insurgency never materialized and Ma never personally came close to the fighting. Instead, he travelled to the various Arab kingdoms soliciting formal recognition and aid for the GMD, which had already been driven off the Chinese Mainland and had established the ROC government in exile on Taiwan. In 1952, a coup overthrew King Farouk I of Egypt (r. 1936–52). President Gamal Abdel Nasr (1918–70) took power on a platform of Pan-Arab Socialism, aligning Egypt with socialist/communist states around the world. At the height of the Cold War in 1957, Nasr established diplomatic relations with the PRC. The ROC thereupon transferred Ma Bufang from Cairo to Saudi Arabia, where he served as Taipei's ambassador to the kingdom for the next four years. While he served as a loyal diplomat for the ROC, he never moved to Taiwan and remained in Saudi Arabia until his death.

The Ma Clique and other Chinese Muslim warlords were soldiers, patriots and patrons – investing not only in defence, technology and infrastructure, but also in education and cultural development. They were not a monolithic group of two-dimensional figures, but represented multiple, nuanced viewpoints and interests. Most were vehemently nationalistic, seeing the future of Muslims as inextricably connected to the destiny of the nation as a whole. They were also staunchly anti-Communist, seeing the ideology as dangerously internationalist and godless, and therefore holding no respect for religion or cultural distinctiveness. Even if many of the Hui warlords were not personally observant of Islamic rituals and norms, they still wanted those rights protected for their community. Consequently, few Muslim warlords remained in Mainland China after the establishment of the PRC. Most remained loyal to the Republic, either following the ROC government into exile on Taiwan, or supporting the GMD from abroad as part of the post-war Chinese Muslim diaspora.

Each of the warlords championed Islam and Muslims in his own way, and also capitalized on religious sentiment among the people in the pursuit of secular goals. Warlords found common cause with notable imams and Muslim intellectuals of the day. Hardly anyone but the warlords had the resources to support the religious, educational, cultural and political activities of the scholars, who in turn conferred religious authority and legitimacy upon the initiatives of their patrons. This symbiosis of military and religious elites was highly effective in the propagandization of new ideas of Chinese Muslim identity and responsibility for building the community and nation.

An early collaboration of soldiers and scholars resulted in the establishment of the most important Chinese Islamic educational institution of the Republican era, Chengda Normal School (Chengda Shifan Xuexiao 成達師範學校). Tang Kesan 唐柯三, a ROC official in Shandong and founder of the Chinese Islamic Progressive Association (CIPA)[12] in 1912, Fa Jingxuan 法鏡軒, a local Muslim businessman and self-taught Islamic scholar, and Mu Huating 穆華亭, a retired military officer, came together to respond to the need for more Muslim teachers who could teach Chinese, Islamic and general courses in modernized Muslim schools.[13] In 1922, they recruited Imam Ma Songting 馬松亭 (1895–1992) to head up the project of opening a school to train such teachers. Originally established in 1925 in Jin'an as the 'first national institution of higher learning for Muslims in China', Chengda 'offered a combination of "modern" (i.e., Western), and Islamic curriculum'.[14] The school became a magnet not only for students from around China, but also for patrons. Ma Fuxiang was the school's 'guardian angel', who helped fund it and, in 1928, relocate it to Beijing (where it was later renamed Chengda College). After Ma Fuxiang's death, his son Ma Hongkui served as the chair of Chengda's Board of Directors and continued to provide funding.[15] Chengda's reformist educational philosophy sought to prepare the next generation for integration into mainstream society and participation in the newly established nation (i.e. Zhonghua Minzu):

> In the minds of the reformers, Chinese Muslims had lived in a closed world for too long, and this self-imposed marginalization had caused the Chinese Muslim community to lag behind other groups in Chinese society. To remedy this marginalization, it was seen as necessary that Muslims learn written Chinese and participate in full in Chinese life.[16]

Imam Ma Songting emphasized that Chengda graduates were groomed to serve as community leaders – 'heads of mosques, heads of schools, and heads of CIPA branches'.[17]

The Chengda modernist word view, advocating a dual commitment to Islamic revival and Chinese nationalism, was further promulgated in the school's own magazine, Yuehua 月華, first published in 1929 with financial backing from Ma Fuxiang. Yuehua was one of approximately thirty Chinese Muslim journals published between 1911 and 1937, many espousing the congruity of patriotism and religious piety. This ideology was reiterated by many leading intellectuals at the time, including the prominent nationalist imam Hu Songshan 虎嵩山 (1880–1955) of Gansu. Hu was an early follower of the Yihewani movement, with its Wahhabi-influenced views opposing any adulteration of 'pure' Islam, such as Sufi 'superstition' or Han Kitab 'syncretism'. However, after he performed the Hajj in 1925 and experienced what he perceived as anti-Chinese discrimination he abandoned the Wahhabi doctrine and devoted himself to uplifting Chinese Muslims by helping build a vibrant Chinese nation, in which they would be full participants. He promoted solidarity between Muslims and non-Muslims, for only together could they fend off the pernicious influence of foreign imperialism. After returning to China, he successfully persuaded many of his Yihewani brothers to follow him to a more nationalist orientation. Hu was aided in his endeavours by the warlords Ma Fuxiang, Ma Bufang and Ma Hongkui who supported the building of schools in which to teach a modern curriculum based on a combination of Western knowledge and Islamic and Confucian principles. He had a brief falling out with Ma Hongkui when he accused the general of polytheism – the cardinal sin of *shirk* (associating partners with Allah), for holding a Chinese New Year celebration in 1935. Naturally, Ma was not pleased and had Hu removed from his position as head of the Ningxia Sino-Arabic School and banished him from the province. Three years later, however, Ma pardoned Hu and made him head of the Sino-Arab Normal School in Wuzhong. During the War of Resistance, Hu strongly supported the cause by preaching anti-Japanese propaganda from the pulpit and in print on the grounds of Chinese nationalism and defence of Islam, including the declaration of jihad against the Japanese.[18]

Under Hu Songshan's influence, the Yihewani became closely aligned with members of the Ma Clique and by extension the GMD, which shared its nationalist agenda for modernization through education. The ROC, intent on modernizing and learning from other nations, encouraged its young elite to venture out into the world. Muslim students also took this opportunity to revive relations with the Muslim world.[19] In addition to travelling to Mecca for pilgrimage, 'one of the new phenomena of the 1920s and 1930s was ... Chinese Muslims who spent large stretches of time in the Arab world, mainly in study at Egypt's Al-Azhar University'.[20] Many of these Hui intellectuals returned from the Middle East with traditional Islamic academic credentials as well as revivalist views and took up leadership positions as imams. They became a new breed of *ahong* – anti-Sufi, anti-syncretic, Chinese Nationalist and modernist (in terms of scientific and technological progress). Wang Haoran 王浩然 (1848–1919) paved the way for this new class of imams by initiating the trend of studying at Al-Azhar in the 1900s. Ha Decheng 哈德成 (1888–1943) and Wang Jingzhai 王靜齋 (1879–1949) followed in the early 1920s, and Ma Songting in the early 1930s. By 1939, at least thirty-three Chinese Muslim students had passed through at Al-Azhar.[21]

Wang Jingzhai, together with Ma Songting, was recognized one of the 'Four Great Ahongs'[22] of the Republican era. He also advocated full participation in the construction of the ROC, based on his particular interpretation of the Hadith, '*ḥubb al-watan min al-īmān*' ('Love of homeland is part of faith').[23] Wang concluded that there was no contradiction between nationalist devotion and Islam, and moreover,

Muslims had a duty to serve their nation. Thus, Muslim identity and Chinese nationalism converged in a new formulation of Chinese Muslim simultaneity that was distilled into the oft-repeated slogan (still cited by the Communist government in the PRC today): 'Aiguo, aijiao' 愛國愛教 ('Love country, love religion'). Wang Jingzhai combined faith, activism and statesmanship as he travelled to the Middle East; Ma Fuxiang sponsored his Hajj in 1921. Then, already in his forties, Wang also went to Al-Azhar.

When he came back to China, Wang made one of the greatest single contributions to Chinese Islamic education and culture. Some fifty generations since the first Muslims entered China, no one had ever rendered the entire Qur'ān in Chinese. The Han Kitab authors had translated some verses here and there to quote in their books. Ma Dexin undertook the monumental task of a complete translation but was executed before he could finish. When the first Chinese version finally appeared in the early twentieth century, it was done by a non-Muslim, based on a Japanese translation of an English one. After returning from Egypt, Wang completed the first Muslim translation of the Qur'ān into Chinese. Moreover, he was strong advocate of Sino-Arabic education, not only to increase religious knowledge, but also to facilitate Chinese Muslims' involvement in relations between China and the Muslim world.

Wang also became politically active after returning to China. During the Second Sino-Japanese War, he went on a mission in Yunnan to rally Muslims for the war effort. Many young Muslims, heeding his call to perform their duty to the homeland, entered government service. Such activities also helped inspire a semi-official citizens' diplomatic mission to the Middle East. With the country strongly united against the Japanese, Muslims in China 'skillfully used the master narrative of anti-imperialism to construct a transnational self (China and the Islamic world) in relation to a transnational other (Western and Japanese imperialism), in order to carefully advance the ethno-religious interests of their own community'.[24] With funding from the ROC government, Wang Zengshan 王曾善, prominent Hui business leader Ma Tianying 馬天英, and others organized the 'Hui Delegation to the Middle East' to solicit sympathy and support for the Chinese cause abroad. The delegation was soon selected, each of the delegates distinguished by his linguistic abilities and expertise. Each had deep social ties to the Chinese Muslim community and strong religious and intellectual ties to the greater Muslim world.[25]

The delegation left Hong Kong on 8 January 1938, arriving in Mecca one month later for the Hajj. After their mission was done, the delegation had travelled more than 10,000 miles over fifteen months, visiting eight countries.[26] They were warmly received by their fellow Muslims wherever they went, and the mission was deemed a success. Upon their return in 1939, the delegation sent a memorandum to Chiang Kai-shek urging the ROC to follow up their efforts by sending ambassadors and consuls to various Muslim countries.[27] In particular, they 'recommended establishing diplomatic posts in Saudi Arabia to protect Chinese pilgrims and Uyghur Muslims living in Mecca'.[28] The GMD opened a consulate in Jeddah that year. These young activists played a significant role in linking China with the Muslim world, which in turn garnered international recognition and support for the ROC. The delegates were the direct products of an era of modernizing reform in China, having been prepared for their mission with an education that combined Chinese, Islamic and Western elements. They were urbane and cosmopolitan, polyglot and polymath, and thus reminiscent of the Huiru of old. But their horizons were even broader than those of their eminent forebears. They were even more worldly and had experienced a living connection with the Muslim world. They were the protégés of the warlords and imams who had seized the opportunity for Muslims in China to get in on the construction of a new nation from the ground floor, a chance to be no longer marginalized in Chinese society. Just as revolutionaries and nation-builders, whether Nationalist or Communist, had broken with imperial tradition and explicitly appealed to and expressed concern for the masses, these Muslim leaders joined the political fray and fought for the interests of Muslim laypeople in a new era, when Muslims were recognized as a critically important segment of the Chinese population.

Chapter 6
Muslims and the state in Communist China

At the height of the Cultural Revolution the following scene was not uncommon in cities and towns across China:

A young man stands silently off to the side as a procession comes down the main street. He had taken off his customary white cotton skullcap to become less conspicuous. The students form four files as they march in lockstep, dressed in blue, grey, and khaki uniforms with the now familiar red bands wrapped around their left arms. Girls, distinguished from the boys by their braided pigtails, shout the slogans just as vociferously as their male counterparts: 'To rebel is justified! Down with the old!' Walking behind them are teachers from the local school, forced to lower their gaze with their heads facing downward in shame. The young man recognises the old man who had taught him Qur'ān and mathematics years ago and instructed him to be a proud member of the Chinese nation, now being paraded as a symbol of anti-revolutionary backwardness. The teacher and the others are forced to confess their ignorant adherence to feudal superstitions while the youngsters deride them. Earlier that month, the young man had watched helplessly as the Red Guards stormed the mosque he used to attend as a child, tossing its carpets and copies of scriptures into the road to be burned. Later, after the prayer hall had been gutted, he heard that livestock had been moved in – sheep, some cattle, and pigs! – but he could not bear to go see the desecration for himself. He is a member of a lost generation, squeezed between tradition and the hope for a brighter future, and this new reality in which his livelihood, his education, his family, and his religion have all been upended seemingly overnight. He dares not speak up lest he also be made an example of obsolescence.

The Xinhai Revolution of 1911 gave birth to twin heirs: The GMD and the CCP. And while they both inherited features from their ideological father, Sun Yat-sen, these twins were anything but identical. Their fundamental differences led to a bitter, internecine struggle that ultimately ended with the Communist victory in the Chinese Civil War, the exile of the GMD-ROC to Taiwan and the establishment of the PRC on the mainland in 1949. Thus, Sun's revolutionary achievements were but a necessary step towards the start of a new revolution based on the principles of Marxist-Leninist philosophy, as interpreted by Mao Zedong 毛澤東 (1893–1976). This Communist Revolution would give birth to a totally new social, economic and political vision – a New China.

Upon founding the PRC, the CCP under Mao attempted to instate an entirely new polity, military and industrial economy. But it also had to contend with issues that had plagued rulers of China for centuries, especially how to provide for and bring under control an enormous population spread over a vast territory. Inhabiting basically the same geographical area and boundaries of the Qing Empire and ROC, this population was also internally diverse, abounding with different ethnic, cultural, linguistic and religious communities. If the CCP wanted to exercise control over those frontier regions inhabited largely by non-Han peoples, and maintain harmony among different groups in ethnically integrated areas, it could not focus on the development of Han society to the exclusion of others. Given the PRC's intention to develop the entire country and uplift the condition of all its citizens, Han and non-Han alike would have to be brought into this new future together.

In the new Communist nation-building project, despite an ostensible principle of equality among all peoples, elements of Han nationalism were inherited from the Republican period and earlier epochs' ethnic and cultural stratification. The Han people were identified by the CCP as the most developed constituency in the country, the exemplar of a nation poised for proletarian revolution. Other groups, by comparison, were regarded, to varying degrees, as backward, feudal, superstitious and needing to be dragged forward to catch up with the Han majority. Actually, the overwhelming majority of China's population at the advent of the PRC, Han and non-Han, were peasants. Because industrialization was underdeveloped nationwide, there was no significant proletariat as Marx had understood the term. And since the majority of peasants were Han, in proportion to the overall population it was the Han who were most in need of being uplifted socially and economically. It is true that most non-Han citizens also lived in underdeveloped conditions, but, as we know, Chinese-speaking Muslims were largely integrated with their Han neighbours. Thus, rural Muslims lived side by side with rural Han, but Muslims and Han also lived together in the more developed cities. The rural–urban (agricultural–industrial) divide in early Communist China was more significant than ethnic division in socio-economic terms.

The CCP pushed development through industrialization and agricultural reform in its first decade in power. This included the takeover of all industry by the state, as well as the collectivization of land across the country. Initially these policies were quite successful in stimulating the economy and promoting rapid social change. At the same time as this progress was being made, the state also engaged in surveying the country's demographic landscape to determine which groups lived where, and which communities required a boost from the government to catch up with the mainstream society. Thus began the massive investigative and theorizing project of dividing, identifying and categorizing the various constituent groups that made up the PRC.

During the early 1950s, the CCP still took its cues from the bastion of communist thought and policy, the Union of Soviet Socialist Republics (USSR). In its own revolution and development process, the USSR under Joseph Stalin (1878–1953) also had to consolidate power over the diverse population and expansive territory of the former Russian Empire. It therefore sought to divide the country into discrete, controllable units based on the different nationalities subsumed under the Soviet Union. Each nationality (Rus. народ, *národ*) was regarded to have its own unique cultural characteristics, especially language and traditional (folk) customs, that distinguished it from others. These differences were identified and highlighted, and each group possessing definable national characteristics, originating from a particular geographic locale, would be allowed a measure of autonomy as one of the Soviet republics that together constituted the USSR.

Under Mao, the PRC pursued a similar programme of national categorization. The CCP assembled a team of Soviet-trained social scientists to identify the PRC's constituent nationalities. These theoreticians used similar criteria to those in the USSR. Each nationality supposedly could be distinguished by four factors: common language, common economic life, common territoriality and psychological makeup, which expresses itself in a common culture. Unlike the Soviet system, however, national groups in the PRC would not be given their own republics, but rather territories that were home to a local majority of non-Han Chinese inhabitants were given the status of 'semi-autonomous region'; the only republic was the unitary People's Republic. The Chinese term designated for 'nationality' under this project was *minzu* 民族, a Japanese neologism (Jap. *minzoku*) coined during reforms of the Meiji era (1868–1911) to approximate Western sociological concepts of race, nation and/or ethnicity. The term was co-opted in China during the Republican era to refer to the entire Chinese nation (Zhonghua Minzu), but in the PRC took on the new meaning of distinct nationalities (today the preferred English translation is 'ethnicities') in a multinational state. The initial phase of the Minzu Project categorized thirty-nine groups, as recognized in the 1954 census. Fifteen more groups were added by the 1964 census, and then two more by 1979, bringing the total to the current figure of fifty-six: fifty-five minorities (*shaoshu minzu* 少數民族) and one great Han majority (Dahan Minzu 大漢民族).

As in the USSR, categorization relied heavily, perhaps disproportionately, on common language, frequently overlooking significant cultural differences. For instance, the Zhuang 'nationality' is composed of a vast array of local groups concentrated in Guangxi but dispersed in Guizhou, Yunnan, Guangdong and Hunan. Zhuang villages often have distinct customs, and speak mutually unintelligible tongues, but because these are all classified linguistically as belonging to one language family (i.e. Tai), the Zhuang are considered a single minzu. Even the Han majority is replete with internal diversity (regional, linguistic, religious, cultural etc.). Another minzu that defies facile categorization are the 'Hui', the name assigned to the Chinese-speaking Muslim population. We have encountered the term 'Hui' before, as it has been used since the Yuan dynasty to refer generally to Muslims in China, while implicitly specifying those whose mother tongue is Chinese in late imperial and Republican China. According to the minzu system, however, the Hui are those Muslims of putative foreign ancestry (Arab, Persian, Turkic etc.), dispersed throughout the country, who speak the local Chinese dialect of their region. In most ways, they are indistinguishable from their Han Chinese neighbours, except wherein their ethnic–religious–cultural traditions differ noticeably. As we can see from this simple description, categorization of the Hui as a single group, distinct from the Han and other minzu, already challenges the established criteria. The Hui do not have their own distinct language, but rather share this with all Han speakers; while there are regions where they may be more concentrated, they clearly do not have their own territory, or homeland, within the borders of the PRC; being well-integrated with their Han counterparts in both rural and urban areas, their economic life parallels that of the Han majority who engage in all manner of occupations to earn their livelihood. This leaves only one criterion – 'psychological makeup which expresses itself in a common culture' – to provide the distinctiveness necessary to identify the Hui as a minzu. Being as dispersed as they are, with different historical roots and attachments to place, there are naturally regional cultural differences among the Hui. So, what then might account for or manifest a unitary 'psychological makeup'? Do Han individuals, or members of any other community for that matter, all share an identical 'psychological makeup'?

It would seem that the only factor that links all Hui to one another is that they, or their ancestors, are Muslims who share an historical connection to the religious tradition of Islam. That is not to presume that all Hui are devout Muslims, or even practise Islam, but it is part of the transmitted tradition of their lineage. Acknowledgement of this fact as relevant, or necessary, to minzu categorization is highly problematic. According to CCP doctrine, based firmly on Marxist philosophy, religion is only an aspect of popular culture, which is not fundamental to the economically determined 'base' of society. Rather, it is an aspect of the insubstantial, illusory, 'superstructure' that develops atop the base as a product of historical class conflict. Marx famously referred to religion as the 'opium of the people', a sort of delusion on which the masses rely to ease the pain resulting from their exploitation by the ownership class. Religion, according to Marxist doctrine, is based on a collectively shared falsehood that there exists some supreme being, a creator who will comfort and redeem those who suffer in this world. But Marx, his followers and interpreters over the generations flatly rejected this belief through their embrace of atheist materialism. Mao and the founders of the PRC similarly rejected the truth of religion, so the notion that this phenomenon could be a valid criterion on which to base national identity is anathema to the Communist ideology. To recognize Islam, qua religion, as the essential feature of the Hui minzu would be to grant it a legitimacy that the Party could not abide.

Minzu Project theoreticians necessarily reduced religion to an aspect of culture, part of the superstructure that the Communist revolution seeks to dismantle. But if Hui identity hinges on this religio-cultural frame, what would become of the Hui people if the revolution reached its successful end of eliminating religion? How would Hui be distinguishable from, say, Han who had renounced Buddhism, Christianity or any other religious faith? And if they would not be distinguishable, is there any real distinction between them now? This question has never been given a satisfactory official answer, for to do so would require questioning some basic assumptions of the party-state and its own principle of eventually eradicating all class distinction. If the purpose of the Minzu Project was to divide segments of the population for the purpose of rendering them subject to state control, this could be done without addressing the logic of its underpinnings. And so, the Hui minzu, or Huizu 回族, has become an irreducible reality in the PRC, alongside fifty-five other reified minzu.

Once the minzu had been identified and categorized, the PRC government could formulate and articulate a 'minzu policy', which it promulgated in the Constitution of 1954. The relevant passages dealing with minzu, or nationalities, begin with the broad statements in the Preamble:

> All nationalities of our country are united in one great family of free and equal nations. This unity of China's nationalities will continue to gain in strength, founded as it is on ever-growing friendship and mutual aid among themselves, and on the struggle against imperialism, against public enemies of the people within the nationalities, and against both dominant-nation chauvinism and local nationalism. In the course of economic and cultural development, the state will concern itself with the needs of the different nationalities, and, in the matter of socialist transformation, pay full attention to the special characteristics in the development of each.[1]

Unity and harmony of the various minzu under the umbrella of the PRC is emphasized, making it clear that any disturbance, whether by the Han majority or members of the minorities, will not be tolerated. Moreover, it is stipulated that the state, which created the minzu, will also be their patron in pursuing the supreme goal of socialist development. Various articles then go on to elaborate on this general principle:

> Article 3. The People's Republic of China is a single multi-national state. All the nationalities are equal. Discrimination against, or oppression of, any nationality, and acts which undermine the unity of the nationalities are prohibited. All the nationalities have freedom to use and foster the growth of their spoken and written languages, and

to preserve or reform their own customs or ways. Regional autonomy applies in areas where people of national minorities exist in compact communities. National autonomous areas are inalienable parts of the People's Republic of China.[2]

So, the citizens of all minzu have equal rights and responsibilities before the law. Among these rights is the preservation, or modification, of the distinct language and customs of each minzu. Limited regional autonomy is granted to minority-majorities, but the notion of regional minzu secession, independence or separatism is unequivocally unacceptable. Article 49, item 10 clearly states that final say and jurisdiction over all 'affairs concerning the nationalities' shall rest with the State Council, while Article 60 indicates that the government shall 'take specific measures appropriate to the characteristics of the nationalities concerned'.[3] In other words, the agent which created the minzu based on the categorization of essentialized characteristics also has the right to treat the minzu on the basis of those characteristics. Finally, the sole mention of religion (which we know in the case of the Hui is pivotal to their minzu status) occurs in Article 88: 'Citizens of the People's Republic of China enjoy freedom of religious belief.'[4] This article appears to be in stark contradiction to the ultimate Communist goal of eradicating false belief, but it is obviously a concession to the incompletion of the revolution at this stage of history.

If religion was going to be tolerated to some extent, then it would also have to be regulated. Islam became one of the five religions officially recognized by the PRC, along with Buddhism, Daoism, Catholicism and Protestant Christianity. Obviously, these monolithic religious categories do not account for the tremendous internal diversity of each of these traditions, but their official status allows the state to exercise control over each of them. An official state-run association has been established to act as a liaison between the religious community and the CCP and to conduct the affairs of each community. In 1953, the China Islamic Association (Zhongguo Yisilan Xiehui 中國伊斯蘭協會) was established in Beijing. As stated in its charter, among its main functions are:

(1) Carrying out activities conducive to religious harmony, national unity, social stability, national reunification and world peace, carrying out socialist rule of law and core values education, uniting and leading the Muslim people to join the cause of reform, opening up, and socialist modernization for the country. Stabilizing and developing overall services;

(2) Assisting the government in propagating and implementing China's religious freedom policy and religious laws and regulations, safeguarding the legitimate rights and interests of the Islamic community and the Muslim people in accordance with the law, reflecting the opinions and demands of Islamic organizations, Islamic people and Muslims, and giving full play to the bridge bonding effect.[5]

The original PRC's Constitution of 1954, in principle, promotes many liberal ideals, guarantees universal equality and provides for ample freedom. The rights put forth in the Constitution promised peace and prosperity for ethno-religious groups like the Hui. But the document has been amended several times since, reflecting both domestic and geopolitical changes, as will be discussed below. To contextualize the evolution of the document over the subsequent decades requires an overview of economic and sociopolitical developments, some of which had a profound effect on the way ethno-religious groups like the Hui have been regarded and treated by the party-state.

Nearly a decade after the establishment of the PRC, the dynamism of the country's initial development surge began to slow dramatically. Projections of catching up to Western industrial economies were proven impossible, while the agrarian base was unable to keep up with population growth. This severe downturn necessitated extreme policy change to provide a stimulus for economic growth and social progress. Thus, Mao Zedong declared the bold initiative known as the 'Great Leap Forward' (Da Yuejin 大躍進, 1958–62). Its policies were often accelerated or intensified forms of existing measures of industrialization and collectivization, but they were also harsher. Gradual collectivization of land was replaced by confiscation and the complete prohibition of private ownership. Recalcitrant landlords were accused of being anti-revolutionaries and summarily executed. Millions upon millions of peasants were displaced and required to move to workers' communes. Many other citizens were sent to forced labour camps. Consequently, as agricultural resources and labour were diverted to factories for massive industrial projects, food production declined, leading to countrywide famine. An estimated ten to twenty million people were killed or died from unintended effects of the Great Leap Forward, and the PRC was plunged deeper into economic catastrophe. Social effects were also felt as the government, in its attempt to eliminate vestiges of feudal traditions, outlawed many Chinese religious and customary practices. By the early 1960s, there was no doubt that the initiative had failed, even though the

CCP issued falsified statistics to propagandize its success. Many party leaders blamed Mao's poor decisions, thus marginalizing his influence as rivals nipped at his heels.

For Mao to survive challenges within the party, he would have to resort to even more radical measures. By the mid-1960s, he claimed that the Great Leap Forward did not achieve its desired outcome because it had not gone far enough in rooting out counter-revolutionary elements in the party and throughout society, and these internal enemies were spreading corruption that betrayed the founding principles of the PRC. These pernicious influences had to be purged once and for all by a renewal of the revolutionary spirit, and re-education of the entire population in the core doctrines of Maoist ideology. The solution crafted by Mao was called the 'Great Cultural Revolution' (Da Wenhua Geming 大文化革命, 1966–76).

The Cultural Revolution was not as concerned with the economic base as it was on re-shaping and 'purifying' social behaviour and cultural practice in order to reform the people's consciousness. This was to be accomplished through even more repressive policies than the Great Leap Forward had enacted, especially targeting any forms of difference and dissent. The declared purpose of the revolutionary revival was to completely destroy any behavioural and cognitive holdovers from before the Communist Revolution, especially what Mao referred to as the 'Four Olds' (Si Jiu 四舊) – old customs, culture, habits and ideas. Mao activated a paramilitary youth corps indoctrinated in revolutionary rhetoric and tactics, the Red Guards (Hong Weibing 紅衛兵), to serve as his ground soldiers in the nationwide purge. They attempted to destroy all relics of the pre-revolutionary past, as well as help round-up and abuse individuals accused of harbouring any of the Four Olds. Such individuals were subjected to public humiliation, physical violence, forced confessions, internment in re-education camps and/or execution. For the re-education of the general citizenry, a programme of forced re-location of urban elites to rural communes was also implemented. The Cultural Revolution impacted all sectors and all levels of PRC society as Mao also used it as a pretext for purging political rivals within the CCP.

Religious institutions, including places of worship and their property, clerics and lay believers were heavily targeted. All religious communities were affected; Red Guards stormed temples, monasteries, churches and mosques with equal fury. But ethno-religious minorities were most vulnerable to attack. Thus, Hui and other Muslim communities suffered greatly in this period. Religious rituals were prohibited and anyone caught practising was subject to punishment. Like other places of worship, mosques were repurposed as factories, administrative offices, community centres or even housing for livestock; adding insult to injury, some mosques were used to house pigs, rendering them ritually unclean according to Islamic norms. The greater the symbolic value of a place, the more likely it was to be desecrated. For example, the Ming dynasty Grand Mosque in Xi'an was turned into a steel factory for years. In addition to these material and physical effects, the Cultural Revolution also led to the closing of religious schools, thus cutting off a generation from traditional knowledge.

These anti-religious policies were implemented in spite of the reiteration of religious freedom in the amended PRC Constitution of 1975. However, the wording of the relevant text, Article 28, reveals some subtle yet profound changes:

> Citizens enjoy freedom of speech, correspondence, the press, assembly, association, procession, demonstration and the freedom to strike, and enjoy freedom to believe in religion and freedom not to believe in religion and to propagate atheism.[6]

The obvious emphasis is on atheism and non-belief, and the right to propagate religious faith is clearly omitted. In fact, few if any of the other rights spelled out in the article were actually held up in practice during the Cultural Revolution. Moreover, while the rights of minzu in a multinational state were affirmed as in the 1954 version, the emphasis also shifted to their collective cooperation towards the goals of the revolution, as averred in the amended Preamble: 'People of all nationalities in our country, unite to win still greater victories!'[7]

There are many tragic stories that come out of this turbulent era. One of these took place at the end of the decade of the Cultural Revolution in the small Yunnan town of Shadian 沙甸. The Hui residents of the town, upwards of 7,000 people, were already hit by anti-religious policies. In 1974, the government issued an order closing all local mosques. In response, devout Muslims began to protest what they saw as a violation of their constitutional rights. Some factions began to arm themselves with homemade weapons in fear of government violence. The PLA realized the Hui community's worst fears in 1975 when some 10,000 troops raided Shadian, reinforced by jet fighters which bombed the town. When the dust had cleared, approximately 1,500 Hui townspeople had been killed and over 4,000 homes destroyed. The 'Shadian Incident' is recorded as the only ethnic uprising during the Cultural Revolution.

Mao Zedong, who had been suffering ill health for years, died in 1976. The PRC had been plunged into a full decade of chaos and destruction when the chairman's death opened up an opportunity to change course. While the CCP leaders did not wish completely to discredit the founder of the country, they found a ready scapegoat in the so-called 'Gang of Four' (Siren Bang 四人幫),[8] the radical leftist faction of the party upon whom all the excesses and atrocities of the Cultural Revolution could be blamed. Out of the rubble of the decade-long social and political turmoil emerged a new, more staid and pragmatic CCP leadership headed by Deng Xiaoping 鄧小平 (1904–97), who effectively ruled the PRC from 1978 to 1992 without ever donning the titles of head of state, head of government or party chairman. Deng ushered in an era of economic reforms, including the introduction of some free-market principles and practices, which he called 'Socialism with Chinese characteristics'. He also loosened the rigid social restrictions of the Mao era and opened the PRC to more extensive trade and cultural relations with the outside world. Collectively, these policies were known as 'Reform and Opening Up' (Gaige Kaifang 改革開放).

The reforms opened tremendous new opportunities for ordinary Chinese citizens. First among these was the ability to earn money through private enterprise, including small businesses. Many people began to enjoy a higher standard of living. But the effects went far beyond economics. The easing of social constraints also allowed people to explore and express ideas outside of the narrow doctrine of the unitary party-state. For those who had lived through the Great Leap Forward and/or the Cultural Revolution, the failure of the government to live up to its promises led to a loss of faith in the CCP. Now they were being told that they could not rely on the state for their welfare, and that their economic prosperity depended on their own private initiative. Given the opportunity to seek solace outside party ideology, many turned to religious faith. The opening of China to foreign influence, as well as permission for Chinese citizens with means to travel outside the PRC also presented previously unknown options.

All of these conditions led to new cultural and individual expressions across society, in all walks of life. The implications for China's Muslims, particularly the Hui, were significant. In 1982, a new version of the

Constitution was ratified. In it, religious and ethnic rights (and restrictions) were enumerated in greater detail than ever before. In the Preamble, the document acknowledges that it is a 'struggle to safeguard the unity of the nationalities', and 'the state does its utmost to promote the common prosperity of all nationalities in the country'. Article 4 lays out the official CCP position on the status of all minzu:

> All nationalities in the People's Republic of China are equal. The state protects the lawful rights and interests of the minority nationalities and upholds and develops the relationship of equality, unity and mutual assistance among all of China's nationalities. Discrimination against and oppression of any nationality are prohibited; any acts that undermine the unity of the nationalities or instigate their secession are prohibited. The state helps the areas inhabited by minority nationalities speed up their economic and cultural development in accordance with the peculiarities and needs of the different minority nationalities. Regional autonomy is practiced in areas where people of minority nationalities live in compact communities; in these areas organs of self-government are established for the exercise of the right of autonomy. All the national autonomous areas are inalienable parts of the People's Republic of China. The people of all nationalities have the freedom to use and develop their own spoken and written languages, and to preserve or reform their own ways and customs.[9]

While the Constitution provides for recognition of the distinctiveness of each minzu, it also clearly states that this distinctiveness can never be used as a justification for separating from the rest of the country or threatening its territorial integrity. At the same time, however, this article introduces the idea that because minority minzu still lag far behind the Han in terms of development, the state must assist them to catch up. To compensate, the minorities benefit from a Preferential Policy (Youhui Zhengce 優惠政策) that privileges them over Han in matters such as school and housing placement, hiring and employment opportunities, especially for government positions (though virtually never in the highest political echelons).

Article 36 gives a definitive statement on the place of religion in the PRC:

> Citizens of the People's Republic of China enjoy freedom of religious belief. No state organ, public organization or individual may compel citizens to believe in, or not to believe in, any religion; nor may they

discriminate against citizens who believe in, or do not believe in, any religion. The state protects normal religious activities. No one may make use of religion to engage in activities that disrupt public order, impair the health of citizens or interfere with the educational system of the state. Religious bodies and religious affairs are not subject to any foreign domination.[10]

Two phrases immediately stand out in this amended clause – 'normal religious activities' and 'foreign domination'. The former leaves a wide opening for the state's interpretation of what is or is not 'normal', leaving religious citizens to wonder where the invisible, arbitrary line is drawn. The latter makes it clear that religious communities with ties to a larger community outside China must know that their first allegiance belongs to the PRC, irrespective of the teachings of their faith.

Hui Muslims took advantage of the reforms and newfound openness. Mosques were repaired, renovated and reopened. Where a mosque had been destroyed a new one was often built in its place. Many old mosques in central China had been built (or rebuilt) with imperial sponsorship during the Ming dynasty following the Chinese architectural style of Buddhist, Daoist or Confucian temples. Their structures are wooden, with tiled rooves, the eaves slightly curved and pointing upwards, like a pagoda. They are often surrounded by a Chinese-style garden, complete with moon gates and large standing rocks reminiscent of mountains – reflecting literati aesthetics. The Grand Mosque of Xi'an and the Niujie Mosque in Beijing are good examples of such architecture. By contrast, the new mosques built in the 1980s and 1990s endeavour to emulate a Middle Eastern, Arab architectural style. Almost all of the structures have narrow, cylindrical minarets and one or more bulbous green domes reminiscent of the Prophet's Mosque (al-Masjid al-Nabawī) in Medina. The ubiquity of the Arab style demonstrates the pervasiveness of Islamic influence coming from the Middle East as China opened up to the world. It also reveals the westward-looking attitude adopted by many Hui during this era; their inspiration, not only in terms of architecture but also fashion, education and devotional practices was coming from the Muslim world. This wave of 'Arabization' reveals a tacit rift between some Chinese Muslims and the state:

> Islam and Arabization posed subtle threats to the Chinese government ... in their capacity to provide [Hui] residents with an index of civilization, a vision of modernization, and the means for achieving civilization and

modernization that differed from those the state provided and existed outside of the state's purview.[11]

Despite misgivings about undue foreign religious influences, the government tolerated these expressions of Islamic religiosity among the Hui, probably to help foster good will within Chinese Muslim communities, but also to demonstrate to Muslim countries with whom it wished to strengthen relations that the PRC was pro-Islam. Besides, from the perspective of the party-state these allowances were mostly of a superficial nature. In 1990, however, a development in China's international relations with Saudi Arabia had a large impact on the lives of many Chinese Muslims. That year, Riyadh broke off diplomatic relations with the ROC on Taiwan and exchanged embassies with Beijing. Prior to this event, any Chinese Muslims wishing to visit the kingdom to perform the pilgrimage to Mecca had to do so unofficially, so very few did. But with newly established relations, the two countries began to engage in 'Hajj diplomacy', whereby the PRC permitted its Muslim citizens – mostly Hui – to travel to Mecca, first very few, but in increasing numbers with each passing year: 'According to statistics, in the ten years from 1985 to 1994 there were just more than 20,000 Chinese Muslims that performed the Hajj.'[12] Hajj diplomacy made many Muslims overseas aware of Chinese Muslims for the first time, and they took great pride in knowing that Islam was alive and well represented in China. It also exposed Chinese pilgrims to new and different interpretations of Islam. Visiting Saudi Arabia ignited a new interest in the Wahhabi doctrines, which had first been introduced to China by the Yihewani movement, and other Salafi groups, in the early twentieth century.

Upon returning from Hajj, many Hui pilgrims spread these teachings within their communities, claiming that they represented 'true' Islam, free from the accretions of Chinese culture over the centuries. They invited Saudi donations and sponsorship to build mosques and Islamic schools, which were then furnished with Chinese translations of the Qur'ān printed in Saudi Arabia as well as Wahhabi-oriented teaching materials. The state did not object to these outside influences, even though, strictly speaking, they rubbed up against the boundaries of constitutional injunctions: 'No one may make use of religion to engage in activities that … interfere with the educational system of the state. Religious bodies and religious affairs are not subject to any foreign domination.'[13]

By the end of the first decade of the Gaige Kaifang, many Chinese citizens had an optimistic outlook on the country's course. Economic policies promoted growth and development that touched the lives of more people in the PRC than ever before. Moreover, the lifting of rigid social constraints provided a breath of fresh air to a previously closed society and gave people a greater sense of personal choice. Many experimented with new fashions and Western-style entertainment. Some had the chance to travel abroad for the first time. Ethno-religious minorities such as the Hui enjoyed these opportunities, as well as the option to revive long-neglected religious traditions. Of course, many among those generations who had lived through or were raised during the Great Leap Forward and/or Cultural Revolution had become thoroughly secularized and had little interest in religion. Thus, in an era when the entire society had a chance to seek out new experiences, it was the younger generation that felt most emboldened and adventurous. Young Chinese Muslims were no exception to the trend.

One episode that created a stir in the Chinese media, but escaped notice internationally, was a Muslim protest in Beijing in April 1989. That year, a book titled *Xing fengsu* 性風俗 (Sexual Customs) was published. The publishers promoted it as anthropological research on sexual practices around the world. When it came to the Muslim world, the book treated various Islamic symbols and rituals in a highly sexualized manner. For example, the authors wrote that the minaret suggests a phallus and the mosque's dome a woman's *mons pubis*. Shockingly, it claimed that the Hajj was akin to an orgy in which pilgrims engaged in bestiality with camels. Muslims throughout China were naturally offended. Small-scale protests broke out in the provinces, but a much larger demonstration hit the streets of the capital. It was staged by university students and also attracted local Hui residents. In total, around 3,000 protesters marched from the Haidian district to Niujie, and finally to Tian'anmen Square. Most of the participants were Hui, but in a rare show of inter-minzu, pan-Islamic bonding Muslims of other ethnicities also joined the march.

In April 1989, other students were testing the limits of the Reform and Opening Up in what has come to be known as the 'Beijing Spring'. Large groups of students were already assembling regularly at Tian'anmen to express demands for democratic reforms. The Muslim march was likely overshadowed by the general pro-democracy gatherings, which grew day by day. Students were aware that the USSR was loosening its hold over the Eastern Bloc countries so they timed their protest to coincide with a state visit by Soviet General Secretary Mikhail Gorbachev.

The Muslim protesters were probably also emboldened by these events. The timing of their public expression of grievances coincided with certain occurrences in China and abroad. Banners at the march called *Xing fengsu* 'China's *Satanic Verses*',[14] referring to the novel by Salman Rushdie that had caused Muslim outrage in the West earlier that year. Protesters in Beijing demanded the government redress the offense by censuring the publishers and banning the book. The Iranian supreme leader Ayatollah Ruhollah Khomeini had publicly condemned *The Satanic Verses* and issued a fatwa (Islamic legal ruling) calling for Rushdie to be executed for blasphemy against the Prophet and Islam. The Muslim protesters were also aware that then Iranian president Ali Khameni (Iran's present-day Supreme Leader) was scheduled for a state visit to Beijing on 11 May. Clearly, they wanted to attract his attention and that of other Muslim world leaders. They were successful in their effort as Khameni made a public statement of his support for the protesters during his visit, thereby putting pressure on his hosts to follow suit.

Perhaps in a gesture to save face the CCP leadership not only met the protesters' demands to ban the book, but also waived prosecution of Muslim protesters around the country who had violated the law. Such lenience may be understood in the context of the government's patient passivity towards the pro-democracy student gatherings at Tian'anmen in the heady weeks leading up to the eventual crackdown on 4 June. But the strategic timing of the protest to coincide with Khameni's visit certainly played a part in the lack of reprisals as the CCP leadership was still courting stronger relations with Iran and other Muslim countries. The state had to appear to treat its Muslim citizens gently and take their grievances seriously or risk offending Muslims abroad. The manner in which the Muslim students carried themselves was also strategically thought out. Even in their anger, they did not criticize the government. Rather, they invoked the state's own rhetoric in their banners and slogans: '"Respect China's Freedom of Religion!' 'Uphold the Constitution!' 'Uphold the Party's Nationality and Religion Policies!' 'Preserve National Unity!' They quoted Wang Jingzhai's famous exhortation, 'Love the Country, Love the Religion', and cried out in religious exultation, '*Allāhu Akbar*' ('God is Great').[15] Simultaneously demonstrating faithful devotion and patriotism, they manifested 'protest *to* the government, rather than *against* it', thereby complying with the state's insistence on 'order versus disorder, rationality versus confusion, law versus criminality, and reward versus punishment'.[16]

In the aftermath of the Tian'anmen crackdown, the CCP was determined to prevent future uprisings and public disturbances. Many of the liberties granted by the government that led up to the Beijing Spring were revoked or severely curtailed. The security state of the PRC began to reassert itself in ways far more subdued than the Cultural Revolution, using more of a scalpel than a bludgeon to excise undesirable elements from society. The targets of domestic surveillance were no longer 'anti-revolutionaries' but rather political dissidents. The majority of the population would be left to enjoy the fruits of the market economy and China's increasing participation in globalization, provided they did not engage in or support political dissent. It was as if the state had made an implicit agreement with its citizens – if the latter did not agitate politically or disturb the peace, the former would provide the means for increased economic prosperity. The state's priority was law and order by means of an obedient populace, who became willing participants in a consumer culture.

Hui and other Muslims would similarly be required to toe the party line along with the Han majority. They were permitted to continue their 'normal religious activities' and ethnic customs, so long as these did not in any way challenge the singular authority of the party-state. In Hui communities, Islamic schools continued to receive support and educational contributions from Saudi Arabia and other Muslim countries. More mosques were built. For example, in Shadian, site of the 1975 PLA raid against Hui protesters, the local community, with aid from the state and outside Muslim donations, built one of the largest mosques in the PRC (capable of holding 10,000 worshippers), complete with four tall minarets and massive green dome. After the Shadian incident, the state issued an apology, began paying reparations to victims and their families and erected a monument to the town's martyrs. The local economy began to flourish in the Gaige Kaifang era with special policies enhancing trade between Muslim countries and merchants in Shadian.

In the 1990s the number of Chinese Muslims permitted to go for Hajj grew each year. In the early part of the decade, roughly 2,000 pilgrims per year were making the trip and 'after 1995, the number of Hajjis were growing by 2,000 people annually'.[17] In the early 2000s the number stabilized to around 4,000 to 5,000 per year, but by 2007 the annual total exceeded 10,000 and continued to rise steadily during the next decade. The Chinese pilgrims given official Hajj exit visas were expected to act as unofficial diplomats for the PRC, representing the country at the international gathering of Muslims in Mecca.[18] In scrutinizing applicants on the waiting list to decide who will be selected to go each year, the government prioritizes people with positive social profiles, who have no record of negative activities. Thus, in its most visible policy affecting the religious life of Muslim citizens, the PRC government distinguishes between 'good' and 'bad' Muslims in a way that is reminiscent of imperial Chinese practices. The vast majority of the successful applicants are Hui, while very few belong to other minzu. Uyghur Muslims in particular have found it increasingly difficult to receive permits to go to Mecca in recent years, due to the state's fraught relationship with perceived extremists in Xinjiang. The Uyghur-Xinjiang issues will be discussed in greater detail in the subsequent chapters.

After the 11 September 2001 (9/11) terrorist attacks, the administration of US president George W. Bush attempted to promote solidarity among world powers in the 'global war on terror'. Even traditional US rivals, Russia and China, were willing to get on board as they also had internal Muslim populations whom they cast as domestic terrorists. The call to fight militant Islamic extremism on a global scale provided justification within the international community for the PRC to deal more sternly with Uyghur and other Muslims whom it assessed to be a threat to national security. In order to avoid being painted with the same brush, many Hui Muslims in the early 2000s made a concerted effort to avoid political controversy and portray themselves as loyal to the party-state.

As the wars in Afghanistan and Iraq, and conflict in Israel–Palestine and Kashmir, among others, waged on, Chinese Muslims remained conspicuously staid in their reactions, too timid to be 'active participants in the protests and seminal debates roiling the larger Islamic world. In that world, they are almost invisible.'[19] Ma Ruxiong, a Hui teacher from Linxia, explained his community's silence when the Danish newspaper *Jyllands-Posten* published caricatures of the Prophet Muhammad in 2005, which drew outrage from Muslims worldwide:

> Obviously, we're different from Muslims in other parts of the world. We just can't go into the streets and protest. You have to have permission from the government. But there are other things we can do. We pray to Allah to protect all Muslims in the world.[20]

The self-censorship and non-political stance taken by such Chinese Muslims is part of the implicit deal they, like other Chinese citizens, have made with the state. As Ma Huiyun, director of an Islamic school in Linxia, said, 'we have to cooperate with the government ... They asked us to be calm. They said they would speak on our behalf and express our unhappiness.'[21] In 2015, after the terror attacks on the Paris offices of Charlie Hebdo in response to another cartoon depicting the Prophet, most of the world came together to condemn the attacks and affirm freedom of speech. In China, however, official sources such as the Xinhua news agency took a different viewpoint, with an editorial stating: 'There should be limits to free speech ... If (people) set limits when venting "freedom" and respect others, there would be fewer tragedies in the world.'[22] In a sentence, the PRC implicitly kept its promise to speak on behalf of Muslim sentiments while promoting its own agenda regarding limits to protected speech.

The state has made good on guarantees written into the 1982 Constitution (which has since been slightly amended, but not in its clauses on religion or minorities). In particular, the government has supported Islamic practice in two key areas, which comprise two of Islam's Five Pillars: Prayer and pilgrimage. The government proudly publicizes gestures of tolerance and solicitude in its published White Papers, including statistics of how many mosques are maintained in the country with state support; how many government-trained imams are serving; and, especially, how many Chinese Muslims have been permitted to make the pilgrimage to Mecca each year.[23] All of these functions are performed by the state-controlled China Islamic Association. A 1997 White Paper summed up the ideal relationship between all religious citizens and the state:

> It is traditional for Chinese religious believers to love their country and religions. The Chinese government supports and encourages the religious circles to unite the religious believers to actively participate in the construction of the country. The various religions all advocate serving the society and promoting the people's well-being, such as ... Islam's 'praying to Allah to give great reward in this world and hereafter'.[24]

It is interesting to note how the CCP has co-opted Wang Jingzhai's Republican-era slogan: '*Aiguo, aijiao*'.

In the pursuit of its main objective – maintaining law and order – the party-state will still make certain concessions to religious interests, especially in regions where minorities outnumber Han residents. Officially, the atheist CCP does not recognize religious law. But the Constitution has justified recognition of 'Hui customary law' (*Huizu xiguanfa* 回族習慣法), that is, rules pertaining to worship, diet and life-cycle rituals, as part of its tolerance for minzu lifestyles. But the term for sharī'a in modern Chinese, *Yisilan jiaofa* 伊斯蘭教法 (literally, Islamic Religious Law), only refers to legal systems in Muslim countries abroad, and never to the lived traditions of Islam in China. PRC law does not permit the implementation of sharī'a as a comprehensive legal code that includes not only religious, but also civil, political and penal rules. So Chinese Muslims have adopted an abridged view of sharī'a. However, in localities where observant Hui Muslims are the majority, CCP authorities sometimes rely on local Muslim leaders to take part in the resolution of legal disputes or even adjudication in the courts. In effect, within parameters set by local officials, the government utilizes authority approved by Muslim communities, including aspects of shari'a, to settle legal cases.

Again, these accommodations usually apply to Hui communities, while conditions in Uyghur and other Muslim minzu areas differ significantly. More rigid restrictions have been put in place in Xinjiang and other Muslim-majority regions since the 2014 terror attacks at the rail station in Kunming 昆明, Yunnan, in which police have charged Uyghur perpetrators. By extension, because Hui Muslims have also been implicated in the investigation of the incident, suspicion and caution have been extended to Muslims in various communities around China. The security situation affecting Chinese Muslims has coincided with a national policy under the administration of President Xi Jinping 習近平 (b. 1953) scrutinizing the role of religion in society, and especially seeking to limit foreign religious influences in the country, whether Buddhist, Islamic or Christian. Under this policy, there is a clear preference for localized, sinicized expressions and interpretations of religion. Thus, Muslims are encouraged to prioritize their allegiance to the PRC and, if they choose to follow religion, to devote themselves to an Islam 'with Chinese characteristics'.

Chapter 7
Muslim diversity in contemporary China

Upon entering the main hall at the Museum of Ethnic Cultures one is confronted by an enormous colourful tapestry that dominates the space. This museum is designed to teach the public about the diversity of their country and the mural is there to emblemize harmony in diversity in stunning fashion. The artistic style of socialist realism is almost belied by colours more vibrant than real life – the red foreground, the swirling ochre and yellow background, and in the middle, figures adorned in many-hued patterns. At the centre foreground stands the figure a handsome young man dressed in Western-style: jeans, a t-shirt and jacket, with a stylish haircut much like one might see on the streets of Beijing in the late 1980s. On either side of him, covering the entirety of the mural are dozens of people, men and women dressed in spectacular costumes, some with flowing gowns, others in long tunics, some in fur hats, turbans, or other ornate headdress, the girls sporting elaborate hairstyles. Each costume is distinct, representing one of the constituent minzu of the People's Republic. The permanent exhibitions re-enforce the cultural diversity – Kazakh men in tall white woollen caps; Uyghur girls in their varicoloured skirts and long braids extending from underneath neat little pillbox hats; Miao women wearing black garments with embroidered patches of red, yellow, orange, blue, and white stripes; bearded Hui elders donning the ubiquitous white skull cap and loose fitting old-fashioned Chinese jacket and trousers. What unites them is their difference from the Han figure at the centre; they represent timeless folk traditions, while he epitomizes the forward progress of modernity. The other common characteristic of the ethnic representatives is that they all appear cheerful, dancing and playing instruments as they look with admiration at the robust Han archetype in their midst. The overarching message: All are happy to be part of the rich tapestry – distinct yet all equally 'Chinese'.

The establishment of the Minzu System paved the way for the ethnic policies that have developed in the PRC over the past seven decades. These policies have in turn girded the reification of ethnic minorities as discrete groups distinguished from the Han majority and from each other. In principle, China's approximately 1.4 billion people are unified under a single state and ruling party. Diversity among this enormous population complicates social and political control endeavours; hegemony craves homogeneity. By dividing the populace into one dominant ethnic group comprising over 90 per cent of the population and fifty-five minority groups, however, the government can better manage the tremendous diversity under its purview. While each shaoshu minzu, or ethnic minority, is considered unique, some may be correlated with each other on the basis of shared characteristics – linguistic, regional, economic, religious etc. For example, ten of the fifty-five shaoshu minzu share a common religio-cultural connection to Islam. This does not mean that all members of these ethnic groups today are practising Muslims (i.e. adherents of the religion of Islam), but simply that historically their ancestors most probably were. The total population of these ten minzu, and therefore of all nominal or affirmed Muslims in the PRC, is officially estimated at around twenty-five million, of which the Hui (approx. 11 million) and Uyghur (approx. 10 million) are the two largest groups. Apart from their relationship to Islam, these ten 'Muslim minzu' may also be grouped together or differentiated along other lines.

Hui and non-Hui Muslims can be divided according to their historical origins in China, which follow divergent trajectories. On the one hand, the formation of the Hui minzu is the outcome of a protracted naturalization process described in the preceding chapters. The putative ancestors of the Hui transplanted in China more than a millennium ago and their descendants have evolved from a diaspora into a distinct minzu through genetic and mimetic hybridization of foreign and indigenous elements in the Chinese socio-cultural environment. That is, the Hui are the product of converging lineages that coalesced into a group with identifiable common characteristics leading to their 'recognition' as a minzu.

The non-Hui Muslim ethnic minorities, on the other hand, were mainly incorporated through a process of annexation of their homelands beyond the central Chinese heartland. Different Chinese Empires had made incursions into the regions of Central Asia beyond China's traditional borders to the West since the Han dynasty, with major inroads made during the Tang period, but they had not incorporated these lands en masse. It was not until the Yuan dynasty that China and Central Asia were joined under a single polity – the unified Mongol Empire at the apogee of its power and expansion. But this period of Eurasian hegemony was short-lived and came to an abrupt end as the Ming dynasty withdrew from the frontier regions and concentrated it jurisdiction over a contracted realm. The Manchu conquerors pursued an expansionist policy and the Qing Empire came to control immense swaths of Inner and Central Asia, including Inner Mongolia to the north, Xinjiang to the northwest, and Tibet to the southwest. The name of Xinjiang literally means 'new frontier', referring to the fact that it was not part of previous Chinese Empires. The territory of Xinjiang actually encompasses a number of sub-regions, which were quite distinct both geographically and demographically before the Qing conquest – places like Dzungaria, the Ili valley, Altishahr (Kashgaria), eastern Turkistan and the vast Taklamakan Desert. When the Qing dynasty assumed control over, or colonized, Xinjiang, the Uyghur and other peoples inhabiting this territory were subsumed within the empire whose geopolitical borders were later inherited by the ROC and then the PRC.

The peoples living within Xinjiang and neighbouring frontier regions already had well-established group identities based on ancient tribal, linguistic and cultural relationships. Their proximity to Chinese civilization paved the way for enduring commercial and intercultural exchanges. These indigenous ethnic groups became Qing subjects, intermingled with Han, Hui and Manchu subjects who came to settle in Xinjiang. They eventually became citizens of the PRC and were then assigned minzu status because of the annexation of their lands in late imperial Chinese history. The two pathways to minzu formation – naturalization and annexation – account for some of the significant differences among the Hui and non-Hui Muslim peoples, especially with regard to their respective degrees of sinicization, or 'Chineseness'.

Apart from the Hui, the other nine Muslim minzu all speak non-Han languages, including members of the Altaic (Turkic and Mongolic) and

Indo-European families. The Uyghur, Kazakh, Kyrgyz, Salar, Uzbek and Tatar all speak Turkic languages, while the Bao'an and Dongxiang speak forms of Mongolian. The Tajik speak dialects of Persian, an Indo-European language. Most of these minzu are distributed geographically in the northwest regions of the PRC. The Uyghurs constitute the majority population of Xinjiang, where there are also smaller populations of Kazakhs, Kyrgyz, Uzbeks, Salars, Tatars and Tajiks. The Bao'an, Dongxiang and Salars live mainly around the border of Qinghai and Gansu provinces. While the Hui also reside largely in the northwest (Gansu, Ningxia, Qinghai and Xinjiang), as we have noted before, they are dispersed throughout China, represented in every province with sizeable enclaves in most big cities. In terms of economic life, some of the Muslim minzu are traditionally agriculturalists (e.g. Uyghur, Bao'an) or pastoralists (e.g. Kazakh, Kyrgyz). Within each of the ethnic groups, some are rural and some are urban. As agriculturalists, the Uyghurs, for example, have been a sedentary people for many centuries and are distributed in villages and towns around the Tarim Basin of Xinjiang. The Hui, who typically live side by side with Han Chinese, pursue agriculture in the countryside and various trades and professions in urban centres; harking back, perhaps, to the occupation of their distant ancestors, many Hui still engage in trade as merchants and shopkeepers.

Such inter-minzu differences are fairly obvious, but intra-minzu diversity also exists and is frequently overlooked by outsiders who tend to essentialize ethnic minorities. Among the Uyghur, for example, who live in cities, towns and villages scattered throughout the expansive Taklamakan Desert, each oasis has its own customs, dialect and distinct identity; Uyghur national unity is a relatively recent notion, which will be discussed later. Hui in different regions across China also have local customs that set them apart from other members of their minzu. One of the most noticeable differences is linguistic. Hui are generally speakers of Han Chinese dialects; just as their Han compatriots speak a wide array of (often mutually unintelligible) dialects, so too Hui communities tend to speak the local dialect of their respective region. In many majority-Hui locales, the vernacular may be peppered with words and phrases derived from Arabic and/or Persian. Depending on where they live, some Hui dialects also incorporate loan words from other languages, such as Mongolian or Tibetan; there are also Tibetan-speaking Muslims, known as Kache, who are considered part of the Tibetan minzu, as well Mongolian-speaking Muslim Bao'an and Dongxiang minzu mentioned above. Then there is the unique case of the 'Hui' community, also known as the Utsul people, living on the island of Hainan, China's southernmost province. The Utsul have their own mother tongue (though they also speak Mandarin and/or Hainanese dialect today). This language, called Tsat, belongs to the Malayo-Polynesian branch of the Austronesian family. Historically, the Utsul were an offshoot of the Cham people of Southeast Asia, who came to Hainan from the Muslim kingdom of Champa (in present-day central Vietnam) during the fifteenth century, escaping after the Vietnamese conquest. Apart from their shared connection to Islam, the Utsul are as different from the Hui of the mainland as any other minzu. However, under the PRC's minzu identification project of the 1950s, they were not considered a significant enough population to be awarded independent minzu status (despite fulfilling all four necessary minzu criteria), so they were grouped with the Hui. Today, many scholars view them as one of over two dozen 'unrecognized ethnic minorities' (*weishibie minzu* 未識別民族) in the PRC. Other unrecognized Muslim minorities include the Guge 古格, Kangjia 康家, and Tomao 托茂 (subsumed under Hui) and the Aynu 艾努 and Keriya 克里雅 (subsumed under Uyghur).

Apart from these linguistic differences and ethnic anomalies, religious distinctions also subdivide the various Muslim minzu. Virtually all of China's Muslims are historically connected to and/or identify with the Sunni branch of Islam (as are the majority, upwards of 80 per cent, of the world's Muslims). One notable exception are the Sarikoli Tajik of western Xinjiang, who follow the Nizārī branch of Ismāʿīlī Shiʿa[1] Islam (as distinguished from the Wahki Tajik, who are Sunni). Most Muslims in China are also traditionally adherents of the Hanafi school (Ar. *madhhab*) of Islamic Law, which is predominant throughout Turkey, Central Asia and South Asia, making it the most populous of the four Sunni legal schools. Yet, beyond these overarching commonalties among the Muslim minzu, religious differences abound.

The first fundamental and perhaps most essential distinction is the divide between religiosity and secularity. As we have seen historically, there have been Chinese Muslims who have lapsed in their observance of Islam, or even discarded their Muslim identity in order to assimilate into Confucian Chinese culture and society. Although there is no documentary evidence, we may speculate that some Chinese Muslims may have embraced other religio-philosophical traditions or faiths (e.g. Buddhism, Daoism etc.). In the nineteenth and early twentieth centuries,

Christian missionaries (mostly Protestant, but also Catholic and Orthodox) specifically targeted Chinese-speaking Muslim communities for proselytization,[2] and so there were some Muslims who left the fold of Islam that way. Secularism as an aspect of modernity contributed greatly to the bifurcation of religiosity and non-religiosity (including atheist, non-theist, agnostic and eclectic/undefined spiritual world-views), especially in the late nineteenth-twentieth centuries.

Karl Marx (1818–83), as one of the leading proponents of modern secularism, bequeathed his atheist views to the socialist-communist philosophical tradition inherited by Leninism and eventually Maoism in China. As we have noted, the CCP ideology is officially atheist, while articles of the PRC Constitution stipulate freedom of religious belief or non-belief for its citizens. During the first two decades of the PRC, especially during the Cultural Revolution, the government actively discouraged or banned religious devotion among the populace. Many people abandoned religion at that time, whether voluntarily or under coercion. During the purge of the 'Four Olds', ethno-religious minorities were barred from their places of worship, or saw them destroyed, and also gave up religious practices in order to avoid persecution. The CCP was thus successful in pushing its atheist agenda and millions of PRC citizens were secularized, many of them never to return to religiosity thereafter. Even when many faith communities experienced a religious revival during the Reform and Opening Up era, some of the older generation upheld their secularity and eschewed religion, including among the Muslim ethnic groups.

Beyond the religious–secular divide, however, among those who identify as believing, practising Muslims, there are also further distinctions in how they interpret, understand and observe Islamic doctrine and ritual. That is to say, there is tremendous sectarian division within Chinese Islam. This is especially prevalent among Hui communities, dispersed as they are throughout China. Regional variation of customs and doctrinal teachings often accompanies these sectarian differences. The basis of these variations may be traced back to the historical origins of regional communities. Whether it is factually true or not, most Hui claim descent from foreign ancestors, mainly Arabs and/or Persians. Hui living in the northwest commonly trace their lineage to merchants and other immigrants who entered China from Central Asia via the overland Silk Roads; therefore, logically, their putative ancestors would have followed a strain of Islam highly influenced by Persianate culture. By contrast, Hui whose ancestors are believed to have come by sea to Southeast

China, were more likely to have carried with them modes of Islam practised around the Gulf. The massive influx of Muslims from the Middle East and Central Asia under Mongol rule re-enforced pre-existing regional differences while adding even more diverse elements to the Muslim melting pot in China: 'Based on the wide distribution of Muslims in China under the Yuan, the evolution of the Sinophone Muslims during the succeeding Ming dynasty took place in a bewildering variety of contexts.'[3]

Over a period of 700 to 800 years, from the Tang period to the Ming period, a transformation from Islam *in* China into 'Chinese Islam' occurred. The earliest sojourners and settlers spawned generations of Muslims of mixed Chinese and foreign heritage. Newcomers from abroad infused new blood into these hybrid lineages, and also brought new ideas from the Muslim world. We have seen how various historical geopolitical circumstances affected the development of Muslim communities in China, and how Chinese Muslims faced the dilemma of acquiescing to assimilative forces in Chinese society with the concomitant risk of losing their distinctive Islamic identities. Many Muslims did assimilate in order to achieve a measure of security or even prosperity. Through their assimilation, or sinicization, they produced expressions of religiosity and interpretations of Islamic teachings that were localized, indigenized, and/or naturalized within the Chinese Confucian context. The product of this centuries-long process is a way of life that is simultaneously Chinese and Muslim.

Hui communities following this pattern and process, whose existence could be traced back, actually or imaginarily, to the origins and founders of Chinese Islam, retrospectively came to be called *gedimu* 各地目, a transliteration of the Arabic word *qadīm*, meaning 'ancient' or 'old'. This adjective referred, of course, to the notion that these were the oldest Muslim communities in China. They are also the most ubiquitous (around 58 per cent of all Hui). Gedimu Islam (also known as Laojiao 老教, or 'Old Teaching') is firmly grounded in the Sunni tradition of the Hanfi legal school. Gedimu communities in villages, towns or city districts tend to be centred around a local mosque with its own ahong (imam) and, depending on its size, some clerical personnel. Typically, a school is attached to or housed within the mosque, where local children receive basic instruction in fundamental Islamic tenets and ritual practice. Gedimu mosques often date back to the Ming or Qing dynasties and are usually constructed in the style of Chinese temple architecture. Gedimu communities tend to be close-knit, though they do engage in commercial transactions and social interactions with their Han neighbours. This contact sometimes results in intermarriage, most commonly between Hui men and Han women, who are often expected to convert to Islam and rear their children as Muslims. In the past, Gedimu families also had a custom of adopting Han children whom they raised as Muslims, often for the purpose of providing Muslim spouses for their sons and/or daughters when they grew up.

The highly assimilated nature of the Gedimu tradition led to the development of practices and institutions peculiar to these communities. One example is the uniquely Chinese phenomenon of 'women's mosques' (nüsi 女寺), which began in the late Ming to early Qing period.[4] These houses of worship are run by women for women of the community. At the head of a nüsi is a nü ahong 女阿訇 (female imam), who leads congregational prayers and instructs female students in ritual practice, basic doctrine and reading the Qur'ān. The nüsi is typically affiliated with, if not attached to, the main mosque of the community, and frequently the nü ahong is the wife of the male ahong. People often assume that the establishment of women-only mosques in China was due to Islam's segregation of the sexes, but this is not the case (or else it might be more common across the Muslim world). It was actually a response to Confucian scruples about wanton mingling of men and women. In order to conform to Chinese social norms, Muslims developed a tradition that exists down to the present day and is now being replicated in other contemporary Muslim societies and communities.

The simultaneity of Gedimu communities also provided the platform for some of the most remarkable achievements by Sinophone Muslims. As we have seen, the shift to Han Chinese as a mother tongue and the evanescence of Arabic and Persian as spoken languages during the Ming period led to a decline in Islamic knowledge. This state of affairs inspired Hu Dengzhou, who was educated in a Gedimu mosque school, to go abroad in pursuit of broader and deeper learning. He returned to China to establish the Jingtang Jiaoyu reforms of Islamic studies in Chinese. The teacher–student network he created served to link previously independent, isolated Gedimu communities across central and eastern China. This network eventually gave rise to the Muslim literati class, the Huiru, who produced the Chinese-Islamic canon of the Han Kitab. The fluidity and adaptability of Gedimu Islam thus helped raise the profile and promote the acceptability of Muslims in China.

Around the same time as the Han Kitab were being written in Muslim centres of central and eastern China, Sufism entered northwest China. While Hu Dengzhou visited and learned from Sufi teachers in Central Asia and the Middle East, and brought back Sufi texts and teachings, there is no record of any initiation or specific devotional practices in which he may have engaged. The Huiru certainly incorporated aspects of Sufi philosophy in the Han Kitab, but these references were highly theoretical. Again, there is no way of knowing whether the Confucian-Muslim literati practised mystical techniques; if they did, it was not publicized, as this could have compromised their agenda to present Islam as a staid, respectable religion that was fully compatible with Confucian norms. The case of Ma Zhu's lawsuit against the Qadiriyya Sufi order in Yunnan on charges of heresy demonstrates a rift between the Huiru theorists and Sufi practitioners.

The Qadiriyya ṭarīqa (Sufi order, lit. 'path') boasts one of the oldest lineages, traced back to the Iranian shaykh ʿAbd al-Qādir al-Jilānī (c. 1077–1166). It has spread throughout the Muslim world. Perhaps the earliest entry of Sufism into China is attributed to the 1674 arrival in Guangzhou of the Qadiri shaykh Khawaja Sayyid ʿAbdullāh (d. 1689). Sayyid ʿAbdullāh preached in northwest and southwest China for fifteen years, and is buried in Langzhou 閬州, Sichuan. One of his close disciples, Qi Jingyi 祁靜一 (1656–1719, also known as Hilāl al-Dīn) became the first Chinese shaykh of the Qadiriyya, establishing its centre in Linxia. Since the transmission from Sayyid ʿAbdullāh to Qi Jingyi was spiritual rather than genealogical, a non-heredity succession became the tradition for Chinese Qadiris; in fact, their shaykhs practise celibacy and personally select their successors from among their disciples.[5] Qi's tomb in Linxia became a site of veneration and pilgrimage, practices also associated with the Qadiriyya in China. Strict Qadiris practice an ascetic form of Sufism, which may include poverty, celibacy and rigorous meditative/devotional exercises such as repeating the names of Allah thousands of times (i.e. dhikr). As a result of its historical distribution, today Qadiri Sufis are found among the Hui in both the northwest and southwest and represent approximately 1.4 per cent of China's overall Hui population.

The Kubrawiyya is a Central Asian ṭarīqa, which was founded by Najm al-Dīn Kubra (1145–1221) in the thirteenth century. According to Chinese Kubrawi oral accounts, the order was introduced to China during the Ming dynasty by Shaykh Muhuyindeni (Muḥyi al-Dīn), who travelled there on three separate occasions: first to Guangdong and Guangxi; then to Hunan and Hubei; and finally to the northwest (Xinjiang, Qinghai and Gansu).⁶ According to the traditional narrative, Muhuyindeni settled in the Dongxiang village of Dawantou 大灣頭, near Linxia. There, he was received by the local Zhang (張) clan, a branch of whom converted en masse to Islam and became his disciples. He thereupon took the Chinese surname Zhang for himself. His spiritual lineage, carried hereditarily through his son, came to be known as the Zhangmen (Zhang menhuan 張門宦). Muhuyindeni's proselytization and conversion of the local Han population drew negative attention from local officials, who suspected him of preaching heresy.⁷ He died in 1221, and his tomb, or gongbei, in Dawantou was the most important Kubrawi shrine in China, before it was destroyed by GMD troops in 1928.⁸ The Kubrawiyya still exist in Gansu today, but they are by far the smallest Chinese Sufi community, just 0.7 per cent of the total Hui population.

The two largest Sufi menhuan, also prevalent in the northwest, are the rival branches of the Naqshbandi ṭarīqa discussed earlier in the context of Qing dynasty Muslim conflicts, namely the Khafiyya and the Jahriyya (see Chapter 4). The Naqshbandiyya are also an order with Central Asian roots, established in the thirteenth century and named after their principal shaykh, Bahā' al-Dīn Naqshband Bukhārī (1318–89). The ṭarīqa and its teachings spread widely throughout Central Asia, the Indian Subcontinent and the Ottoman Empire. It was brought to China in 1672 by the shaykh Afāq Khoja, who preached in the northwest among Chinese-speaking Muslims. One of his disciples, Ma Tai Baba spread the teachings and opened a school in Linxia. One of his students, Ma Laichi, went to Mecca in 1728, and returned to open his own school in Linxia, where he taught devotional practices including the veneration of deceased shaykhs and their tombs, and a meditative dhikr performed silently. His Khafiyya menhuan followed a hereditary succession and attracted many Gedimu followers, whose donations enriched the order greatly. The Khafiyya eschew asceticism and believe in active engagement with the wider society. They have used Confucian philosophy to interpret Islamic scripture and doctrines (yiru quanjing 以儒詮經), akin to the methodology of the Huiru.⁹ The Khafiyya still reside in Gansu (especially Linxia and Lanzhou) and remain under the authority of a shaykh from the Ma lineage. They account for approximately 7 per cent of the Hui in the PRC today.

The Jahriyya branch of the Naqshbandiyya in China was founded by Ma Mingxin after he returned from Arabia in 1761. His teacher, 'Abd al-

Khāliq, taught him an ecstatic, vocalized form of *dhikr* and was against the veneration of saints, accumulation of wealth and lavish expenditure on religious buildings – basically the complete opposite of Ma Laichi's Khafiyya teachings. The Khafiyya branded the Jahriyya 'Xinjiao' (New Teaching) and themselves the 'Laojiao' (Old Teaching, not to be confused with the same title applied to the Gedimu), as a way of saying the latter were heretical upstarts whereas they themselves were the authentic establishment. Khafiyya–Jahriyya internecine struggle was at the root of the Jahriyya Revollt in Gansu (1781) and the First (1862) and Second (1895) Dungan Revolts. In the Republican era various warlords of the Ma Clique belonged to one or the other of the Naqshbandi sub-orders, putting aside old rivalries. While they are no longer engaged in armed conflict, however, the feud between the two sub-orders can still be felt nowadays in cities like Lanzhou, where some members of one group avoid worshipping with the other. The Jahriyya is the largest of the four Chinese Sufi groups today, constituting around 11 per cent of all Hui.

Besides the Sufi menhuan, a number of other Hui sectarian groups have emerged since the start of the twentieth century. One of these was Ma Qixi's Xidaotang 西道堂, founded in 1901. This so-called 'Hall of the Western Way' is also known as the Hanxue Pai 漢學派 (Chinese Studies Sect) because of its synthesis of Confucian and Islamic teachings. In this regard, Ma Qixi, who came from a Gedimu background, was also heavily influenced by the Han Kitab canon, especially the writings of Liu Zhi, which became the movement's core source and a major component of its curriculum. Based on the Han Kitab, Xidaotang teachings are infused with mystical ideas of philosophical Sufism, such as union with God, and they have also absorbed some Jahriyya influences, including opposition to the veneration of saints. Both of these elements made Ma Qixi a target of Khafiyya purists, including the warlord Ma Anliang, who accused the Xidaotang of heterodoxy. Ma Qixi was nearly killed and the sect almost wiped out. Despite this conflict with a pro-Republican general, Ma Qixi backed the GMD and participated in the building of the nation. The movement developed into a closely knit community based in Gansu and then dispersed throughout the northwest. Communalism and the pooling of resources, mostly derived from the trade network run by followers, are hallmarks of the Xidaotang, which survives today as a small solidarity, perhaps 1 per cent of Hui Muslims in total.

Yihewani (a Chinese transliteration of the Arabic *Ikhwān*, short for al-Ikhwān al- Muslimūn, or 'Muslim Brotherhood') was another movement that developed around the end of the Qing period. Its founder, the imam Ma Wanfu, was Dongxiang by ethnicity and came from a village called Guoyuan 果園 near Linxia. He also went to Mecca to study and was influenced by Saudi Wahhabism, which taught that Islam, as practised by most Muslims, had been corrupted by a plethora of cultural accretions, popular superstition and custom, and heterodoxies like Sufism. Wahhabism is based on the teachings of Ibn Taymiyya (1263–1328) and his later follower Ibn 'Abd al-Wahhāb (1703–92), both adherents of the Hanbali school of Islamic law and theology. Ma Wanfu nevertheless followed the Hanafi madhhab, like most Chinese Muslims. The Yihewani emphasize their strict compliance with the Sunna, the living example of the Prophet, and therefore call themselves Sunnaiti 孫奈提 in Chinese.

Like other Salafi movements, Wahhabism promotes a revival of 'true' Islam, the pure faith and practice of the pious Muslim ancestors (Ar. *salaf*), based strictly on the Qur'ān and Ḥadīth, as interpreted from a literalist perspective; for this reason, Wahabbis/Salafis are commonly referred to as Muslim 'fundamentalists'. When Ma Wanfu returned from Arabia to Gansu, he began to preach this doctrine among Gedimu communities, whom he accused of following an Islam adulterated by excessive accommodation to Chinese culture. While not opposed to Sufism in principle, he denounced the Sufi menhuan that practised religious innovations and excesses like the 'worship' of shaykhs and idolization of their tombs. For this reason, General Ma Anliang, a defender of the Khafiyya menhuan, called Ma Wanfu and followers of his 'new teaching' (again a derogatory term) *kuffār* (sing. *kāfir*), or infidels. After Ma Wanfu fought alongside the Muslim rebels in the Second Dungan Revolt, Ma Anliang, a Qing loyalist, sought his arrest and execution. These plans, however, were thwarted when Ma Qi helped Ma Wanfu to escape.

The Yihewani, as originally conceived by Ma Wanfu, was part of a global pan-Islamic revivalist movement, and therefore did not espouse nationalist sentiments or ambitions. Yet, when faced with a choice during the Chinese Civil War, the movement's leadership after Ma Wanfu decided to give their full support to the GMD. Imam Hu Songshan had already begun to transform the Yihewani from within, steering away from pan-Islamism and mere revivalism toward a more progressive and Chinese nationalistic ideology. After these reforms, Ma Qi's son, General Ma Bufang, embraced the Yihewani as the most viable group to support his aspirations for social, educational, religious and cultural modernization. The 'partnership' of Ma Bufang and Hu Songshan led to the ascendancy of the Yihewani in the Northwest during the Chinese Civil War. General Ma further promoted the Yihewani by repressing rival sects, including non-Yihewani Salafis (those who had not subscribed to Hu Songshan's reforms) as well as Sufi menhuan and traditional Gedimu communities. Despite clashes with other Muslims and having supported the GMD against the Communists, the Yihewani have survived in the PRC. In fact, the CCP has supported the Yihewani more than any other Hui group, harnessing its Chinese nationalism in much the same way as the GMD had previously done. Today, the Yihewani are the second largest group (after the Gedimu), representing an estimated 21 per cent of the Hui population.

When the Yihewani were becoming more moderate and mainstream, some of the movement's followers broke away to perpetuate the more puritanical, fundamentalist and pan-Islamic ideology of Wahhabi-influenced Salafism. These Chinese Salafis were hostile towards and isolated from nearly every other Muslim solidarity in China. For decades, the Salafis were forced to subsist on their own, having very limited contact with the Muslim world outside the PRC. With the Gaige Kaifang reforms of the 1980s, however, China opened to greater foreign contact and influence, and the Chinese Salafis were able to use this opportunity to increase their engagement with Salafis abroad. In particular, they were able to receive Saudi financial support to build mosques and schools, which taught a strongly Wahhabi-influenced curriculum. These outside contributions were tolerated by the PRC government, which was courting Arab and Muslim countries to enhance political and commercial relations. More recently, however, within the past decade, the government has been attempting severely to limit the scope of foreign religious influence in the PRC, and this has affected the Salafi communities. Nowadays, Chinese Salafis have been forced by the political climate to blaze their own path, free of Saudi-Wahhabi support. Consequently, they have made greater accommodations to Chinese society, whereas previously they accused other groups (Gedimu, Yihewani, Xidaotang, Sufis etc.) of being overly accommodating. The insularity of Salafi communities in China prevents research that would allow us to estimate their numbers, let alone glean more about their activities.

The fissures among different Chinese Muslim groups can be in some ways even more divisive than the rifts between Muslims and non-Muslims. We have seen intra-Muslim rivalry dating back to the Ispah Rebellion, which pitted Shi'a against Sunni Muslims and the Yuan dynasty. There were no more bitter and bloody conflicts than the Khafiyya–Jahriyya feud that erupted in several revolts against the Qing dynasty. The Khafiyya menhuan proved to be an equal-opportunity antagonist against other Chinese Muslim groups, such as the Xidaotang and the Yihewani. The latter, when given the chance, manifested its own intolerance against other Muslims groups, including the Gedimu population (from which its own members were drawn), Sufi menhuan, and especially schismatic Salafis. And, as just mentioned, the Salafis bear animosity towards virtually all other communities. In the worst cases, these sectarian and ideological contentions devolved into mutual rebuke or even the extreme measure of *takfīr*, the act of accusing another of being an infidel. It is a major sin, according to Islam, for a Muslim to kill another Muslim, so takfīr has been used throughout Islamic history to justify intra-Muslim warfare. It is thus a most grave charge, which, if brought irresponsibly, can condemn the accuser to God's punishment, as the Prophet said: 'If a Muslim declares his brother to be a disbeliever, then verily the accusation is true of one of them. Either the accused is as claimed, or the charge is returned against the accuser.'[10]

Apart from such religious infighting, Muslims in China have also altercated based on ethnic and cultural differences. The most notable division has historically been between the two largest Muslim ethnic groups in China: Hui and Uyghur. The Uyghur people have a long history independent of China but have also had close relations with Chinese civilization since at least the Sui dynasty (see Chapter 1). The Tarim Basin of present-day Xinjiang has been their homeland since at least the ninth century when they were forced into diaspora after the fall of the Uyghur Khaganate. As such, they became a dominant presence along eastern stretches of the overland Silk Roads, providing hospitality for caravans of traders in the various oasis settlements in the Taklamakan Desert.

The majority of the Uyghurs, like other Turkic peoples, converted to Islam, but due to their geographical dispersion, the Islamization process occurred gradually in different oases over a period of almost 500 years (tenth–fifteenth century). Most Uyghur communities are agricultural, growing different kinds of produce in the various oasis settlements. Each of these towns and cities was, moreover, politically independent. For example, the Karakhoja state, based in Turfan and Ürümqi, was a centre of traditional Uyghur culture, whose residents were mainly Buddhist and Manichaean originally. The Karakhoja were invaded by the Mongols in 1209 and put up a lengthy resistance before finally submitting in 1335. They did not embrace Islam until the fifteenth century. By contrast, the Uyghurs in the Chu River valley converted to Islam in 934, whereupon they founded the Islamic Kharakhan state (940–1212), which maintained close ties with the Samanid Emirate of Samarkand. In the early thirteenth century they too were conquered by the Mongols. Kashgar, the Kharakhan capital, became an important centre of Turkic Islamic culture and learning, on par with Samarkand and Bukhara. The entire Tarim Basin was conquered by the Mongols, who incorporated it into their empire thus uniting the majority of Uyghurs under a single ruler for the first time since the ninth century. This unification expedited the spread of Islam among the Uyghur settlements. By the fifteenth century, most of the Uyghur lands had been thoroughly Islamized.

Uyghurs were counted among the Semu class of Yuan society, so they were present in China during that period, but maintained their own independent culture. When the Ming dynasty contracted the territorial boundaries inherited from the Yuan, the part of Central Asia known as East Turkistan found itself once again outside the Chinese Empire. The Uyghur oases reverted to separate states, which vied with each other for primacy, while also trying to resist being absorbed into the Timurid Empire (1370–1507) to the west. By the seventeenth century, most of the region had fallen under the control of the Dzungar Khanate (1634–1758), a confederation of Buddhist Oirat Mongols. After the Manchus conquered China and established the Qing dynasty, they commenced a military expansion into Inner Asia. The Kangxi emperor began the invasion of the Dzungar domains, which continued until his grandson, the Qianlong emperor, completed the annexation of Dzungaria and the Tarim Basin in 1759. The entire territory thereupon received its new name, Xinjiang, after it was incorporated into the Qing Empire.

At first, many among the Uyghur welcomed the overthrow of the Dzungars and supported the Manchus. The Manchus attempted to control Xinjiang first by installing local puppet rulers. The Kangxi emperor elevated a Uyghur chief to rule Hami in the early eighteenth century. The Qianlong emperor attempted to do the same throughout Xinjiang by dividing it into four satellite states. Beginning in the mid-eighteenth century, the Qing government embarked on a policy of colonization, encouraging Han and Hui migration and settlement in Xinjiang with incentives of economic opportunity and social mobility. This policy was intended to offset the Uyghur majority of the region and ease its incorporation within the Chinese sphere of influence; this process continues to this day. But this strategy was a failure as local Uyghur populations resisted both imposed rulership and population transfer. Due to the rebellions of the 1760s, the Qing were forced to occupy Xinjiang militarily from the late eighteenth century onward. The occupation diverted resources and manpower to maintain security in the territory and was therefore a drain on the Qing regime, weakening its ability to repel foreign incursions in the eastern parts of China. Xinjiang was officially made a province of the empire in 1884.

After the fall of the Qing dynasty in 1911, the ROC inherited the territory and borders of the empire and sought to pacify volatile areas. Political factionalism and squabbles within the government disabled the ROC from consolidating centralized rule, thereby allowing the rise of warlords in more remote border regions. Xinjiang thus became an embattled region throughout the Republican and Civil War eras. After hundreds of years of being divided and conquered by foreign regimes – Mongol, Manchu and Chinese –Uyghurs, exposed to Western ideas of self-determination between the world wars, began to conceive of themselves as a single nation. And like many other nations in that era, they aspired to have an independent state of their own.

In 1933, at the height of the first phase of the Chinese Civil War, Uyghur nationalists established a short-lived, independent East Turkistan Republic (ETR, 1933–4), centred in Kashgar. Uyghur independence from the ROC was supported by the USSR, who hoped to bring the western part of the territory into their own orbit (much like Mongolia, or other Central Asian republics). The name 'East Turkistan' obviously drew upon the notion of pan-Turanianism (the unity of all Turkic peoples), which regarded the Uyghur homeland as the easternmost part of 'Greater Turkistan', extending to Anatolia in the west. This conception, espoused by Uyghur nationalists, meant turning away from Chinese political domination and cultural influence and looking westward, to Samarkand, Bukhara, and even Istanbul, for ethnic and religious brotherhood.

The ETR was soon conquered by a Chinese warlord, Sheng Shicai 盛世才 (1895–1970), who ruled Xinjiang for a decade. Sheng, who had originally been backed by the USSR, changed allegiances on favour of the ROC in 1946. Once the ROC was internally unified under Chiang Kai-shek, however, it attempted once again to assert control over Xinjiang, but it faced Uyghur resistance in the Soviet-supported Ili Rebellion (1944). The same year saw the creation of a second East Turkistan

Republic as a puppet state of the USSR. This new iteration of the ETR opposed both the GMD and the CCP. It fell in 1949 when the PLA entered Xinjiang. The CCP declared the final liberation of Xinjiang and its inhabitants from foreign imperialism, claiming thereby to have completed the Uyghur people's struggle on their behalf. From that time until today, the PRC has maintained that Xinjiang is an inalienable part of China, albeit with semi-autonomy for its non-Han citizens guaranteed; this notion has been contested by many Uyghurs themselves. The Xinjiang Uyghur Autonomous Region was officially established in 1955. Ironically, incorporation into the PRC and the newly established Minzu System provided the Uyghur people across Xinjiang with a national identity and a unity they had not shared for over a millennium. This reinforced a burgeoning Uyghur nationalism that would become a lingering problem for the PRC government down to the present day.

Xinjiang was hit hard by the failed policies of the Great Leap Forward, leading to the mass emigration of some 60,000 Uyghur refugees to the USSR in 1962. At the same time, the PRC had begun a population transfer of Han Chinese into Xinjiang, promising them economic opportunity and other benefits, in order to improve (from the government's perspective) the ratio of Han to Uyghur residents. Over the course of two decades, beginning in the 1950s, the percentage of Han living in Xinjiang rose from 7 per cent to nearly 40 per cent, while the percentage of Uyghurs has fallen to 45 per cent. In the provincial capital of Ürümqi, Han residents came to outnumber local Uyghurs nearly 76 per cent to 13 per cent (the remainder are Hui and other minzu). This policy naturally increased ethnic tensions, primarily between Uyghur and Han, though Hui and other minorities have also been drawn into the regional conflict. The government has tried to encourage the collective assimilation of Uyghurs into the mainstream, Han-dominant culture of the PRC. It has implemented policies such as mandatory Mandarin-language classroom education for children, and restrictions on using the Uyghur language in official, public contexts. Certain traditional customs and religious practices were also restricted during the first several decades of the PRC.

Since the incorporation of Xinjiang into the PRC, some Uyghurs have embraced the idea of a shared national destiny and development. Many have enjoyed the benefits of the Preferential Policy that privileges non-Han minzu in school and housing placement and certain employment opportunities, but this has only earned them the resentment of Han residents of Xinjiang who regard this as reverse discrimination. Yet, even with these measures to win the hearts and minds of non-Han populations, the majority of Uyghurs cling tenaciously to their ethnic and cultural distinctiveness, and many of them desire even greater autonomy than the PRC Constitution provides. And then there is a minority who would prefer complete independence for Xinjiang from China, which the Constitution and the party-state reject outright.

Since 1933, in one form or another, organized activists have pursued Uyghur independence and self-rule invoking 'East Turkistan', a term abhorred by both the ROC and PRC for its anti-Chinese implications. This cause has included several separatist factions, most of them nationalist and secular in nature. Others, however, invoke jihad and religious affiliation with foreign Islamists. Their struggle for independence is combined with the goal of the global ascendance and domination of a particular interpretation of Islam. By far, most Uyghur activists who promote greater autonomy or independence are in fact secular, albeit culturally Muslim; they consider Islam to be an integral part of the Uyghur national identity, but do not pursue their grievances against the PRC in religious terms. The Islamist fringe movements, however, have taken an extreme position, advocating and/or using violent means. Most prominent among these factions is the East Turkistan Islamic Movement (ETIM), which is believed to have morphed its identity and changed its name to the Turkistan Islamic Party (TIP). Over the past three decades, the ETIM/TIP has used terrorist tactics, claiming responsibility for dozens of attacks in Xinjiang and elsewhere in the country. While the ETIM/TIP and secular, nationalist movements have separate agenda and different goals, they are often conflated in both government policy and public opinion. This conflation serves to justify wide-reaching policies for dealing with the 'Xinjiang Problem', though the reality of internal factionalism among Uyghur separatists actually benefits the party-state by preventing a unified resistance.

Uyghur cultural politics has proven to be a persistent threat to PRC national security and unity, while Islamic identity has undeniably played a role in the ongoing conflict. But, of course, not all Muslims in China share the same antagonistic views of the party-state. The majority of Hui see themselves and their fortunes to be tied to the overall strength and prosperity of the PRC and tend to fall in line with government policies. Therefore, Hui often side with the state and their Han compatriots concerning the Xinjiang problem and Uyghur agitation in general. For centuries, Chinese-speaking Muslims have distanced themselves from their non-Han co-religionists. In the twentieth and twenty-first centuries, many Hui have spoken out against Uyghur separatism and extremism making a clear distinction between themselves and the radical, 'unruly' Muslims in China's western frontier region, just as Chinese Muslims in the past regarded themselves as part of the civilized centre of the empire, in contrast to western 'barbarians'. Today Hui go to great lengths to demonstrate to the public and the state that they are not extremist, radical Muslims. Hui and Uyghur, the PRC's two biggest Muslim ethnic minorities, are unmistakably distinct from each other, largely due to their distinct historical origins and their current outlooks.

As we have seen, the Hui, among all ethnic groups, have the most in common with the Han ethnically, linguistically, historically and culturally. Indeed, Hui are often highlighted as a shining example of minority integration into mainstream society, as well as the PRC's commitment to respect of ethno-religious rights. Hui–Han relations, however, are still marred by mutual misunderstanding, mostly based on age-old cultural perceptions and stereotypes. While many Hui have been thoroughly assimilated and secularized, and often resemble Han not only in physical appearance but also in lifestyle, those who maintain aspects of religious and cultural distinctiveness sometimes have difficulty socializing with their Han counterparts. Hui and Han alike cite mutually irreconcilable differences based on Islamic custom, if not belief and practice.

Anti-Muslim sentiment since the beginning of the twentieth century has caused many Chinese Muslims to flee China, creating a Hui Muslim diaspora in places such as Central Asia (where they are still referred to as 'Dungan'), Southeast Asia and the Middle East (especially in the Gulf States). Ironically, the Muslim emigrants often find themselves clustered together with overseas Chinese communities of the greater Chinese diaspora.

Perhaps the greatest and most persistent obstacle to Hui–Han conviviality, today as in imperial times, is the difference in dietary habits. The pork taboo in Islamic law and practice is well known around the world. Yet, many Han cannot grasp why Hui and other Muslims would abstain from this staple, and to them delicious, meat. For centuries, ignorant hypotheses about the reason for Muslims' avoidance of pork have circulated. Some Han have speculated that it is because the pig is a kind of totem to the Hui, their revered ancestor.[11] Hui Muslims, for their part, maintain a belief that pork is filthy, so those who consume it are also ritually impure. Those who observe the dietary restrictions would be reluctant to eat in the home of Han neighbours, even if they did not serve pork, because their cooking and eating utensils, indeed their very kitchen and house, is believed to be contaminated by this impurity. The notion of being *qingzhen* ('pure and true') is so fundamental to the identity of religious Hui that the taboo creates a boundary between the sacred and the profane that they dare not cross.[12] Observance of such boundaries can affect all parts of life, from the home, to school, to the workplace, to public space. Hui have solved this problem by opening their own shops and restaurants, specializing in mutton and beef dishes, such as Lanzhou *lamian* 蘭州拉麵 (spicy beef noodle soup) found across China and heartily enjoyed by Han patrons as well.

Given the obstacles to ethno-religious intermingling, partaking of ethnic cuisine in the context of a cosmopolitan society is perhaps one step in the process of lowering barriers. But there remains a big difference between cultural appropriation and genuine appreciation of another culture. The popularity and ubiquity of lamian restaurants does not bespeak a profound understanding of the Islamic cultural and religious traditions behind the noodles. And while the PRC promotes bold rhetoric about respect for and the equality of all minzu in China, it also delivers mixed messages about its attitude towards multi-culturalism and the viability of a multinational state. On the one hand, the official policy is and always has been to uphold the sanctity of minzu distinctiveness. But the functional reality appears to be government endorsed practices to downplay ethnic difference and encourage homogenization through sinicization (or Hanification) of minorities. The official policy has resulted in such regulations as Mandarin language education for all ethnic groups, obligatory training in CCP doctrine and civics, but also the benefits of the Preferential Policy. Minority individuals may join the Party, and some even serve in government positions. These achievements are upheld by the state as tokens of the success of integration initiatives, which attempt to embrace diversity while downplaying difference. Removing boundaries between minzu is an unspoken correlative to the Marxist ideal of eradicating class distinction. Even as diversity is 'protected', there is a sense in which it is simultaneously being phased out. Ethnic heritage may be 'celebrated', but only within parameters specified by the state. Material cultures are vestiges of a bygone era, pre-revolutionary relics.

The preservation of minzu distinctiveness has been symbolized by the establishment of state-run institutions to honour the various ethnic groups in their native regions as well as similar associations in the capital. One of the most notable institutions recognizing the place of ethnic minorities is Minzu University of China (MUC, Zhongyang Minzu Daxue 中央民族大學), originally founded in Beijing in 1951 as the Central Institute for Nationalities (Zhongyang Minzue Xueyuan 中央民族學院). In 1993 it became the country's pre-eminent university for ethno-linguistic, sociological and anthropological studies. The faculty and student body are integrated, comprised of both Han and minorities (with quotas for the various minzu). Other regional universities catering to local minority students and professors exist in various provinces, but the Beijing campus is by far the most prestigious and renowned. While MUC certainly fulfils the PRC goal of minority representation at the national level, it nevertheless contributes to an essentialization and objectification of ethnic communities, similar to the way indigenous peoples have been treated by colonial powers around the world.

These perspectives are literally on display at the university's Museum of Ethnic Cultures (Minzu Bowuguan 民族博物館), described at the head of this chapter. The museum is a trove of ethnic material culture, exhibiting thousands of hand-crafted objects of the ethnic minorities meticulously catalogued. Of note, Han ethnic culture is not included in the collection. It is, therefore, a de facto museum of minority heritage curated, for the most part, by outsiders to the various cultures preserved therein. While members of various ethnic groups populate the university and museum, most of them live a largely Han-ified lifestyle while the artefacts of their cultural patrimony lie lifeless in vitrines. In another part of Beijing there is the spectacle of the Chinese Ethnic Culture Park (Zhonghua Minzuyuan 中華民族園), a 50-hecatre ground dedicated the re-creation of the daily life and architecture of various minzu, providing 'facility and base for the protection, presentation and exchange of ethnic culture heritage. It is the window of ethnic policy of the government, harmony and progress of 56 nationalities in China.'[13] The Culture Park in the capital is replicated in other cities across the PRC, giving the (mostly Han) general public a 'taste' of how ethnic minorities live through cultural performances, celebrations and concession stands in a theme park atmosphere. The lived culture of the shaoshu minzu can scarcely be found in most parts of China today. Instead we find sterile displays: costumes worn for photo opportunities; religious ceremonies presented for entertainment; and reproductions of material culture for ethnological study and touristic consumption.

Beyond such essentialized displays, inter- and intra-Minzu life is far more complex in real communities where boundaries alternate between rigidity and fluidity. Among those Hui who have set aside strict religious scruples, mixing with their Han compatriots is not at all uncommon, as they study and work side by side. Hui–Han intermarriage also occurs, especially in bigger cities, and is encouraged by the state. Miscegenation has contributed to the emergence a new kind of Chinese Muslim – the Han convert to Islam. Some Han partners will convert in order to placate their spouse's family. Other Han have embraced Islam for reasons of belief and conscience, but since the PRC census only counts citizens by minzu status and not religious affiliation there is no way to know how many Han Muslims live in China.

In the contemporary PRC, Han perceptions of Muslims are impacted by the worldwide phenomenon of Islamophobia – fears of terrorism, 'creeping sharī'ā', the belief that Muslims are plotting to conquer and convert the world, Islamic misogyny, etc. Antiquated stereotypes and current events, including the public and government perceptions of the Xinjiang problem, have resulted in growing prejudice against Hui, Uyghurs, and other Muslims in China and abroad. Chinese social media abounds with Islamophobic content, some of it translated from Western sources, but increasingly home-grown as well. Yet, the government seeks to quell this animus both to promote domestic socio-political harmony and to court and maintain friendly relations with Muslim countries overseas, as we shall see in the final chapter.

Chapter 8
Chinese Muslims, global Islam and the global power of China

Every day people migrate from the Pakistani countryside to the largest city, Karachi, in search of work and economic opportunity. Yet, with this massive influx, the already sweltering, congested city becomes ever more crowded with fewer and fewer well-paid jobs available. As migrant workers arrive, they find virtually no one hiring and are relegated to the ranks of the urban under- or un-employed. Securing anything more than the most menial jobs requires skills, including proficiency in English, which many migrants lack. In this increasingly desperate situation, some hear about the burgeoning job market at the new deep-water port of Gwadar on the Arabian Sea and decide to leave the big city for the distant boomtown. Upon arriving in Gwadar, many are astounded by the level of development proceeding in the former fishing village. Seeking work at the new dockyard, one might take the bus that drives the length of the isthmus, which bisects the mammoth port. Looking back, one would see the jagged red cliffs rising up from the coastline and realise how vastly different this scene was from Karachi. This is the new Special Economic Zone built largely upon Chinese investment. The China-Pakistan Economic Corridor initiative brings many Chinese businessmen to Karachi and other cities in the interior, but the Chinese presence in Gwadar far exceeds anything found elsewhere in the country. Despite the rapid development of the port, rumours abound that the whole project is behind schedule or even grinding to a halt. Some extremists regard

China as just another foreign, non-Muslim power ready to exploit Pakistan. Gunmen recently attacked a new hotel in Gwadar, but this has not deterred migrants from arriving day after day. Amidst the cranes and forklifts at the dock, there are Pakistani labourers but the foremen and managers are mostly Chinese. Among the job applicants one can hear many languages: Urdu, Punjabi, Baluchi, even Pashto. On top of that clamour one hears office workers speaking to each other in Chinese and to Pakistani employees in English with a heavy Chinese accent. As difficult as it may be to find work in Karachi without a strong command of English, those wishing to advance their careers in Gwadar might be advised to learn Mandarin as well.

During nearly three decades since the early 1990s, the number of Muslims permitted by the PRC to go to Mecca for the Hajj rose steadily from roughly 2,000 per year to a peak of 14,500 in 2016. In 2017, however, the numbers dropped to 12,800, and then 11,500 in 2018.[1] The reasons behind this long, steady rise and sharp decline reveal much about China's relationship to its internal Muslim population as well as its foreign relations with Muslim countries abroad, and the balancing act it attempts between these interrelated interests. Since the time of the Reform and Opening Up of the late 1970s to early 1980s, Hajj diplomacy was a means for the PRC government to reward (especially Hui) Muslim citizens for their political loyalty and social compliance, while cultivating closer ties with the Muslim world (Saudi Arabia, in particular). This double-edged policy continued into the new century but has changed like so many other geopolitical realities post-9/11.

As discussed earlier, the PRC's struggle with Uyghur pro-independence activists and separatists in Xinjiang was subsumed under the Global War on Terror and created a starker division between Uyghur and Hui Muslims. Hui participation in Hajj increased alongside Uyghur travel restrictions. The disparity in policies directed at the two largest Muslim minzu widened in the 2000s. Uyghur CCP members avowed, 'Uyghurs enjoy the same religious freedoms as Hui Muslims do',[2] but conditions on the ground suggested otherwise. The difference was no more pellucid than in the case of Islamic education in China. A nationwide boom in the construction and opening of mosque-based schools took place in Hui communities, while tight restrictions were imposed on religious education in Xinjiang in order to prevent the spread of extremism (as defined by the party-state).

The US-led wars in Afghanistan and Iraq continued apace, while Western governments and NGOs repeated their criticism of PRC human rights violations. China and other countries pointed out the hypocrisy of US rights advocacy in light of the revelations coming out of Abu Ghraib[3] and Guantanamo Bay. The United States and its allies had ceded much of the moral high ground while the PRC watched the unfolding, or unravelling, of American Middle East policy. The PRC government used that time as a spectator to grow its economy and impose strict control over sources of political dissent and agitation such as separatist movements in Xinjiang and Tibet. At the same time, China pursued a foreign policy of increased investment in Asian and African countries, including strategic and economic partnerships with a number of Arab and other Muslim countries. In the post-9/11 environment, relations between the US sphere of influence and many parts of the Muslim world became fraught with mutual unease. Western countries hurled human rights and terrorism-related accusations at Arab and Muslim regimes, which only made partnership with the PRC more appealing to them, since neither partner need peddle in recriminations to transact with each other. Thus, many Arab/Muslim countries began a slow pivot towards the growing power of the PRC, which in turn began to focus increasingly on its Central Asian neighbours, the Indian Ocean region, Middle East and Africa further abroad.

China's Xinjiang problem was not going away, however. In fact, it was worsening. So, a looming question was how the PRC's treatment of its own Muslim populations would affect its desire to build stronger ties with the Muslim world. How would Muslim governments, in response to domestic public opinion, address the Xinjiang issue, if at all? Would they overlook it and focus instead on the mutual benefits, economic and otherwise, in their relations with Beijing? Above all, how would the PRC address the issue, if at all, with Muslim regimes and with the international community in general?

The PRC's response to questions or criticisms about its handling of the Xinjiang issue was generally to downplay problems and divert international attention. In terms of addressing the global Muslim community, one strategy was also to highlight the successful integration of Hui Muslims into Chinese society and emphasize the government's beneficence towards them in terms of religious freedom and state support. The jewel of this policy was the Hajj diplomacy that permitted more and more Hui pilgrims to visit Mecca, even as the number of Uyghurs decreased precipitously. This frequently had the side effect of driving a wedge between Hui and Uyghurs (and other Muslims in the PRC), while marginalizing Uyghur concerns.

Uyghur agitation, protest and incidents of violence continued during the first decade of the 2000s. There had been several bus bombings in the previous decade (1992, 1997) but these were treated as isolated crimes orchestrated by Uyghurs in exile. At first, the government publicly attached little importance to what appeared to be random incidents and denied that there was an organized domestic terrorism problem. Yet, attacks increased in severity and frequency, forcing authorities to recognize self-avowedly Islamist groups like TIP (the successor to ETIM) as serious threats to national security. As the PLA and local police used increasingly harsh tactics to combat these groups, extremist violence was also ramped up. From 2007 to 2009 there were nearly a dozen attempted or successful attacks. ETIM/TIP claimed responsibility for many of them or praised the initiative taken by sympathetic but non-affiliated individuals or groups.

A wave of protests followed the death of Mutallip Hajim, a wealthy Uyghur merchant who died in police custody in Khotan on 3 March 2008. While the precise circumstances of his death are unknown, Uyghurs across Xinjiang rose up. They also demonstrated against newly implemented policies restricting public expressions of religiosity, such as the wearing of headscarves (Ar. *ḥijāb*) by women in Xinjiang. The protests happened to coincide with unrest in Tibet, though no direct connection has ever been established. In the summer of 2008 authorities were also maximizing security in preparation for the Beijing Olympic games. The Olympic torch was scheduled to make its journey through Kashgar in June, and the government wanted to avoid any untoward incidents. Arrests of suspected terrorists plotting attacks occurred, followed by a spate of attacks on local police stations in several Xinjiang cities in which officers and civilians were injured and killed.

The violence appeared to have died down towards the end of 2008 but began to escalate again the following summer. In June 2009, a fight between Han Chinese factory workers and Uyghur migrant workers in the Guangdong city of Shaoguan 韶關 broke out. The Han workers accused some Uyghur men of having sexually assaulted a young Han woman, and proceeded to attack Uyghur co-workers. Over 100 people were injured and two Uyghur men died as a result. Local officials said that ethnic conflict was unfortunately common in such work environments and a police investigation discovered no evidence of the alleged sexual assault. The government position is that the incident was overblown by Uyghur separatist groups operating in exile, in order to stir unrest. On 5 July 2009 a mass protest in Ürümqi, putatively against the Shaoguan incident, turned into several days of rioting involving violence between local Uyghur and Han (and Hui) residents, destruction of property and fighting with police attempting to control the situation. The numbers of casualties are disputed among various media sources, but the official toll reported by Xinhua that August was 197 killed, 156 of them civilians among whom 134 were Han, eleven Hui, ten Uyghur and one Manchu; over 1,600 were injured.[4] In the aftermath of the riots, as smaller ethnic skirmishes and protests continued to erupt, the central government imposed strict restrictions on citizens' movements and communication, temporarily shutting down the internet for days, in order to restore calm. The Ürümqi riots ushered in a new state of securitization in the PRC, especially in Xinjiang.

It then remained to be seen how the Muslim world would to respond to the event. Pre-empting any potential censure, Beijing petitioned the Organization of Islamic Cooperation (OIC) headquartered in Saudi Arabia not to issue a statement of condemnation. The OIC complied. Saudi Arabia remained conspicuously silent about Xinjiang. This was likely due to the growing business relationship between the kingdom and the PRC. Saudi trade with China exceeded $43 billion in 2010, and oil giants Aramco and Sinopec had recently made deals to collaborate on building infrastructure, such as the massive refinery in the Saudi city of Yanbo. The reaction from Muslim countries was overwhelmingly unperturbed, suggesting that most were willing to accept the PRC's account of events and justification for its actions. Only two (non-Arab) Muslim governments offered criticism: Iran and Turkey.

Iran's foreign minister, Manouchehr Mottaki, expressed 'concerns among Islamic countries' in a conversation with the foreign minister of the PRC, Yang Jiechi.[5] It is noteworthy that the riots in Xinjiang took place approximately one month after the Iranian presidential elections in 2009, the results of which were contested and led to protests that the government also suppressed. To criticize the PRC not only would have offended Iran's principal trading partner, which supplies the Islamic Republic with nuclear and military technology, but it would also have highlighted its own popular uprising and subsequent crackdown. There was, however, a high-ranking cleric who criticized both China and his own government, as Grand Ayatollah Youssef Saanei proclaimed,

'Silence and indifference toward such oppressions on the people is an unforgivable vice.'[6] And yet, the Supreme Leader Khameni remained silent. Iran's muted official response attests to the strong ties the PRC and Iran developed over the previous two decades.

Turkey's reaction to the situation in Xinjiang was the harshest of any Muslim country. Prime Minister (now President) Recep Tayyip Erdoğan invoked the most severe of terms: 'The incidents in China are, simply put, a genocide. There's no point in interpreting this otherwise.'[7] Such strong language was likely intended for a domestic audience, because the Turkish public is deeply emotional about the perceived plight of the Uyghur people. There is a large Uyghur diaspora community in Turkey whose members are regarded as political and religious refugees. The Uyghur exodus from Xinjiang in the mid-twentieth century deposited diaspora communities in Central Asia as well as in Turkey, which welcomed Uyghur immigrants as Turkic Muslim brethren. Indeed, a popular belief among many in Turkey holds that the Uyghur people are the ancestors of all Turks and that East Turkistan is the cradle of Turkic culture. Turkish people protested against PRC policies in Xinjiang, and the government had to support such popular sentiment without alienating the PRC, with whom it had built up strong bilateral relations in recent years.

In 2010, erstwhile Turkish foreign minister Ahmet Davutoğlu walked back the hard line taken by Erdoğan by affirming Turkey's respect for Chinese sovereignty and territorial integrity, which would prevent it from ever interfering in the domestic affairs of the PRC. He expressed hope that the Xinjiang problem could be solved peacefully and that the region and its people could serve as a crucial link between the two countries. In October of that year, en route to an official visit to Beijing, Davutoğlu stopped over in Kashgar and Ürümqi. By permitting his landing in Xinjiang, Beijing allowed Davutoğlu to display Turkey's commitment to the Uyghurs before entering into high-level talks about foreign trade, mutually beneficial infrastructure projects and increased strategic co-operation.

At that time, Turkey, a member of the North Atlantic Treaty Organization (NATO) and applicant for membership in the European Union (EU), volunteered to act as a broker between China and the West. The PRC had numerous ongoing disputes with the United States in matters relating to Xinjiang, among them the disposition of Uyghur detainees picked up by US-led forces in Afghanistan. After years of detention at Guantanamo Bay, these men were exculpated and scheduled to be released. The Chinese government wished them to be extradited to the PRC to face trial. The United States instead made arrangements with third countries (Bermuda and Palau) to grant them residence. Beijing also protested the United States granting asylum to Rebiya Kedir (b. 1946), a Uyghur businesswoman and activist in exile who led the Uyghur World Congress and whom the PRC considers to be at the forefront of separatist, extremist interference in Xinjiang.

Attacks continued intermittently over the next several years (2010–13), leading to mass arrests of Uyghur suspects. Increasingly, ETIM/TIP claimed responsibility forcing the central government to take the domestic terrorist threat more seriously than in previous decades. Reports came out of Xinjiang in non-Chinese media of intensifying measures to surveil Uyghur citizens and restrict the observance of cultural and especially religious customs and practices that the government believed to contribute to extremism. These restrictions included the prohibition of forms of Islamic dress, including headscarves for women and beards for men in certain public contexts, as well as lingering around mosques after congregational prayers, unsanctioned religious study, and fasting during Ramadan for civil servants and other public employees, including teachers and students.

A change at the top of the CCP signalled a sterner position against crime, national security threats and any activities that jeopardize the unity and stability of the PRC. Xi Jinping became general secretary of the Party in 2012, and immediately implemented strict policies to rid the government and society of corruption, to rein in political dissent through measures like policing the internet, and to regulate compliance to social norms within a rigid legal framework. His regime also began to pursue a more aggressive foreign policy, using both soft and hard power to assert China's global position and advance its geopolitical and economic agenda. In 2013, Xi assumed the office of president of the PRC and in the autumn of that year unveiled his administration's most ambitious flagship plan for international relations and trade, the so-called 'One Belt, One Road' (*Yidai Yilu* 一帶一路), or 'Belt and Road Initiative' (BRI).

The BRI was predicated on China's millennia-long history of (East–West) international trade and diplomacy along the ancient networks of the overland and maritime Silk Roads (hence the reference to land-based 'one belt' across Eurasia, and the 'one road' traversing the Indian Ocean into the China seas). Invoking this glorious past, going back to the Han and Tang dynasties, the PRC was declaring that it was prepared to reclaim China's position as a global power, extending its reach deep into Afro-Eurasia and beyond. In addition to its traditional scope, which has included Central and Inner Asia, China was now also going to be a player in South and Southeast Asia and, harking back to Zheng He's Ming dynasty 'treasure fleet', would also project its maritime power all the way to Africa. Through the BRI, the PRC hopes to secure strategic access to vital resources and markets. The BRI is, at its core, a conglomeration of massive infrastructure projects in partnership with many countries. It seeks to build roads and railways, airports and seaports, along which goods will flow bidirectionally. The building of naval and air force bases in the Indian Ocean region will also help secure shipping lanes, on which China depends, against possible military blockades by other global powers.

Of special interest in terms of economic opportunities are access to fuel and mineral resources in Central Asia, Middle Eastern oil and natural gas (as well as petrodollars from trade), and various natural resources and new markets in Africa. In all of these cases, the PRC will inevitably encounter Muslim countries, societies and cultures. In addition to these far-reaching collaborations and exchanges, the PRC shares borders with fourteen countries, five of which are Muslim-majority,[8] borders which have historically been permeable. For the BRI to pass its first hurdle, it must assure friendly relations with its Muslim neighbours. A major concern for the PRC is that for the overland 'belt' segment of the BRI to be viable, the situation in Xinjiang must be stable since virtually all roads westwards pass through it. Yunnan, which also has a large (Hui) Muslim population with connections to neighbouring Muslim diaspora populations, provides access to South East Asia. Terrorism, or even the public perception of problems involving China's Muslim populations, could result in a lapse of confidence regarding the initiative. Moreover, opening Xinjiang to contact with the greater Muslim world carries the risk of the 'wrong' Islamic influences entering the PRC.

While the governments of most Muslim countries involved in the BRI have enthusiastically embraced it, not everyone has been fully sold on the initiative. Economists have voiced concerns that the PRC is setting 'debt traps' for developing countries by luring them into deals for expensive infrastructure projects with promises of dividends that will not easily be realized. The PRC is providing loans that these struggling economies will not be able to repay in time, forcing them to default and allowing China to collect the debt by taking full control over the infrastructure, especially ports and bases. Others have criticized the BRI as being tantamount to soft power neo-colonialism whereby the PRC will extend its political power around the world through economic control. Some people on the ground where the BRI will lay its tracks have even objected to the incursion of Chinese influence on cultural and religious grounds. They argue that because the balance of economic power is so lopsided in China's favour, weaker countries will be dominated and overwhelmed not only by Chinese goods, but by the influx of Chinese nationals and cultural influences. Opponents to the BRI worry that the PRC will run roughshod over local ecologies, both physical and cultural, without showing respect to the customs and traditions of indigenous populations. A major concern is that the initiative will inundate recipient societies with Chinese cultural values that run counter to their own.

An example of how these criticisms, concerns and objections to BRI play out may has been witnessed in Pakistan, where the China-Pakistan Economic Corridor (CPEC) represents one of the most ambitious regional branches of the BRI at a total value of $62 billion. CPEC aims to build a network of infrastructure (rail lines, highways, ports etc.) running the length of Pakistan from its borders with Xinjiang in the north to a brand new deep-water seaport in Gwadar, on the Arabian Sea. It promises to bring commerce and employment to vitalize the Pakistani economy, which is why former prime minister Nawaz Sharif (b. 1949) first signed the agreement and his successors, including current prime minister Imran Khan (b. 1952), continue to support it heartily.

However, factions within Pakistan oppose it just as vehemently and have expressed their opposition violently. Among them are separatists in the province of Baluchistan, where the CPEC terminus of Gwadar is located, and where a gas pipeline from Iran is being constructed. Baluchi separatists have been active for decades, ever since the territory was incorporated into Pakistan in 1958, maintaining their cultural and national independence. They see CPEC as yet another example of Islamabad's disregard for their self-determination, allowing Chinese colonialists to exploit Baluchistan's resources and eventually outnumber the local population and deprive them of employment. Insurgent groups such as the Baluchi Liberation Front (BLF) and the Baluchi Liberation Army (BLA) have served warning that Chinese interests, including Chinese nationals, will be targets of violence. The BLA has already claimed responsibility for a suicide bombing on a bus carrying Chinese workers in Dalbandin, an attack on the Chinese Consulate in Karachi in 2018 and an attack by gunmen at an international hotel in Gwadar in 2019.[9]

A more explicitly religious form of opposition to CPEC has come from militant organizations affiliated with global jihadist networks. Tehrik-i-Taliban Pakistan (TTP), a group with ties to the Taliban in Afghanistan, has declared that any foreign ally of the Pakistani government may be targeted. TTP has already waged its self-proclaimed jihad against the United States and its allies for over a decade, citing the invasion by foreign imperialists with anti-Muslim, secular values as motivation. As the United States increasingly withdraws its support for the Pakistani state, China has come in to fill the void. As early as 2012, TTP justified attacks on Chinese nationals in Pakistan on the grounds of revenge for the PRC's treatment of Uyghurs in Xinjiang.[10] Other Islamist militants with ties to the Islamic State of Iraq and Syria (ISIS), now active in Afghanistan and northwest Pakistan, have also invoked the Uyghur cause in kidnappings and slayings of Chinese nationals in 2017. ISIS had already added the PRC to a list of countries, including the United States, Israel and India, guilty of the oppression of Muslims.[11]

China's ascendancy as global power not only ramps up its rivalries with other powers, most obviously the United States, but also places it within the crosshairs of extremist non-state actors intent on doing it harm. In 2012, a jihadist website called for retaliation against China for injustices against Uyghurs, threatening Chinese nationals in the Middle East: 'Chop off their heads at their workplaces or in their homes to tell them that the time of enslaving Muslims has gone.'[12] The call to action recalls Osama bin Laden's fatwa in 1998, which declared that American civilians would be targets of al-Qaeda's future attacks. As the PRC challenges the United States for superpower supremacy in the twenty-first century, it can only expect an escalation in such threats. And as it pursues closer relations with Arab and Muslim regimes despised by militant Islamist groups, it can also expect to receive more calls for jihad against it. Ties between global jihadist networks and extremists within Xinjiang have been growing for more than a decade. ISIS and al-Qaeda-related groups have actively been recruiting foreign fighters among Chinese Muslims. In 2015, an ISIS website posted a video with a song in Mandarin exhorting Muslims to join the jihad against the 'shameless enemy' after a 'century of slavery'.[13] The PRC is not mentioned by name in the video, but it was posted only a few weeks after ISIS claimed responsibility for the execution of a Han Chinese hostage in Iraq, freelance consultant Fan Jinghui 樊京輝 (1965–2015). The fact that the song lyrics are in Mandarin suggests that the video may have been intended to appeal to Hui Muslims, or more likely younger

Uyghurs whose education has mainly been in Mandarin. Judging from the appearance of Uyghur fighters on battlefields in Syria, such recruitment and propaganda efforts have been effective. Realizing the PRC's worst fears, many Uyghur militants in the Middle East have admitted that they became radicalized after the 2009 riots and subsequent crackdown in Xinjiang and later joined the fight in Syria and Iraq in order to acquire weapons and training to use back in their homeland.[14]

Rather than eliminate the domestic terrorism threat within the PRC, the security measures imposed in Xinjiang after the 2009 Ürümqi riots seem to have caused extremists to seek out soft targets elsewhere in China. On 1 March 2014 an attack of unprecedented brutality, called by many 'China's 9/11', took place at the main railway station in Kunming. Eyewitnesses have described a group of as many as eight people dressed in black rampaging through the station wielding knives and cleavers, striking at anyone within their reach. By the time police had finally shot or subdued the perpetrators, the official count was thirty-one killed and 143 wounded. Authorities identified the assailants as Uyghurs from Xinjiang who had allegedly attempted to flee the PRC to participate in jihad abroad, but when turned back at the border with Laos decided to attack civilians within Yunnan. Local and central government authorities limited reporting of the attack, its aftermath and the trial that saw the surviving attackers sentenced to death and executed in 2015.

Word of the incident did spread, however. Popular sentiment within the PRC favoured harsh measures to crackdown on Uyghurs in Xinjiang, and on Muslims throughout the country. Islamophobic posts proliferated on Weibo and other Chinese social media, conflating Muslims in China, whether Uyghur, Hui or other, with Islamist terrorists worldwide. No official link has ever been established between the Kunming attackers and any global jihadist group. Authorities in Yunnan deported Uyghur residents back to Xinjiang and imposed greater scrutiny on Hui activities within local Hui communities, such as Shadian, though again no connection has been made between the attacks and non-Uyghur Muslims.

In the wake of the Kunming attack, with its obvious implications for domestic stability as well as the potential alarms it could set off in connection with the BRI, the government decided to implement even stronger measures in Xinjiang. In May 2014, the Xi administration announced the 'Strike Hard' campaign (Yanli Daji 嚴厉打擊)[15] to combat all forms of terrorism in the PRC, but with a special focus on Xinjiang. The expressed goal of the campaign was to combat extremism by continuing to repress cultural and religious practices associated with radicalization in combination with enhanced techniques of surveillance of suspected extremists amidst the general population by means of genetic and biometric data, closed-circuit television cameras, voice recognition technology and mandatory digitally encoded identification cards. Checkpoints and sweeping round-ups of Uyghur citizens became common in Xinjiang as part of the crackdown.

Since 2016, reports have surfaced of facilities used to house those detained in the round-ups. The PRC government has described these as camps whose main purpose is vocational training and education in PRC national ideology and civics. The vast majority of those held in the camps are Uyghur with some Kazakh and Kyrgyz as well. As word spread of the camps, the PRC faced growing criticism from foreign governments and media over their suspected nature and the lack of transparency about them. Throughout 2018, mainly Western countries called on China to open the camps to journalists and foreign inspectors as they began to cite human rights abuses. By 2019, the rhetoric turned to outright condemnation. Most Muslim governments, including Turkey, had remained silent up until that point. With the Turkish public becoming increasingly vocal about the camps, the Turkish Ministry of Foreign Affairs in February 2019 issued a statement acknowledging and rebuking the PRC for the interment of over one million Uyghurs and other Muslims.[16]

In March 2019, the State Council Information Office of the PRC responded to the charges, issuing a White Paper titled 'The Fight against Terrorism and Extremism and Human Rights Protection in Xinjiang'. The paper affirms China's historical claim to Xinjiang dating back to the Han dynasty. It then provides an analytical history of the region and its peoples, concluding that for centuries Xinjiang was a relatively harmonious melting pot of cultures and religions. According to the paper, Islam is not the indigenous religion of the Uyghur people but rather it was historically imposed upon them from outside. The paper explains that religious extremism in Xinjiang may be traced to the relatively recent introduction of an intolerant form of Islam that is exploited by separatists to justify defiance of government authority. Enumerating and recounting recent episodes of terrorist violence, the paper states that extremists are in fact the worst culprits of human rights abuses. By contrast, it claims that the PRC government defends human rights by combatting extremism and terrorism. The paper identifies the root causes of the 'three evil forces' of ethnic separatism, religious extremism and violent terrorism as exploitation and brainwashing by those with intentions to destroy the social and political cohesion of Chinese society. The perpetrators of these evils are able to succeed in their exploitation and brainwashing because the local population is economically underdeveloped and poorly educated. Therefore, in addition to removing the detrimental influence of criminals spreading extremist ideas, the PRC must invest in lifting the people of Xinjiang out of poverty and providing them with both a modern education and a proper understanding of religious teachings. In light of the White Paper, the camps are presented as part of an initiative to provide practical training to help especially Uyghur civilians acquire the skills needed to participate in the modern economy, to learn the knowledge necessary to be a good citizen of the PRC and to block any pernicious influences from extremist religious teachings. The PRC's explanations and justifications of its policies did little to silence international critics. On 12 July 2019, a joint statement[17] was drafted at the United Nations Human Rights Council (UNHRC) and signed by ambassadors from twenty-two countries[18] condemning the arbitrary detention of Uyghurs and other minorities in Xinjiang. The following day, another joint letter was signed by representatives of thirty-seven countries[19] and sent to the UNHRC. The second letter opens with a rebuke of the politicization of human rights concerns. It then explicitly supports the PRC's policies for restoring peace and security in Xinjiang and for combating extremism and terrorism within the sovereign rights of a nation preserving its territorial integrity. The letter further affirmed the PRC's claim of safeguarding human, ethnic and religious rights in Xinjiang and throughout China. All of these are, of course, PRC talking points. The list of signatories is notable because of who is and is not included. Because the letter is a response to the previous day's statement signed by mostly Western countries, it is no surprise to see traditional adversaries of the West (e.g. Russia, North Korea, Cuba, Venezuela etc.). But the list includes representatives of more than a dozen Muslim-majority countries, including the members of the Gulf Cooperation Council (GCC) led by Saudi Arabia, and leading members of the OIC, such as Pakistan and Egypt. Most of the signatories have also signed lucrative deals with the PRC as part of the BRI. A few major Muslim countries did not sign the letter, including Indonesia, Iran, Malaysia and Turkey. Weeks earlier, however, according to Chinese media, Turkish president Erdoğan reversed his foreign ministry's February condemnation of PRC policy in Xinjiang during a visit to Beijing – a far cry from his 2009 accusation of genocide.[20]

The United States was conspicuously absent from the signatories to the first letter because the administration of President Donald Trump (b. 1946) withdrew from the UNHRC in 2018. The US State Department had already issued numerous statements denouncing the PRC's actions in Xinjiang and calling for the release of the detainees and closure of the camps. On 18 July 2019, US Secretary of State Mike Pompeo called the treatment of Uyghurs the 'stain of the century'.[21] The following day, a letter signed by nearly 100 scholars, professors and religious leaders from Xinjiang publicly refuted Pompeo's claims about the camps, allegations of religious and cultural persecution, and invasions of privacy. First, the letter describes amenability of living conditions in the camps, the quality of their educational programmes, and the fact that 'trainees' are permitted to leave for regular and special visits home. The letter explains that the PRC is simply trying to prevent terrorism by stamping out extremism, which includes education in the camps to address the root problems of ignorance and poverty. It affirms the PRC's efforts to preserve the unique languages and culture of ethnic minorities and support lawful religious practices and institutions that do not promote extremist ideas. Finally, it states that security measures installed in Xinjiang are no different than those used to maintain public safety in any modern society, including the United States.[22] The irony of criticism coming from an administration whose leader campaigned for election on a promise of banning all Muslims from entering the United States, and which currently maintains detainment camps at the country's southern border, where children are separated from their parents, cannot be lost on the PRC and its supporters.

The letter notes that since the opening of the camps and implementation of extreme restrictions there have been no incidents of terrorism or ethnic violence in Xinjiang. Thus, the PRC justifies these actions for achieving the state's main objective of securing the region. Much of the rest of the world, however, is unconvinced by this justification. Reports and perspectives on the situation inside Xinjiang diverge drastically from, some diametrically opposed to, the official Chinese narrative, especially among Western media, governments and non-governmental organizations. Chinese media coverage on Xinjiang is scant and foreign journalists have mostly been barred from the camps and the region in general so direct reporting on the conditions of Uyghurs detention and internment is limited. Nevertheless, a coherent and comprehensive narrative has been assembled from a variety of reliable non-Chinese state and non-state sources – foreign intelligence, leaked internal PRC documents on government policies and practices, victims' testimonies and eye-witness accounts from unnamed Chinese individuals, dissidents in exile and/or asylum seekers.

After the eventful summer of 2019 with its many diplomatic exchanges between the PRC, its allies and its critics, the Office of International Religious Freedom of the US Department of State published a comprehensive report on Xinjiang, drawing upon many of the sources enumerated above.[23] The report constructs a lengthy narrative of draconian policing and widespread human rights violations. The abuses described include random police and paramilitary searches of Uyghur and other Muslim homes, systematic seizure of religious materials and destruction of houses suspected of being used for 'unofficial' religious practices; many mosques and religious schools have also been razed. Civilians are reportedly detained for suspicions of religious extremism based on such probable causes as men growing beards, women starting to wear headscarves and veils, and people giving up smoking and/or drinking alcohol. It would seem that behaviours previously considered 'normal religious activities', in the words of the PRC Constitution, have now become criminalized.

Uyghurs have been put in camps, by their own accounts against their will, for indefinite periods without release or contact with anyone outside. Others have apparently been 'disappeared' without any trace, leaving family members asking for proof that their loved ones are still alive. The arrests and disappearances have given rise to forced family separations and a crisis of Uyghur children whose parents are detained being placed in orphanages. Despite the protests of extended family, these 'orphans' are held in institutions where they may be educated by the state in the mandatory Chinese curriculum and CCP civics and where they may remain until they reach the age of majority. Among those imprisoned have been prominent academics and other professionals who were in no need of vocational training. Descriptions of conditions inside the camps include brutal practices such as forced labour, unwanted reproductive interventions (e.g. abortions and sterilizations), physical torture and psychological and sexual abuse, and come cases of extra-judicial killings. A striking example of de-humanization evocative of other historical human atrocities is a report that human hair forcibly removed from prisoners has been used in the manufacture of cosmetic products.

The official response to such reports has been a summary denial and repudiation, claiming their contents have 'disregarded the facts, slandered and attacked China with unwarranted accusations, flagrantly politicized human rights issues, and grossly interfered in China's internal affairs'.[24] The difference in perspectives between the PRC's narrative and that of its Western critics is more than just mutual allegations of the all-too-common 'fake news' variety, or state manufactured propaganda. There seems to be an even more alarming dilemma in evidence here – a crisis of truth plaguing the world today. As an oft-repeated adage (probably erroneously attributed to Chinese tradition) goes, 'There are three truths: Your truth, my truth, and *the* truth.' The meaning, of course, is that our apprehension of truth is always subjective and perspectival, and objective or absolute truth will therefore always elude us. That principle is certainly operative in the case of the present situation in Xinjiang. There are some facts that are undisputed by either side of the divide. The international community is aware that there has been extremist violence in China and the PRC acknowledges that the camps exist. That, however, appears to be where agreement ends. In this case, the truth has become no longer a matter of differing perspectives, but an intransigent ideological and highly politicized standpoint. Our word has become so polarized that the pursuit of truth has become a dangerous enterprise.

The blurring of truth has become an instrument of politics as never before. Some say that ideological intransigence and global hyper-nationalism are leading us to a new Cold War between the PRC and United States. But even the apparent polarities of such a conflict are unclear. At the time of the writing of this book the two superpowers are engaged in a bitter trade war. In its opposition to the rise of Chinese power, the US government has taken a strong stand against human rights abuses in Xinjiang, leading to the passage of the Uyghur Human Rights Policy Act by the US Congress. However, on 17 June 2020, the same day that President Trump signed the act into law, former US National Security Advisor John Bolton claims that Trump also personally told Xi Jinping that he 'should go ahead with building the camps, which Trump thought was exactly the right thing to do'.[25] When the PRC's strongest adversary equivocates on the Xinjiang situation, the support of Chinese policy by Muslim countries, even against the interests of their Uyghur co-religionists, becomes normalized. Among other things, this situation allows the BRI to proceed apace, as the PRC's allies and partners remain steadfast and committed. China thus appears poised to withstand the international controversy over Xinjiang, its relations with most major Muslim countries intact.

The number of Chinese pilgrims going to Mecca may have declined in recent years, but it appears that Hajj diplomacy is no longer as important as it had been before because the PRC has solidified its economic and strategic ties with Saudi Arabia and other Muslim countries. Beijing remains just as committed as before to wooing Muslim partners and collaborators. An example of this commitment is the nearly $4 billion invested in the construction of an Islamic theme park in Yinchuan 銀川, the China Hui Village Culture Park (Zhonghua Huixiang Wenhuayuan 中華回鄉文化園). The project was started in 2001, with portions opened in 2005, though final completion is scheduled for 2020. It is advertised as 'the only theme-park in China that displays ethnic Hui culture, religion and traditions' where visitors 'can fully enjoy Hui folk culture, religion, dances, songs and movies and food'.[26] The park 'includes an ethnic Hui museum, a ritual palace, a Hui ethnic customs village and a Hui catering and performance center as well as a Muslim restaurant and art craft shopping street' but the 'main attraction of the park is a white Islamic-style building, which is surrounded by a long and round corridor'.[27] It is perhaps ironic that while the PRC, in its effort to sinicize all religious expressions in China, encouraging all new mosques to be built in a Chinese style, is nonetheless sponsoring the construction of this arabesque 'palace' with multiple domes and minarets. The park is intended to lure Muslim tourists from around the world. Direct flights from Dubai to Yinchuan have been established. Foreign Muslims, especially from Arab countries, are welcomed to experience Chinese Islam in a manner and venue fully sanctioned by the PRC government. This Islam is Hui, with emphasis on the ethnic aspects of Hui identity and culture: food, costume, performance, and arts and crafts. This is clearly the face of Islam that China wishes to show the world.

So far, the park has not nearly attracted the volume of overseas visitors it has expected. In the meantime, however, tens of thousands of Muslims are coming to China every year. Many come for business. Some even stay for lengthy sojourns reminiscent of the Tang dynasty merchants who first brought Islam to China. The cities of Yiwu 義烏 (Zhejiang province) and Guangzhou have become magnets for Arab and other Muslim traders. Guangzhou has also attracted large numbers of Muslim visitors to its important Islamic heritage sites. The Huaisheng Mosque and especially the tomb of Saʻd ibn Abī Waqqāṣ are destinations for religious tourism, both domestic and international. Hui and Uyghur domestic tourists from other parts of China and foreign visitors flock to Waqqāṣ's graveside to offer prayers, turning the site into a kind of shrine, or site of religious visitation (Ar. *mazār*). This phenomenon has put Guangzhou on the map as a place of importance to Muslims worldwide. Guangzhou is a hub in the maritime portion of the BRI and has the history to substantiate the PRC's claim that the initiative is indeed reviving the glory of the ancient Silk Roads.

Yet even as the Islamic legacy of China is showcased for the world to see, the recent Chinese instantiation of Islamophobia tears at the fabric of ethno-religious harmony in the PRC. The Xinjiang problem has put Islam in a negative light for much of the Han Chinese public, who do not necessarily discern the nuances of minzu politics, nor the differences between domestic Muslim populations and those abroad. For many, Islam and Muslims are irredeemably alien to the Chinese culture and way of life. Some Han Chinese resent what they regard as the privileges the government has bestowed on ethnic minorities despite their inability or unwillingness to integrate into mainstream Han society. Every marker of Islamic identity is reminder of these perceived irreconcilable differences. A new ordinance in Beijing requires Muslim businesses, especially restaurants, to remove Arabic signs from their storefronts[28] and what happens in the capital is usually replicated throughout the country in short order. This is in line with the government's sinicization of religion campaign, but it runs counter not only to the letter of the PRC Constitution but also to the spirit of seeking to strengthen relations with the Muslim world. As China attempts to rise to the next level as a global superpower, it must strike a balance between domestic and foreign affairs with Chinese Muslims inevitably finding themselves caught in the middle.

Notes

Introduction

1   Jeff Diamant, 'The Countries with the 10 Largest Christian Populations and the 10 Largest Muslim Populations', *Pewresearch.org*, 1 April 2019. https://www.pewresearch.org/fact-tank/2019/04/01/the-countries-with-the-10-largest-christian-populations-and-the-10-largest-muslim-populations/, accessed 2 August 2020.

Chapter 1

1   Mircea Eliade, *The Sacred and the Profane: The Nature of Religion*, New York: Harcourt, 1987, p. 95.
2   The body of water that lies between the eastern coast of the Arabian Peninsula and the western coast of Iran has traditionally been called the Persian Gulf in Western sources. However, today conflict between the Arab states of the region and Iran has challenged this taxonomy, with one side claiming the waters as the 'Arab Gulf' and the other opting for the name 'Persian Gulf'. Remaining neutral amid this controversy, it shall be referred to herein simply as 'the Gulf'.
3   See George F. Hourani, *Arab Seafaring in the Indian Ocean in Early Medieval Times*, Expanded Edition, Princeton, NJ: Princeton University Press, 1995, pp. 46–50.
4   Khānfū خانفو is an Arabic transliteration of Guangfu 廣福, an earlier name for Guangzhou.
5   See the *Old Tang History*, juan 198 (舊唐書, 198 卷), *Jiu Tangshu*, Beijing: Zhonghua Shuju, 1975.
6   The Uyghurs at this time were not Muslims, but rather followed a variety of religions. At the height of its power, the Uyghur Kaghanate made Manichaeism its official religion. The conversion of the Uyghurs to Islam was a gradual process that occurred between the tenth and fifteenth centuries.
7   Medina is an abbreviated version of the city's full name given after the arrival of Muhammad, *Madīnat al-Nabī*, the 'City of the Prophet'.
8   622 CE is the year of the Hijra, the migration of the Prophet and the Muslims of Mecca to their new home in Medina. This event is recognized

within Islam as the start of the Islamic era, so the year 622 CE is contemporaneous with the year 1 AH (after Hijra).

9 The Arabic term for a successor is *khalīfa* (pl. *khulafā'*), from which the English rendering 'caliph' is derived; the institution of successorship, or the state presided over by the Caliph is known as the Caliphate (Ar. *khilāfa*). The first four successors to the Prophet Muhammad, selected by the Muslim community from among his Companions (Ar. *ṣaḥaba*), are collectively referred to in Islamic tradition as *al-Khulafā' al-Mahdī'ūn al-Rāshidūn*, the 'Rightly Guided Caliphs': Abu Bakr; 'Umar; 'Uthman; and 'Ali.

10 Donald Leslie, *Islam in Traditional China: A Short History to 1800*, Canberra: Canberra College of Advanced Education, 1986, pp. 16, 31.

11 *Dashi* is presumed to be a transliteration of term by which the Sasanian Persians referred to the Arabs, Tāzī, which is in turn believed to be derived from the name of an Arab tribe, the Ṭayyi'. See Guangda Zhang 張廣達, 'Dashi 大食', in *Zhongguo da baike quanshu* 中國大百科全書, *Zhongguo lishi* 中國歷史, vol. 1 (Beijing/Shanghai: Zhongguo da baike quanshu chubanshe), 1992, pp. 144–54.

12 In present-day Turkmenistan.

13 The Amu Darya river today runs through the Central Asian countries of Uzbekistan, Turkmenistan, Afghanistan and Tajikistan.

14 The rule of the 'Rightly Guided Caliphs' ended with the assassination of 'Ali (r. 656–61), part of an internal power struggle within the Muslim community. 'Ali's rival, Mu'āwiyah ibn Abī Sufyān (602–80) declared himself Caliph, thereby establishing his family, members of the Umayya clan of the Quraysh tribe of Mecca, as dynastic rulers of the Caliphate.

15 This extended period of military and political conflict in the early years of Umayyad rule is referred to as the 'Second Fitna' (*c*. 680–*c*. 692). *Fitna* فتنة is an Arabic term meaning 'trial', 'strife', 'ordeal' etc., and has been used to refer to conditions of civil disorder. Several distinct periods of '*fitna*' mark early Islamic history. The 'First Fitna' (656–61) refers to the conflict between the fourth 'Rightly Guided Caliph 'Ali and Mu'āwiyah, which resulted in the death of the former and the ascendance of the latter as founder of the Umayyad Caliphate. The 'Second Fitna' arose after the death of Mu'āwiyah and began with the struggle of the Shi'a faction, under the leadership of Husayn, son of 'Alī (and grandson of the Prophet), against Yazīd (r. 680–3), the son and successor to Mu'āwiyah. This conflict culminated in the Battle of Karbala (680) with the martyrdom of Husayn and the decimation of his army. The 'Second Fitna' also included a rebellion against Yazīd by 'Abdallah ibn al-Zubayr (624–92), who challenged the Caliph's political legitimacy on religious grounds. Ibn al-Zubayr propped himself up as a rival caliph and continued his struggle against the Umayyad line in Damascus even after Yazīd's death in 683 CE. His rebellion was ultimately put down under the regime of the fifth Umayyad Caliph, 'Abd al-Malik (r. 685–705) in the year 692 CE. The 'Third Fitna' refers to the various uprisings of the 740s that lead to the fall of the Umayyad dynasty and its replacement by the 'Abbasid Caliphate (750–1258).

16 Percy Molesworth Sykes, *A History of Persia*, London: Macmillan, 1915, p. 53.

17 See, e.g., Charles William Previté-Orton, *The Shorter Cambridge Medieval History*, Cambridge: Cambridge University Press, 1971.

18 As the Umayyad Caliphate expanded in all directions, various non-Arab peoples, including Persians, Byzantines, Copts, Berbers, Azeris, Turks, Kurds etc., were incorporated into the population. Many of them embraced Islam, while others did not. Arabs, retaining the social hierarchy of Arabian tribes, became the upper class, even in majority non-Arab regions. Non-Muslims were relegated to a lower social position, but even non-Arab converts to Islam were not able to share equal status with their Arab co-religionists. To address this problem the Umayyad leaders created social contract called *wala'* (literally a master–servant or patron–client relationship) whereby non-Arab Muslims (*mawālī*) were required to have an Arab patron (*mawla*), and continued to pay a tax like that paid by non-Muslims citizens (*dhimmi*) while being similarly excluded from government and military service.

19 The Banu Hashim were one of the leading clans of the Quraysh, the ruling tribe of Mecca, from which the prophet Muhammad was descended.

20 Carl von Clausewitz, *On War* (*Vom Krieg*, 1832), eds. Michael Howard and Peter Paret, Princeton, NJ: Princeton University Press, 1984, p. 87.

21 From the seventh to ninth century, Central Tibet (known in the indigenous language as Bod) was the seat of an independent empire stretching over a vast territory from Kashmir in the west, to the Uyghur Kaghanate in the north (present-day Inner Mongolia), to the border of present-day Myanmar in the south, and encompassing the present-day Chinese regions of Ningxia, Gansu, Qinghai and significant portions of Sichuan and Xinjiang. It abutted the 'Abbasid Caliphate to the northwest.

22 The Turkic people in this case were constituents of the Turgesh Empire, allies of the Tibetan Empire, which occupied the region in between the Uyghur Khaghanate and the 'Abassid Caliphate.

23 The Syr Darya river originates in the Tian Shan mountains of present-day Kyrgyzstan and runs westwards through Tajikistan, Kazakhstan and Uzbekistan.

24 Gao Xianzhi (Go Seonji 고선지) was a Tang dynasty general of Korean descent.

25 The Talas river flows east to west from headwaters in the Tian Shan mountains, near the border of present-day Kyrgyzstan and Kazakhstan. The precise location of the battlefield of 751 is unknown but is believed to lay somewhere between the modern cities of Taraz, Kyrgyzstan and Talas, Kazakhstan.

26 *Jiu Tangshu*, juan 198, p. 5316; *Xin Tangshu*, juan 6, p. 166.

27 Hajji Yusuf Chang, 'An Historical Overview: The Hui (Muslim) Minority in China', *The Muslim World League Journal*, vol. 17, nos. 3 & 4, 1987, p. 12.

28 Ibid.

29 This hadith, narrated by Anas, is cited by al-Bayhaqi in *Shu'ab al-Imaan* and *al-Madkhal,* Ibn 'Abd al-Barr in *Jami' Bayaan al-'Ilm*, and al-Khatib through three chains of transmission in *al-Rihla fi Talab al-Hadith*, though it was later deemed 'weak' (*da'īf*) by some scholars.

30 Marshall Broomhall, *Islam in China: A Neglected Problem*, London: Darf, 1987, p. 9.
31 Clyde Ahmad Winters, *Mao or Muhammad: Islam in the People's Republic of China*, Hong Kong: Asian Research Services, 1979, p. 9.
32 Broomhall, *Islam in China*, p. 78.
33 Ibid., p. 63.
34 Ibid., p. 64.
35 Ibid., p. 68.
36 Ibid.
37 Later Arabic sources do not mention the Saʿd narrative either. The thirteenth-century CE Arab traveler, Ibn Batutta, omits it in accounts of his journey to China, indicating that the Chinese Muslim origin myths that refer to it come from the Yuan period (1279–1368) or later, when a distinctly indigenized Chinese Muslim community began to form.
38 S. Maqbul Ahmad, *Arabic Classical Accounts of India and China*, Shimla: Indian Institute of Advanced Study, 1989, pp. 37–8.

Chapter 2

1 Morris Rossabi, 'Islam in China', in Joseph M. Kitagawa, ed., *The Religious Traditions of Asia. Religion, History and Culture*, New York: Macmillan, 1989, p. 357.
2 The East Central district, in addition to housing foreigners, was also home to the greatest concentration of Chang'an's homosexual population, many of the city's courtesan houses and brothels. See Charles Benn, *China's Golden Age: Everyday Life in the Tang Dynasty*, Oxford: Oxford University Press, 2002.
3 Cited in T.V. Philip, *East of the Euphrates: Early Christianity in Asia*, Delhi: CSS & ISPCK, India, 1998, p. 125.
4 Rafiq M. Khan, *Islam in China*, Delhi: National Academy, 1963, pp. 4–5.
5 The current structure was built during the Ming period in the seventeenth century.
6 Rossabi, 'Islam in China', p. 358.
7 Wei Meng, 'The Advent of Islam in China: Guangzhou Fanfang during the Tang-Song Era' (2010). All Theses and Dissertations (ETDs). 814. http://openscholarship.wustl.edu/etd/814, p. 31.
8 Ibid.
9 Ibid., p. 32.
10 Ibid., p. 20.
11 Ibid., p. 22.
12 Ibid., p. 21.
13 Cases involving Muslims and non-Muslims automatically reverted to Chinese jurisdiction.

14 Ahmad, *Arabic Classical Accounts*, pp. 37–8.
15 Meng, 'The Advent of Islam in China', p. 34.
16 Ibid., p. 22.
17 Yu Zhu, *Pingzhou ketan*, juan 2, p. 19, cited in Meng, 'The Advent of Islam in China', p. 24.
18 *Song shi*, 'Dashi Zhuan', juan. 490, p. 14119, cited in Meng, 'The Advent of Islam in China', p. 24; Jon W. Chaffee, *The Muslim Merchants of Premodern China: The History of a Maritime Asian Trade Diaspora, 750–1400*, Cambridge: Cambridge University Press, 2018, pp. 71–4.
19 Rossabi, 'Islam in China', p. 359.
20 Khan, *Islam in China*, p. 5.
21 Hajji Yusuf Chang, 'Chinese Muslim Mobility in Sung-Liao-Chin Period', *Journal, Institute of Muslim Minority Affairs*, vol. 5, no. 1, January, 1984, pp. 167–80.
22 Raphael Israeli, *Islam in China: Religion, Ethnicity, Culture, and Politics*, Lanham, MD: Lexington Books, 2002, pp. 283–4.
23 Chang, 'Overview', p. 13.
24 Khan, *Islam in China*, p. 6.
25 Ibid.
26 Ibid.
27 Chang, 'Chinese Muslim Mobility', p. 156.
28 Ibid.
29 Ibid.
30 Ibid.
31 Ibid.
32 Ibid.
33 Rossabi, 'Islam in China', p. 359.
34 Chang, 'Chinese Muslim Mobility', p. 161.

Chapter 3

1 Donald Daniel Leslie and Ahmad Youssef, '"Islamic Inscriptions in Quanzhou," a Review', *T'oung Pao*, vol. 74, no. 4/5, 1988, pp. 255–72 (p. 268). JSTOR, www.jstor.org/stable/4528421. See also Wenliang Wu, *Quanzhou zongjiao shike* (Religious inscriptions of Quanzhou), revis, by Wu Youxiong, Beijing: Kexue Chubanshe, 2005, 1957 (1st ed.); Dasheng Chen, *Quanzhou Yisilanjiao shike* (Islamic inscriptions of Quanzhou), Yinchuan: Ningxia Renmin Chubanshe, 1984.
2 Ke Fan, 'Maritime Muslims and Hui Identity: A South Fujian Case', *Journal of Muslim Minority Affairs*, vol. 21, no. 2, 2001, pp. 309–32, p. 407.
3 There is no record or evidence of olive cultivation in Quanzhou. The name Zaytūn therefore has an obscure derivation. Apparently, it is a calque

based on a Chinese nickname for the city, Citong Shi 莿桐市 (Tong Tree City). The tung tree, of the genus *Vernicia* has been cultivated in East and Southeast Asia for its seeds (also known as candlenut), which are a source of tung oil, used in paint and varnish. These trees had been introduced to Quanzhou and planted throughout the city by the general Liu Congxiao 留從效 (906–62). Citong became conflated with Zaytūn in Arabic pronunciation and transliteration, even though the olive and candlenut are not related apart from the fact that they both produce a kind of oil (Yingsheng Liu, 'A Lingua Franca along the Silk Road: Persian Language in China between the 14th and the 16th Centuries', in Ralph Kauz, ed., *Aspects of the Maritime Silk Road: From the Persian Gulf to the East China Sea*, Wiesbaden: Harrassowitz Verlag, 2010, p. 145.)

4   E. Gibbon, *The History of the Decline and Fall of the Roman Empire*, ed. J.B. Bury, 7 vols., London, 1906, p. 4 and n.8; David Morgan, *The Mongols*, London: Basil Blackwell, 1986, p. 41.

5   C.J. Tornberg, ed., Ibn al-Athir, *Al-kamil fi'l-ta'rikh*, vol. 12, Leiden, 1853, p. 234; Morgan, *The Mongols*, p. 17.

6   E.G. Browne, *A Literary History of Persia*, 4 vols., Reprint, vol. 2. London: Cambridge University Press, 1969, p. 439; R.E. Dunn, *The Adventures of Ibn Battuta*, Berkeley: University of California Press, 1986, p. 83.

7   See Ch'un Ch'ang, *The Travels of an Alchemist*, trans. A. Waley, London: Routledge & Kegan Paul, 1931, London: Routledge, 2014.

8   Dunn, *Ibn Battuta*, p. 84.

9   Morgan, *The Mongols*, p. 41.

10 Ibid.

11 The Mongolian slaughtering procedure is almost antithetical to that of Muslims. In the latter, the animal is stood upright, and its throat is cut across the jugular vein and carotid artery whereupon all blood is drained from the body. The Mongol butcher lays the animal on its back, restrains it, then slices the chest open and tears out the aorta to cause lethal internal bleeding while retaining all blood inside the carcass. Only after the internal organs are removed is the blood drained and used to make a kind of sausage (Thomas T. Allsen, *Culture and Conquest in Mongol Eurasia*, Cambridge: Cambridge University Press, 2001, pp. 128–9).

12 Morgan, *The Mongols*, p. 125.

13 Morris Rossabi, *Khubilai Khan: His Life and Times*, Berkeley: University of California Press, 1988, p. 13.

14 Ibid.

15 *Semu* may be translated as 'miscellaneous categories', though its literal meaning of 'coloured eyes' has led to the etymological interpretation that it referred to the diverse eye colouring of Westerners.

16 Ibid., p. 71.

17 Ibid.

18 Shamanism, Manichaeism, Buddhism, Nestorian Christianity etc.

19 In contrast to the transliteration Weiwu'er 維吾爾 used in the PRC today.

20 See Dru C. Gladney, *Muslim Chinese: Ethnic Nationalism in the People's Republic*, Cambridge, MA: Harvard University Press, 1991, p. 18; Jonathan Neaman Lipman, *Familiar Strangers: A History of Muslims in Northwest China*, Seattle: University of Washington Press, 1997, pp. xxiii–xxiv. An alternative theory, coming from Chinese Muslim tradition, states that Sayyid Safar (Su Fei'er) coined 'Huihuijiao', literally the 'Religion of the Double Return', to refer to Islam in the eleventh century (Israeli, *Islam in China*, p. 284).
21 Ibid.
22 Chang, 'Overview', p. 14.
23 Khan, *Islam in China*, p. 7.
24 Rossabi, 'Islam in China', p. 360.
25 Ibid.
26 Khan, *Islam in China*, p. 8.
27 Ibid.
28 Ibid., p. 9.
29 Rossabi, 'Islam in China', p. 360.
30 Ibid.
31 Khan, *Islam in China*, p. 8.
32 Ibid., p. 9.
33 Ibid. This is due in large part to the fact that when the Mongols sacked Baghdad in 1258, they destroyed many of the great institutions of learning in the city.
34 Rossabi, *Khubilai Khan*, p. 141.
35 Ibid., p. 179.
36 Rossabi, 'Islam in China', p. 359.
37 Ibid.
38 Ibid., p. 360,
39 Rossabi, *Khubilai Khan*, p. 182.
40 Ibid.
41 Ibid., p. 201.
42 Israeli, *Islam in China*, p. 285.
43 The ratio was consistent with the global Sunni–Shi'a split of around 5:1.
44 Chang, 'Overview', p. 14. Chang writes that Zhu was the son of a Semu officer in the Mongol Tammachi Garrison of Anhui. He makes the further claim that Hongwu's empress, Ma Hou, was also a Muslim and that a number of their children were wed to Muslim spouses and that the emperor had two Muslim cousins.
45 While Bai Shouyi and other Chinese Muslims claim him as a Muslim, non-Muslim scholars question whether Mu Ying was from a Muslim background, let alone a practising Muslim. See Michael Dillon, *China's Muslim Hui Community: Migration, Settlements and Sects*, London: Routledge, 1999, p. 33 and Lipman, *Familiar Strangers*, p. 22.

46 Maria Jaschok and Jingjun Shui, *The History of Women's Mosques in Chinese Islam: A Mosque of Their Own*. Richmond, Surrey: Curzon Press, 2000, p. 77.
47 Rossabi, 'Islam in China', p. 361.
48 James D. Frankel, *Rectifying God's Name: Liu Zhi's Confucian Translation of Monotheism and Islamic Law*, Honolulu: University of Hawaii Press, 2001, p. 23.
49 Ibid.
50 Chang, 'Overview', p. 14. This policy is similar to the case of the European Jews who were required by the Holy Roman emperor, Joseph II, to take German surnames in the late eighteenth century.
51 Cited in Lipman, *Familiar Strangers*, n.12, p. 297.
52 Lipman, *Familiar Strangers*, p. 292. Because of the Islamic prohibition against Muslim women marrying outside the faith and the shortage of eligible Muslim bachelors, many of these adopted sons were intended as future mates for the daughters of these families (Rossabi, 'Islam in China', p. 362).
53 Rossabi, 'Islam in China', p. 361.
54 Ibid.
55 Ibid., p. 362.
56 Ibid.
57 Ibid., p. 361.
58 According to local Islamic records in Quanzhou, cited in Louise Levathes, *When China Ruled the Seas: The Treasure Fleet of the Dragon Throne, 1405–33*, New York: Simon and Schuster, 1994, p. 148.
59 Dated 16 June 1407, the decree is signed by the emperor and appears on a stone tablet outside the Aṣḥāb mosque in Quanzhou (ibid.).
60 Both his father and grandfather were called Ḥājji, meaning that they had performed the pilgrimage to Mecca (Yifu Sun, et al., eds., *The Silk Road on Land and Sea*, trans. Cui Sigan, et al. Beijing: China Pictorial Publishing, 1989, p. 231).
61 On Zheng He's family background and youth see Levathes, *When China Ruled*, pp. 61–5.
62 Sun, *The Silk Road*, p. 231.
63 For a detailed description of Zheng He's trade and diplomatic achievements see Sun, *The Silk Road*, pp. 235–40.
64 Ibid., p. 231.
65 Levathes, *When China Ruled*, p. 172.

Chapter 4

1 Lipman, *Familiar Strangers*, p. 290.
2 Ibid.
3 Frankel, *Rectifying God's Name*, p. 24.

4   Rossabi, 'Islam in China', p. 361.
5   Han Hua Jennifer Chiang, 'Crossing Culture in the Blue-and-White with Arabic or Persian Inscriptions under Emperor Zhengde (r. 1506–21)', Diss., University of Hong Kong, Department of Fine Arts, Hong Kong, 2007, p. 1.
6   For more about the Gedimu, see Chapter 7.
7   Frankel, *Rectifying God's Name*, p. 17.
8   *Kitāb* is also used in Persian, Turkish and other Islamicate languages.
9   Ibid., p. 15.
10 Despite his reference to Arabia (Tianfang), Wang Daiyu was more likely of Persian ancestry (Sachiko Murata, *Chinese Gleams of Sufi Light: Wang Tai-yü's Great Learning of the Pure and Real and Liu Chih's Displaying the Concealment of the Real Realm*, Albany: State University of New York Press, 2000, p. 20).
11 Jianming Fu, et al., eds., *Yisilanjiao jianming cidian* (Concise Dictionary of Islam). Jiangsu: Ancient Books Press, 1993, p. 294.
12 Daiyu Wang, *Zhengjiao zhenquan* (True Explanation of the Orthodox Religion), ed. Yu Zhengui, Yinchuan: Ningxia People's Press, 1987, p. 17.
13 Fu, *Yisilanjiao*, p. 294.
14 Rossabi, 'Islam in China', p. 364.
15 Zhu Ma, *Qingzhen zhinan* (Guide to Islam), Reprint, Tianjin: Huizu Zhongguo Yisilanjiao, 1987, p. 76.
16 See Jonathan Lipman, 'A Proper Place for God: Ma Zhu's Chinese-Islamic Cosmogenesis', in Jonathan Lipman, ed., *Islamic Thought in China: Sino-Muslim Intellectual Evolution from the 17th to the 21st Century*, Edinburgh: Edinburgh University Press, 2016, pp. 15–33.
17 James D. Frankel, 'Islamisation and Sinicisation: Inversions, Reversions and Alternate Versions of Islam in China', in A.C.S. Peacock, ed., *Islamisation: Comparative Perspectives from History*, Edinburgh: Edinburgh University Press, 2017, p. 505.
18 Leslie, *Islam in Traditional China*, p. 122.
19 Xia Wang, ed., *Beijing Niujie Libaisi* (Beijing Ox Street Mosque), Beijing: China Today Press, 1996, p.40.
20 Leslie, *Islam in Traditional China*, p. 126.
21 Ibid., p. 128.
22 On the Qing conquest, occupation and administration of Xinjiang, see James A. Milward, *Eurasian Crossroads: A History of Xinjiang*, New York: Columbia University Press, 2007, pp. 97–115, and Hodong Kim, *Holy War in China: The Muslim Rebellion and State in Chinese Central Asia, 1864–1877*, Stanford, CA: Stanford University Press, 2004, pp. 7–18.
23 Frankel, 'Islamisation and Sinicisation', p. 505.
24 Ibid., p. 507.
25 Ibid.
26 *Dungan* is a term used by Turkic-speaking Central Asians to refer to Chinese-speaking Muslims.

27 *Panthay* is a Burmese term referring to Chinese-speaking Muslims.
28 Lipman, *Familiar Strangers*, p. 219.
29 Ibid., p.132.

Chapter 5

1. Zvi Ben Dor Benite, 'Taking 'Abduh to China: Chinese-Egyptian Intellectual Contact in the Early Twentieth Century', in James L. Gelvin, Nile Green, eds., *Global Muslims in the Age of Steel and Print*. Berkeley: University of California Press, 2014, p. 252.
2. Based on the older Wade-Giles system of romanization the name of the part is rendered 'Kuomintang', which most older texts abbreviate as 'KMT'.
3. *Minzu* is a neologism coined by and borrowed from Japan, where it was devised as an equivalent of the European concept of 'nation' or 'people' that had become central to nineteenth-century political discourse. For more on the *minzu* concept, see Chapters 6 and 7.
4. Songting Ma, 'Zhongguo huijiao yu chengda shifan xuexiao' [Chinese Islam and the Chengda Teachers School], *Yugong*, vol. 5, no. 11, 1 August 1936, pp. 1–14, cited in Yufeng Mao, 'A Muslim Vision for the Chinese Nation: Chinese Pilgrimage Missions to Mecca during World War II', *The Journal of Asian Studies*, vol. 70, no. 2, May 2011, pp. 373–95, p. 378.
5. Ma Qianling so respected his commanding officer Dong Fuxiang that he named his son after him.
6. Although going by the same name and also an Islamic revival movement, the Chinese Yihewani should not be confused with the later Ikhwān al-Muslimīn (Muslim Brotherhood) founded and still active in Egypt and elsewhere in the Middle East (see Chapter 7).
7. For more on the Xidaotang, see Chapter 7.
8. Yufeng Mao, 'Muslim Educational Reform in 20th-Century China: The Case of the Chengda Teachers Academy', *Extrême-Orient Extrême-Occident*, vol. 33, 2011, pp. 143–70, pp. 151, 172.
9. The CCP is often also referred to in English as Communist Party of China (CPC).
10. The First East Turkestan Republic (1933–4) was established in response to calls for self-determination among Xinjiang's Uyghur/Turkic population, who enjoyed brief independence from China before being defeated by Chinese Muslim (Hui) warlords (see Chapter 7).
11. Mao, 'Muslim Educational Reform', p. 152.
12. Chinese Islamic Progressive Association (CIPA) was the first nationwide organization of its kind, predating the GMD-sponsored Chinese Muslim Association, established in 1938 as the Chinese Muslim National Salvation Association (Zhongguo Huimin Qiuquo Xiehui 中國 回民救國中國) then renamed the Islamic National Salvation Association (Huijiao Qiuquo Xiehui 回教救國協會) in 1939, to Chinese Islamic Association (Zhingguo Huijiao Xiehui 中國回教協會) in 1942, which still operates in Taiwan today. These

should not be confused with the Islamic Association of China (Zhongguo Yisilanjiao Xiehui 中國伊斯蘭教中國) established by the PRC in 1953 (see Chapter 6).

13 Ibid., p. 148.
14 Lipman, *Familiar Strangers*, p. 176.
15 Mao, 'Muslim Educational Reform', p. 152.
16 Ibid., p. 150.
17 Ibid., p. 152.
18 Stéphane A. Dudoignon, Hisao Komatsu, and Yasushi Kosugi, *Intellectuals in the Modern Islamic World: Transmission, Transformation, Communication*, Abingdon: Taylor & Francis, 2006, pp. 135–336.
19 Zvi Ben-Dor Benite, 'From "Literati" to "Ulama": The Origins of Chinese Muslim Nationalist Historiography', *Nationalism and Ethnic Politics*, vol. 9, no. 4, 2004, p. 95.
20 Ibid.
21 Benite, 'Taking ʿAbduh to China', p. 252.
22 The so-called 'Four Great Ahongs' (Si Daming Ahong 四大名阿訇) were Nūḥ Da Pusheng 達浦生 (1874–1965), Yaʿqūb Wang Jingzhai, Hilāl al-Dīn Ha and ʿAbd al-Raḥīm Ma Songting.
23 Aḥmad Narāqī, *Khazāʾin bi saʿī va ihtimām-i Zain al-ʿĀbidīn ibn Muḥammad-i Khunsārī* (Tehran, 1878), digitized by Columbia University, vol. 1, New York, 2009, pp. 487, 528.
24 Benite, 'Taking ʿAbduh to China', p. 252.
25 Mao, 'A Muslim Vision', p. 382.
26 Saudi Arabia, Egypt, Lebanon, Syria, Iraq, Iran, India and Turkey.
27 Ibid., p. 389.
28 Ibid.

Chapter 6

1 https://web.archive.org/web/20170721140805/ and http://e-chaupak.net/database/chicon/1954/1954bilingual.htm
2 Ibid.
3 Ibid.
4 Ibid.
5 http://www.chinaislam.net.cn/about/xhgk/about132.html#, accessed 19 July 2019.
6 https://web.archive.org/web/20170725061003/ and http://www.e-chaupak.net/database/chicon/1975/1975e.htm, accessed 19 July 2019.
7 Ibid.
8 The faction's leader was Mao's wife, Jiang Qing 江青, who worked with fellow members Zhang Chunqiao 張春橋, Yao Wenyuan 姚文元 and Wang Hongwen 王洪文.

9   http://en.people.cn/constitution/constitution.html, accessed 19 July 2019.
10 Ibid.
11 Maris Gillette, *Between Mecca and Beijing*, Stanford, CA: Stanford University Press, 2000, pp. 235–6.
12 Song Niu, 'China's Hajj Affairs under the Perspective of National Security', *Istanbul Gelisim University Journal of Social Sciences*, vol. 5, no. 1, April 2018, pp. 101–13, p. 107.
13 http://en.people.cn/constitution/constitution.html, accessed 19 July 2019.
14 Dru C. Gladney, 'Salman Rushdie in China: Religion, Ethnicity and State Definition in the People's Republic', in Charles F. Keyes, ed., *Asian Visions of Authority: Religion and Modern States of East and Southeast Asia*, Honolulu: University of Hawaii Press, 1994, p. 256.
15 Ibid.
16 Ibid., p. 259.
17 Niu, 'China's Hajj Affairs under the Perspective of National Security', p. 107.
18 It should be noted that some Chinese Muslims wishing to perform the Hajj but denied an exit visa opt for an 'unofficial Hajj', joining a pilgrimage group in a third country. From the perspective of the PRC, this is illegal.
19 Jim Yardley, 'A Spectator's Role for China's Muslims', *New York Times*, 19 February 2006, http://nytimes.com/2006/02/19/weekinreview/19yardley.html?_r=1&pagewanted=all&oref=slogin, accessed 18 July 2019.
20 Ibid.
21 Ibid.
22 Qiang Ying, '短評: 新聞自由要有限度' (Brief Commentary: Freedom of the Press Must Have Limits), Xinhuanet, 11 January 2015, http://www.xinhuanet.com//world/2015-01/11/c_1113952852.htm, accessed 18 July 2019
23 'White Paper – Freedom of Religious Belief in China', Embassy of the People's Republic of China to the United States of America, October 1997. http://www.china-embassy.org/eng/zt/zjxy/t36492.htm, accessed 18 July 2019.
24 Ibid.

Chapter 7

1   The Ismāʿīlī Shiʿa, or Ismailis, are a minority within the Shiʿa community, who broke off from the majority 'Twelvers' (Ithnāʿashariyya) during the succession controversy after the death of the sixth Shiʿa Imam (*c.* 700–765 CE). They are the only Shiʿa group that currently recognize a living Imam (descendant of ʿAlī), the Aga Khan IV (1936–).
2   See Broomhall, *Islam in China: A Neglected Problem*, London: Morgan and Scott, 1910; London: Darf, 1987 (reprint); Piscataway, NJ: Gorgias, 2007 (reprint).
3   Lipman, *Familiar Strangers*, p. 39.

4 See Maria Jaschok and Jingjun Shui, *The History of Women's Mosques in Chinese Islam*, Richmond: Curzon, 2000.
5 Gladney, *Muslim Chinese*, p. 44.
6 Michael Dillon, *China's Muslim Hui Community: Migration, Settlement and Sects*, London: Curzon, 1999, p. 127.
7 Ibid., p. 128.
8 Ibid.
9 David Lee, *Contextualization of Sufi Spirituality in Seventeenth- and Eighteenth-Century China*, Eugene, OR: Wipf and Stock, 2015, p. 189.
10 Sahih al-Bukhari, vol. 8, Book 73, Number 125d.
11 See Emile Durkheim, *Elementary Forms of Religious Life*, trans. Carol Cosman, Oxford: Oxford University Press, 2001, pp. 87–153.
12 See Mary Douglas, *Purity and Danger: An Analysis of the Concepts of Pollution and Taboo*, London: Routledge and Kegan Paul, 1966; London: Routledge, 2002, pp. 8–51.
13 http://emuseum.org.cn/en, accessed 26 August 2020.

Chapter 8

1 Rosie Perper, 'China Is Tracking Muslims Embarking on the Annual Hajj Pilgrimage in What Experts Say Is Likely Part of Widespread Government Surveillance', *Business Insider*, 10 August 2018. https://www.businessinsider.com/china-gps-tracking-muslims-on-hajj-part-of-government-surveillance-2018-8, accessed 2 August 2019.
2 Rukiye Turdush, 'A Muslim Divide in China: Uyghur Muslims Face Stricter Controls on Religion than Hui Muslims' (Trans. Mamatjan Juma, written in English by Rachel Vandenbrink), *Radio Free Asia*, 30 November 2012. http://www.rfa.org/english/news/uyghur/hui-11302012172354.html, accessed 13 April 2013.
3 The US military prison near Baghdad.
4 Xinhua, 'Innocent Civilians Make Up 156 in Urumqi Riot Death Toll', Embassy of the People's Republic of China to the United States of America, 5 August 2009. http://www.china-embassy.org/eng/xw/t577165.htm, accessed 3 August 2019.
5 Associated Press, 'Muslim Countries Mostly Silent on China Unrest: Ethnic Clashes, Crackdown on Uighur Minority Draws Muted Reaction', *Asia-Pacific* on NBC News, 10 October 2012. http://www.nbcnews.com/id/31893032/ns/world_news-asiapacific/#.UWtlg79DJzo, accessed 4 August 2019.
6 Ibid.
7 Ayla Jean Lackey, 'Turkish Leader Calls Xinjiang Killings "Genocide"', *Reuters*, 10 July 2009. https://www.reuters.com/article/us-turkey-china-sb/turkish-leader-calls-xinjiang-killings-genocide-idUSTRE56957D20090710, accessed 4 August 2019.

8 North Korea, Russia, Mongolia, India, Nepal, Bhutan, Myanmar, Laos, Vietnam, Kazakhstan, Kyrgyzstan, Tajikistan, Afghanistan, and Pakistan (the latter five are Muslim-majority countries).

9 Sarah Mahmood, 'Why Is China Vulnerable to Terrorism in Pakistan?' *The Diplomat*, 12 January 2019. https://thediplomat.com/2019/01/why-is-china-vulnerable-to-terrorism-in-pakistan, accessed 5 August 2019.

10 Ibid.

11 Ibid.

12 Associated Press, 'Muslim Countries Mostly Silent on China Unrest: Ethnic Clashes, Crackdown on Uighur Minority Draws Muted Reaction', *Asia-Pacific* on NBC News, 10 October 2012. http://www.nbcnews.com/id/31893032/ns/world_news-asiapacific/#.UWtlg79DJzo, accessed 4 August 2019.

13 Josh Chin, 'ISIS Releases Slickly-Produced Mandarin Song Seeking Chinese Recruits', *Wall Street Journal*, 12 December 2015. https://blogs.wsj.com/chinarealtime/2015/12/07/isis-releases-slickly-produced-mandarin-song-seeking-chinese-recruits/, accessed 4 August 2019.

14 Gerry Shih, 'Uighurs Fighting in Syria Take Aim at China', *Associated Press*, 22 December 2017. https://www.apnews.com/79d6a427b26f4eeab226571956dd256e, accessed 5 August 2019.

15 Formally called *Yanlidaji baolikongbuhuodong zhuanxiang xingdong* 嚴厲打擊暴力恐怖活動專項行動 (Strike Hard Campaign against Violent Terrorist Activities).

16 Republic of Turkey Ministry of Foreign Affairs, 'Statement of the Spokesperson of the Ministry of Foreign Affairs, Mr. Hami Aksoy, in response to a question regarding serious human rights violations perpetrated against Uighur Turks and the passing away of folk poet Abdurehim Heyit', 9 February 2019. http://www.mfa.gov.tr/sc_-06_-uygur-turklerine-yonelik-agir-insan-haklari-ihlalleri-ve-abdurrehim-heyit-in-vefati-hk.en.mfa, accessed 5 August 2019.

17 https://www.hrw.org/sites/default/files/supporting_resources/190712_joint_counterstatement_xinjiang.pdf, accessed 5 August 2019.

18 Australia, Austria, Belgium, Canada, Denmark, Estonia, Finland, France, Germany, Iceland, Ireland, Japan, Latvia, Lithuania, Luxembourg, the Netherlands, New Zealand, Norway, Spain, Sweden, Switzerland and the UK.

19 Algeria, Angola, Bahrain, Belarus, Bolivia, Burkina Faso, Burundi, Cambodia, Cameroon, Comoros, Congo, Cuba, Democratic Republic of the Congo, Egypt, Eritrea, Gabon, Kuwait, Laos, Myanmar, Nigeria, North Korea, Oman, Pakistan, Philippines, Qatar, Russia, Saudi Arabia, Somalia, South Sudan, Sudan, Syria, Tajikistan, Togo, Turkmenistan, United Arab Emirates, Venezuela and Zimbabwe.

20 Jeremy Goldkorn, 'Chinese Media: Turkey President Erdoğan Says Uyghurs "Living Happily In Xinjiang"', *Supchina*, 2 July 2019. https://supchina.com/2019/07/02/chinese-media-erdogan-says-uyghurs-living-happily-in-xinjiang/, accessed 6 August 2019.

21 Al-Jazeera, '"Stain of the Century": US Denounces China's Treatment of Uighurs', *Aljazeera.com*, 18 July 2019. https://www.aljazeera.com/news/2019/07/century-denounces-china-treatment-uighurs-190718134228281.html, accessed 5 August 2019.

22 China Daily, 'Joint Letter to Mike Pompeo Secretary of State, the United States of America From Scholars and Religious Personnel in Xinjiang', *ChinaDaily.com*, 19 July 2019. http://www.chinadaily.com.cn/a/201907/19/WS5d31e404a310d83056400015.html, accessed 5 August 2019.

23 '2019 Report on International Religious Freedom: China – Xinjiang', *State.gov*, 10 June 2020. https://www.state.gov/reports/2019-report-on-international-religious-freedom/china/xinjiang/, accessed 31 August 2020.

24 Ibid.

25 Michael Crowley, 'Trump Says He Avoided Punishing China over Uighur Camps to Protect Trade Talks', *Nytimes.com*, 9 July 2020. https://www.nytimes.com/2020/06/21/us/politics/trump-uighurs-china-trade.html/, accessed 31 August 2020.

26 'China Hui Culture Park', *China.org.cn*, 5 January 2011. http://www.china.org.cn/travel/Ningxia/2011-01-05/content_21678148.htm, accessed 6 August 2019.

27 Ibid.

28 Huizhong Wu, 'Sign of the Times: China's Capital Orders Arabic, Muslim Symbols Taken Down', *Reuters*, 31 July 2019. https://www.reuters.com/article/us-china-religion-islam/sign-of-the-times-chinas-capital-orders-arabic-muslim-symbols-taken-down-idUSKCN1UQ0JF, accessed 6 August 2019.

Bibliography

Ahmad S, Maqbul. *Arabic Classical Accounts of India and China*. Shimla: Indian Institute of Advanced Study, 1989.

Akasoy, Anna. *Islam and Tibet – Interactions along the Musk Routes*. London: Routledge, 2016.

Allès, Elisabeth. 'Muslim Religious Education in China'. *China Perspectives* (2003), 45: 21–33.

Allès, Elisabeth, Leila Chérif-Chebbi, and Constance-Hélène Halfon. 'Chinese Islam: Unity and Fragmentation'. *Religion, State and Society* (2003), 31 (1): 7–36.

Allsen, Thomas T. *Culture and Conquest in Mongol Eurasia*. Cambridge: Cambridge University Press, 2001.

Ashiwa, Yoshiko, and David L, eds. Wank. *Making Religion, Making the State: The Politics of Religion in Modern China*. Stanford, CA: Stanford University Press, 2009.

Atwill, David G. *The Chinese Sultanate: Islam, Ethnicity, and the Panthay Rebellion in Southwest China, 1856–1873*. Stanford, CA: Stanford University Press, 2006.

Atwill, David G. *Islamic Shangri-La: Inter-Asian Relations and Lhasa's Muslim Communities, 1600 to 1960*. Berkeley: University of California Press, 2018.

Beller-Hann, Ildiko. *Community Matters in Xinjiang, 1880–1949: Towards a Historical Anthropology of the Uyghur*. Leiden: Brill, 2008.

Ben-Dor Benite, Zvi. 'From "Literati" to "Ulama": The Origins of Chinese Muslim Nationalist Historiography'. *Nationalism and Ethnic Politics* (2004), 9: 4.

Ben-Dor Benite, Zvi. 'Taking 'Abduh to China: Chinese-Egyptian Intellectual Contact in the Early 20th Century'. In James A. Gelvin, and Nile Green, eds., *Global Muslims in the Age of Steam and Print*. Berkeley: University of California Press, 2014.

Benn, Charles. *China's Golden Age: Everyday Life in the Tang Dynasty*. Oxford: Oxford University Press, 2002.

Benson, Linda K. *The Ili Rebellion: Muslim Challenge to Chinese Authority in Xinjiang, 1944–49*. London: Routledge, 1989.

Benson, Linda K. *China's Last Nomads: History and Culture of China's Kazaks: History and Culture of China's Kazaks*. London: Routledge, 1997.

Bovingdon, Gardner. *The Uyghurs: Strangers in Their Own Land*. New York: Columbia University Press, 2020.

Broomhall, Marshall. *Islam in China: A Neglected Problem*. London: Morgan and Scott, 1910; London: Darf, 1987 (reprint); Piscataway, NJ: Gorgias, 2007 (reprint).

Brophy, David. *Uyghur Nation: Reform and Revolution on the Russia-China Frontier*. Cambridge, MA: Harvard University Press, 2016.
Brown, Tristan G. 'A Mountain of Saints and Sages: Muslims in the Landscape of Popular Religion in Late Imperial China'. *T'oung Pao* (2019), 105 (3–4): 437–91.
Browne, E.G. *A Literary History of Persia*, 4 vols. Reprint. London: Cambridge University Press, 1969.
Chaffee, Jon W. *The Muslim Merchants of Premodern China: The History of a Maritime Asian Trade Diaspora, 750–1400*. Cambridge: Cambridge University Press, 2018.
Ch'ang, Ch'un. *The Travels of an Alchemist*. Trans. A. Waley. London: Routledge & Kegan Paul, 1931, London: Routledge, 2014.
Chang, Hajji Yusuf. 'An Historical Overview: The Hui (Muslim) Minority in China'. *The Muslim World League Journal* (1987), 17 (3 & 4).
Chang, Hajji Yusuf. 'Chinese Muslim Mobility in Sung-Liao-Chin Period'. *Journal, Institute of Muslim Minority Affairs* (January 1984), 5 (1): 167–80.
Cheltenham, Edward Elgar, and Leor Halevi. 'Is China a House of Islam? Chinese Questions, Arabic Answers, and the Translation of Salafism from Cairo to Canton, 1930–1932'. *Welt des Islams* (2019), 59 (1): 33–69.
Chen, John. 'Islamic Modernism in China: Chinese Muslim Elites, Guomindang Nation-Building, and the Limits of the Global Umma, 1900–1960'. PhD Diss., Columbia University, 2018.
Chen, Dasheng. *Quanzhou Yisilanjiao shike*. Yinchuan: Ningxia Renmin Chubanshe, 1984.
Chiang, Han Hua Jennifer. 'Crossing Culture in the Blue-and-White with Arabic or Persian Inscriptions under Emperor Zhengde (r. 1506–21)'. Diss. University of Hong Kong, Department of Fine Arts, Hong Kong, 2007.
Cieciura, Wlodzimierz. 'Chinese Muslims in Transregional Spaces of Mainland China, Taiwan, and beyond in the Twentieth Century'. *Review of Religion and Chinese Society* (2019), 5 (2): 135–55.
Cliff, Tom. *Oil and Water: Being Han in Xinjiang*. Chicago, IL: University of Chicago Press, 2016.
Cone, Tiffany. *Cultivating Charismatic Power: Islamic Leadership Practice in China*. New York: Palgrave Macmillan, 2018.
Curtis, Emily Byrne. *Chinese-Islamic Works of Art, 1644–1912: A Study of Some Qing Dynasty Examples*. New York: Routledge, 2019.
Dautcher, Jay. *Down a Narrow Road: Identity and Masculinity in a Uyghur Community in Xinjiang China*. Cambridge, MA: Harvard University Asia Center, 2008.
Dillon, Michael. *China's Muslim Hui Community: Migration, Settlement and Sects*. London: Curzon, 1999.
Dudoignon, Stéphane A., Hisao Komatsu, and Yasushi Kosugi. *Intellectuals in the Modern Islamic World: Transmission, Transformation, Communication*. Abingdon: Taylor & Francis, 2006.
Dunn, R.E. *The Adventures of Ibn Battuta*. Berkeley: University of California Press, 1986.
Eden, Jeff. *Warrior Saints of the Silk Road Legends of the Qarakhanids*. Leiden: Brill, 2018.
Elverskog, Johan. *Buddhism and Islam on the Silk Road*. Philadelphia: University of Pennsylvania Press, 2010.

Erie, Matthew S. *China and Islam: The Prophet, the Party, and Law*. New York: Cambridge University Press, 2016.

Eroglu Sager, Z. Hale. 'Islam in Translation: Muslim Reform and Transnational Networks in Modern China, 1908–1957'. Ph.D. diss., Harvard University, 2016.

Fan, Ke. 'Maritime Muslims and Hui Identity: A South Fujian Case'. *Journal of Muslim Minority Affairs* (2001), 21 (2): 309–32.

Frankel, James D. *Rectifying God's Name: Liu Zhi's Confucian Translation of Monotheism and Islamic Law*. Honolulu: University of Hawaii Press, 2011.

Frankel, James D. 'Islamisation and Sinicisation: Inversions, Reversions and Alternate Versions of Islam in China'. In A.C.S. Peacock, ed., *Islamisation: Comparative Perspectives from History*. Edinburgh: Edinburgh University Press, 2017.

Frankel, James D. 'Sharia in China: Compromising Perceptions'. In Timothy P. Daniels, ed., *Sharia Dynamics: Islamic Law and Sociopolitical Processes*. Cham: Springer International, 2017.

Fu, Jianming, et al., eds. *Yisilanjiao jianming cidian*. Jiangsu: Ancient Books Press, 1993.

Gibbon, E. *The History of the Decline and Fall of the Roman Empire*. Ed. J.B. Bury, 7 vols. London: 1906.

Gillette, Maris. *Between Mecca and Beijing*. Stanford, CA: Stanford University Press, 2000.

Gladney, Dru C. 'Salman Rushdie in China: Religion, Ethnicity and State Definition in the People's Republic'. In Charles F. Keyes, ed., *Asian Visions of Authority: Religion and Modern States of East and Southeast Asia*. Honolulu: University of Hawaii Press, 1994.

Gladney, Dru C. *Muslim Chinese: Ethnic Nationalism in the People's Republic*. Cambridge, MA: Harvard University Press, 1996.

Gladney, Dru C. Dislocating China: Muslims, Minorities, and Other Subaltern Subjects. Chicago, IL: University of Chicago Press, 2004.

Grose, Timothy. *Negotiating Inseparability in China: The Xinjiang Class and the Dynamics of Uyghur Identity*. Hong Kong: Hong Kong University Press, 2019.

Harris, Rachel. *The Making of a Musical Canon in Chinese Central Asia*. London: Routledge, 2008.

Hillman, Ben and Gray Tuttle. *Ethnic Conflict and Protest in Tibet and Xinjiang: Unrest in China's West*. New York: Columbia University Press, 2016.

Israeli, Raphael. *Islam in China: Religion, Ethnicity, Culture, and Politics*. Lanham, MD: Lexington Books, 2002.

Jacobs, Justin. *Xinjiang and the Modern Chinese State*. Seattle: University of Washington Press, 2017.

Jaschok, Maria, and Hau Ming Vicky Chan. 'Education, Gender and Islam in China: The Place of Religious Education in Challenging and Sustaining "undisputed Traditions" among Chinese Muslim Women'. *International Journal of Educational Development* (2009), 29 (5): 487–94.

Jaschok, Maria and Jingjun Shui. *The History of Women's Mosques in Chinese Islam*. Richmond, VA: Curzon, 2000.

Jenco, Leigh K. 'Can the Chinese Nation Be One? Gu Jiegang, Chinese Muslims, and the Reworking of Culturalism'. *Modern China* (2019), 45 (6): 595–628.

Khan, Rafiq M. *Islam in China*. Delhi: National Academy, 1963.
Kim, Hodong. *Holy War in China: The Muslim Rebellion and State in Chinese Central Asia, 1864–1877*. Stanford, CA: Stanford University Press, 2004.
Klime, Ondrej. *Struggle by the Pen: The Uyghur Discourse of Nation and National Interest, C.1900–1949*. Leiden: Brill, 2015.
Lane, George A. *The Phoenix Mosque and the Persians of Medieval Hangzhou*. London: Gingko Library, 2019.
Lee, David. *Contextualization of Sufi Spirituality in Seventeenth- and Eighteenth-Century China*. Eugene, OR: Wipf and Stock, 2015.
Leslie, Donald Daniel. *Islam in Traditional China: A Short History to 1800*. Canberra: Canberra College of Advanced Education, 1986.
Leslie, Donald Daniel, and Ahmad Youssef. '"Islamic Inscriptions in Quanzhou," a Review'. *T'oung Pao* (1988), 74 (4/5): 255–72.
Levathes, Louise. *When China Ruled the Seas: The Treasure Fleet of the Dragon Throne, 1405–33*. New York: Simon and Schuster, 1994.
Lipman, Jonathan N. 'Hyphenated Chinese: Sino-Muslim Identity in Modern China'. In Gail Hershatter, Emily Honig, Jonathan N. Lipman, and Randall Stross, eds., *Remapping China: Fissures in Historical Terrain*, Stanford, CA: Stanford University Press, 1996.
Lipman, Jonathan N. *Familiar Strangers: A History of Muslims in Northwest China*. Seattle: University of Washington Press, 1997.
Lipman, Jonathan N., ed. *Islamic Thought in China: Sino-Muslim Intellectual Evolution from the 17th to the 21st Century*. Edinburgh: Edinburgh University Press, 2016.
Lipman, Jonathan N. 'A Proper Place for God: Ma Zhu's Chinese-Islamic Cosmogenesis'. In Jonathan Lipman, ed., *Islamic Thought in China: Sino-Muslim Intellectual Evolution from the 17th to the 21st Century*. Edinburgh: Edinburgh University Press, 2016.
Liu, Yingsheng. 'A Lingua Franca along the Silk Road: Persian Language in China between the 14th and the 16th Centuries'. In Ralph Kauz, ed., *Aspects of the Maritime Silk Road: From the Persian Gulf to the East China Sea*. Wiesbaden: Harrassowitz Verlag, 2010.
Ma, Zhu. *Qingzhen zhinan*. Reprint. Tianjin: Huizu Zhongguo Yisilanjiao, 1987.
Mao, Yufeng. 'Muslim Educational Reform in 20th-Century China: The Case of the Chengda Teachers Academy'. *Extrême-Orient Extrême-Occident* (2011), 33: 143–70.
Mao, Yufeng. 'A Muslim Vision for the Chinese Nation: Chinese Pilgrimage Missions to Mecca during World War II'. *The Journal of Asian Studies* (May 2011), 70 (2): 373–95.
Matsumoto, Masumi. 'Rationalization Patriotism among Muslim Chinese: The Impact of the Middle East on the Yuehua Journal'. In A. Dudoignon Stephane, Komatsu Hisao, and Kosugi Yasushi, eds., *Intellectuals in the Modern Islamic World: Transmission, Transformation, Communication*. London: Routledge, 2006.
Meng, Wei. '*The Advent of Islam in China: Guangzhou Fanfang during the Tang-Song Era*'. M.A. Thesis, Washington University, St. Louis, 2010.
Milward, James A. *Eurasian Crossroads: A History of Xinjiang*. New York: Columbia University Press, 2007.

Murata, Sackiko. *Chinese Gleams of Sufi Light: Wang Tai-yü's Great Learning of the Pure and Real and Liu Chih's Displaying the Concealment of the Real Realm*. Albany: State University of New York Press, 2000.
Murata, Sackiko. *The First Islamic Classic in Chinese: Wang Daiyu's Real Commentary on the True Teaching*. Albany: State University of New York Press, 2017.
Murata, Sackiko, William Chittick, and Wei-ming Tu. *The Sage Learning of Liu Zhi: Islamic Thought in Confucian Terms*. Cambridge, MA: Harvard University Asia Center, 2009.
Narāqī, Aḥmad. *Khazā'in bi saī va ihtimām-i Zain al-'Ābidīn ibn Muḥammad-i Khunsārī*. Tehran, 1878. Digitized by Columbia University, New York, 2009.
Niu, Song. 'China's Hajj Affairs under the Perspective of National Security'. *Istanbul Gelisim University Journal of Social Sciences* (April 2018), 5 (1): 101–13.
Park, Hyunhee. *Mapping the Chinese and Islamic Worlds: Cross-Cultural Exchange in Pre-modern Asia*. Cambridge: Cambridge University Press, 2015.
Perdue, Peter C. *China Marches West: The Qing Conquest of Central Eurasia*. Cambridge, MA: Harvard University Press, 2005.
Petersen, Kristian. *Interpreting Islam in China: Pilgrimage, Scripture, & Language in the Han Kitab*. New York: Oxford University Press, 2018.
Philip, T.V. *East of the Euphrates: Early Christianity in Asia*. Delhi: CSS & ISPCK, India, 1998.
Previté-Orton, Charles William. *The Shorter Cambridge Medieval History*. Cambridge: Cambridge University Press, 1971.
Rong, Gui, Hacer Zekiye Gonul, and Xiaoyan Zhang, eds. *Hui Muslims in China*. Leuven: Leuven University Press, 2016.
Rossabi, Morris. *Khubilai Khan: His Life and Times*. Berkeley: University of California Press, 1988.
Rossabi, Morris. 'Islam in China'. In Joseph M. Kitagawa, ed., *The Religious Traditions of Asia. Religion, History and Culture*. New York: Macmillan, 1989.
Smith Finley, Joanne. *The Art of Symbolic Resistance: Uyghur Identities and Uyghur-Han Relations in Contemporary Xinjiang*. Leiden: Brill, 2013.
Starr, S. Frederick. *Xinjiang: China's Muslim Borderland*: London: Routledge, 2004.
Steinhardt, Nancy Shatzman. *China's Early Mosques*. Edinburgh: Edinburgh University Press, 2016.
Sun, Yifu, et. al., eds. *The Silk Road on Land and Sea*. Trans. Cui Sigan, et. al. Beijing: China Pictorial Publishing, 1989.
Sykes, Percy Molesworth. *A History of Persia*. London: Macmillan, 1915.
Thum, Rian. *The Sacred Routes of Uyghur History*. Cambridge, MA: Harvard University Press, 2014.
Tontini, Roberta. *Muslim Sanzijing: Shifts and Continuities in the Definition of Islam in China (1710–2010)*. Leiden: Brill, 2016.
Tornberg, C.J. ed. Ibn al-Athir, *Al-kamil fi'l-ta'rikh*. Leiden: 1853.
von Clausewitz Carl, *On War* (*Vom Krieg*, 1832). Eds. Michael Howard and Peter Paret. Princeton, NJ: Princeton University Press, 1984.
Wang, Daiyu. *Zhengjiao zhenquan*. Ed. Yu Zhengui. Yinchuan: Ningxia People's Press, 1987.

Wang, Ke and Carissa Fletcher. *The East Turkestan Independence Movement, 1930s to 1940s*. Hong Kong: The Chinese University of Hong Kong Press, 2018.

Wang, Xia, ed. *Beijing Niujie Libaisi*. Beijing: China Today Press, 1996.

Wang, Yuting. 'Reimagining Chinese Islam and Muslims in Transregional Spaces'. *Review of Religion and Chinese Society* (2019), 5 (2): 131–4.

Winters, Clyde Ahmad. *Mao or Muhammad: Islam in the People's Republic of China*. Hong Kong: Asian Research Services, 1979.

Wu, Wenliang. *Quanzhou zongjiao shike*. Revis. by Wu Youxiong. Beijing: Kexue Chubanshe, 2005, 1957 (1st ed.).

Zhang, Guangda. 'Dashi'. In *Zhongguo da baike quanshu, Zhongguo lishi*, vol. 1. Beijing/Shanghai: Zhongguo da baike quanshu chubanshe, 1992.

Index

'Abbasid Caliphate 16–17, 42, 164 n.15. *See also* Umayyad Caliphate
  and Tang dynasty 18–20, 28
'Abd al-Khāliq 80, 132–3
Abu 'Alī (Pu) 43–5, 60–1
  descendants of 54
Abū Bakr 14, 43
Abū Ḥamīd (Pu Ximi) 41
acculturation 12, 37, 39, 59–60, 68–9
Afāq Khoja 80, 132
Afghanistan 147, 150, 154
Africa 2, 10, 147, 152
Aḥmad Fanakātī 55
  accusations against 56
Akhbar al-Sin w'al-Hind (Accounts of China and India) 25, 34, 38
Ali Khameni 118
Allah (God) 4, 23, 60, 74, 76, 80, 131
American Middle East policy 147
ancestor/ancestry 43, 64, 68–70, 124, 128, 134
An Lushan 19–20, 28, 31
An-Shi rebellion 31, 34, 40
anti-foreign bias 31–2, 36
anti-intermarriage policy 37. *See also* intermarriage
anti-Muslim sentiment 66, 68, 75, 82, 141
Arab Gulf 163 n.2
Arabian Peninsula 9, 14, 163 n.2
Arabian Sea 10, 48, 145, 153
Arab Muslims 15, 20, 25, 42. *See also* non-Arab Muslims
Arabs 10–11, 29, 40, 42, 165 n.18
Asia
  Central Asia 2, 9–11, 15–20, 29, 34, 42, 48, 62, 125, 128–9, 137, 141, 150, 152
  Southeast Asia 2, 48, 141, 152
  Southwestern Asia 14
assimilation 3, 31, 59–62, 66, 69–70, 129, 139
Ayatollah Youssef Saanei 149–50

Bai Shouyi 169 n.45
Baluchistan 153
Banu Hashim 165 n.19
barbarian(s) 12, 50, 58, 60, 141
Battle of Nahawand 14–15
Battle of Talas (Artlakh) 18–19, 28
Beijing 1, 52, 74, 88–9, 109, 115, 118, 143, 149–51, 161–2
Beijing Spring 117, 119
Beiyang Army (Beiyangjun) 89
Belt and Road Initiative (BRI) 2, 151–3, 155, 157, 160, 162
Boxer Rebellion (1899–1901) 88, 91, 93
Broomhall, Marshall 24
Buddhism/Buddhists 11, 20, 24, 32, 52–4, 57, 63, 74, 76, 108–9, 115, 136
  Wuzong on 32–3
Bukhara 15, 42, 49, 51, 137–8
Byzantine Empire 10, 13–15, 29

Caliphs/Caliphate (*khalīfa*) 14–18, 23, 25, 28, 38, 42, 164 n.9. *See also* specific Caliphates
caravan/trade route 9–11
  camel 29
  maritime 10–11, 34
  Overland (*see* overland trade routes)
Catholicism 109
Central Asia 2, 9–11, 14–20, 29, 34, 42, 48, 52, 55, 62, 66, 68, 71, 80, 125, 127–9, 131–2, 139, 141, 150, 152

Central Institute for Nationalities (Zhongyang Minzue Xueyuan) 143
chain migration 34. *See also* migration
Chang'an 11, 13, 15, 19–20, 25, 29, 36, 40
  city plan of 29–30
  foreign merchants in 30
  marketplaces of 30
  Muslim community of 34
  Uyghurs in 31
Chang Chun 51–2
Chang, Hajji Yusuf 169 n.44, 170 n.50
Chang Yuchun 59–60
Chengda Normal School (Chengda Shifan Xuexiao) 98–9
  Yuehua magazine 99
Chiang Kai-shek 92–5, 97, 102, 138
China Hui Village Culture Park (Zhonghua Huixiang Wenhuayuan) 161
China Islamic Association (Zhongguo Yisilan Xiehui) 109, 121
China-Pakistan Economic Corridor (CPEC) 145, 153–4
China's 9/11. *See* Kunming attack 2014
Chinese Civil War 94, 104, 134–5, 138
Chinese Communist Party (CCP) 94, 104–5, 109, 111, 113–14, 119, 121–2, 128, 139, 142, 146, 151, 159
Chinese Empires 17, 42, 125, 137. *See also specific dynasties*
Chinese Ethnic Culture Park (Zhonghua Minzuyuan) 143
Chinese-Islamic relations 2–3, 67
  during Tang/ʿAbbasid period 20, 28
Chinese Muslims 1, 3, 8, 22–4, 59, 62, 66, 68–9, 72–3, 76–80, 85, 89, 92–3, 99–101, 115–17, 119–21, 127, 129, 134–6, 141, 144, 154, 162. *See also* Hui Muslims
  education 93, 146
  history of 23
  oral tradition 24
  pilgrimage 121
  privileges 63
  religious tradition 4, 11, 21, 24, 27, 33, 49
  sharīʿa 122
  students 87
  warlords 98, 138
Chinese Salafis 135. *See also* Salafis

Chinggis Khan 50–3. *See also* Mongolia/Mongols
Christian/Christianity 51, 108–9, 128. *See also* Catholicism; Nestorian Christianity/Nestorianism; Protestant Christianity
  missionaries 128
citizen(s) 37, 101, 109–14, 116, 119, 125, 128, 144, 157
  Chinese 1, 113, 117, 121
  Muslim 116, 118, 120, 146
  non-Han 105, 139
  non-Muslim 165 n.18
  religious 115, 121
  Uyghur 151, 156
civilization, Chinese 1–2, 9, 12, 34, 45, 73, 125, 136
commerce 2, 10, 12, 28–9, 36–7, 41, 153. *See also* trade/traders
commodities 9–10, 12, 27, 30
Communist China 105
Communist Revolution 104, 107, 111
Confucian/Confucianism 52, 57, 63, 67, 69–70, 72, 74–8, 82, 85–6, 115, 127, 129–30, 133
  ideology 11–12, 32, 43, 72
  oneness 75
  Ru (Confucian literati) 73
Confucian-Muslim literati 131. *See also* Huiru (scholars)
Cultural Revolution 103, 111–13, 117, 119, 128
culture 105, 107, 143, 161
  Chinese 1, 3, 9–12, 54, 60–2, 64, 116, 134
  foreign 12–13, 33, 60
  material 61, 67, 69, 142–3
  shaoshu minzu 143
  Turkic 150
  Uyghur 136

Dadu (present-day Beijing) 52, 55–6, 58
Da Minglü (Great Ming Law) 61
Daoism/Daoists 33, 51–3, 74, 76, 109, 115
Dashi 15, 164 n.11
dhikr 80, 131–3
diasporic/diaspora community 3, 25, 38, 48–9, 57, 69, 98, 141, 150, 152

dietary habits/restrictions 4, 69, 141–2
al-Dīn, Amīr 55, 57
al-Dīn, Jamāl 55
al-Dīn, Kamāl 43
al-Dīn ʿUmar, Sayyid Ajal Shams 43, 54
diversity 4, 9, 123–4, 126, 142
    cultural 53, 123
    internal 3, 106, 109
Dong Fuxiang 91, 172 n.5
Dongxiang minzu 126
dual heritage 3, 65. *See also* heritage
Dungan 141, 171 n.26
Du Wenxiu 82, 87
Dzungar Khanate 137

East Turkistan 137, 140, 150
East Turkistan Islamic Movement (ETIM) 140, 148, 151
East Turkistan Republic (ETR) 138–9
economy/economics 1–2, 11, 13, 19, 28, 32–3, 55–6, 63, 68, 88, 104, 110–11, 113, 117, 119, 126, 137, 139, 147, 152–3, 157, 161
edicts 31–3, 56, 67, 78–9
Egypt 14, 97
emigration/emigrants 139, 141
Erdoğan, Recep Tayyip 150, 157
ethnic policies 96, 124, 143
ethno-religious group 69, 93, 101, 110–12, 117, 124, 128, 142, 162. *See also* minzu
Eurasia 9–10, 13, 125, 151
extremism/extremists 120, 141, 145–6, 151, 154–60

fanfang (foreign quarter) 36–43, 49
fanke (foreign guests) 33, 36–7, 39–40, 43
fanzhang (religious leader) 38–9, 41
fatwa (Islamic legal ruling) 118
    Osama bin Laden's 154
First Dungan Revolt (Donggan Bian) 81, 87, 91, 133. *See also* Second Dungan Revolt
First Fitna 164 n.15. *See also* Second Fitna; Third Fitna
Fitna 164 n.15. *See also specific Fitna*
Five Dynasties and Ten Kingdoms period 40
Four Olds (Si Jiu) 111, 128

Gaige Kaifang 117, 119. *See also* Reform and Opening Up
Gang of Four (Siren Bang) 113
Gansu 79, 81, 87, 91–2, 95, 97, 126, 132–3
Gansu Braves (Ganjun) 87–8, 91, 93
Gao Xianzhi (Go Seonji) 17–18, 165 n.24
Emperor Gaozong 7, 14, 43
Gedimu (*qadīm*) 68, 96–7, 129, 132, 134–6
Gedimu Islam (Laojiao/Old Teaching) 129–30, 133
genealogy 8, 24
genocide 150, 157
geopolitics 1–2, 13, 16, 110, 125, 129, 146, 151
Global War on Terror 120, 146
Golok Rebellion (1917–49) 95
goods, trade 29, 34
    Chinese 2, 9, 27
    foreign 11, 27, 30, 35
    luxury 10, 35
Grand Mosque in Xi'an 112, 115
Great Cultural Revolution (Da Wenhua Geming) 111. *See also* Cultural Revolution
Great Leap Forward (Da Yuejin) 110–11, 113, 117, 139
Guangzhou 11, 22–5, 27, 29, 34–7, 40, 43, 47–8, 161–2
    foreign quarters 41
    Muslim community of 38
Gulf 10, 20–1, 34, 48, 129, 163 n.2
Guomindang (GMD) 88, 90–2, 94–8, 100, 102, 104, 133–4, 139. *See also* Kuomintang (KMT)
Gwadar 145–6, 153

Ḥadīth 21–2, 134, 165 n.29
Ḥajj (pilgrimage) 63, 71, 80, 116–17, 119–20, 146–7, 161. *See also* Mecca; Medina
    unofficial 174 n.18
Ḥalāl 62
    method of slaughtering animals 52
Hall of the Western Way (Hanxue Pai) 133. *See also* Xidaotang
Han Chinese 1, 3–4, 58, 60–1, 68, 72, 81, 87, 90–1, 93, 96, 104–8, 114, 119, 122, 125–6, 130, 139, 141–2, 144, 148, 154, 162

Han dynasty (206 BCE–221 CE) 9–10, 12, 29, 125, 151, 156
'Han Kitab' 71–3, 75–8, 82, 92, 99, 101, 130–1, 133
Hanxue Pai. *See also* Xidaotang
Hanren (Northern Chinese and Jurchens) 53. *See also* Yuan dynasty
Hangzhou 29, 41, 43, 49
heritage 3, 8, 23, 31, 60, 65, 129, 142–3, 161
    dual 3, 65
    ethnic 142
Hijra 163–4 n.8
Hongwu emperor 58–60
    'Hundred-Word Elegy' (Baizizan) 60
Huaisheng Mosque 22–4, 161
Huang Chao 40
Hu Dengzhou 65–6
    Islamic learning 70–1, 131
    Jingtang Jiaoyu reforms of Islamic studies in Chinese 130
    language of instruction 71
    teacher–student network 130
Hui customary law (*Huizu xiguanfa*) 122
Huihe 53–4
Hui/Huihui 53–4, 62, 73, 79, 100
Hui minzu/Huizu 90, 107–9, 124, 139
Hui Muslims 4, 25, 79, 90, 106–7, 110, 112–17, 119–20, 122, 124–6, 128–9, 131–3, 135–6, 140–2, 146–8, 152, 161
Huiru (scholars) 73, 75, 77–8, 82, 86, 92, 102, 130, 132
Hu Songshan 97, 99–100, 134–5

Ibn ʿAbd'al-Wahhāb (Ibn Wahhāb) 25, 134
Ibn alʿArabī 77
Ibn al-Athīr 50
Ibn Batutta 166 n.37
Ibn Taymiyya 134
Ibn Yaʿqūb (Bai Yan) 43–4, 54
al-Ikhwān al- Muslimūn (*Ikhwān*/Muslim Brotherhood) 133, 172 n.6
Ili Rebellion (1944) 138
imams/*ahong* 68, 70, 85, 100
    nü ahong (female imams) 130
    Yihewani 97
Indian Ocean 2, 10, 34, 48, 147, 152
Indonesia 48

Inner Asian trade routes 29. *See also* overland trade routes; Silk Roads
insurgency, Muslim 15, 83, 97
insurgent groups 153
intermarriage 31, 37, 61, 130, 144. *See also* anti-intermarriage policy
intra-Muslim rivalry 38, 135–6
Iran 118, 149–50, 157, 163 n.2
Iraq 14, 147, 154–5
Islamic Religious Law (*Yisilan jiaofa*) 122. *See also* Sharīʿa
Islamic State of Iraq and Syria (ISIS) 154
Islamophobia 1, 144, 162
Ismāʿīlī Shiʿa/Ismailis community 127, 174 n.1
Ispah (Sepoy) Rebellion 57, 135

Jahriyya (aloud) 80–1, 132–3, 136. *See also* Naqshbandi Sufi order
    'New Teaching' (Xinjiao) 80, 133
Jahriyya Revolt in Gansu (1781) 133
Jews 29, 34, 40, 170 n.50
jihad 83, 100, 140, 154–5
al-Jīlānī, ʿAbd al-Qādir 131
Jingtang jiaoyu educational system (scripture hall education) 71–3
Judaism 11, 51
Jurchen Jin dynasty (1115–1234) 52

Kaifeng 29, 34, 41–2, 49
Kangxi emperor 78–9, 137
Kashgar 15, 17, 125, 137–8, 150
Khafiyya (silent) 80–1, 91, 132–4, 136
    'Old Teaching' (*Laojiao*) 80, 133
khaganates 13, 19, 31–2, 136
khanates 51–2, 54
Khanbaliq 52. *See also* Beijing; Dadu
Khānfū (Guangzhou) 11, 25, 163 n.4. *See also* Guangzhou
Khubilai Khan 48, 52, 54. *See also* Mongolia/Mongols; Yuan dynasty
    Imperial Institute of Muslim Astronomy 55
    privilege for Muslims 55–6
    punishment of Muslim community 56
    ritual animal slaughter 52, 56
    ruling policies 52–3
al-Khulafāʾ al-Mahdīʾun al-Rāshidūn (Rightly Guided Caliphs) 164 n.9, 164 nn.14–15

Kubrawiyya 131–2
Kunming attack 2014 82, 122, 155
Kuomintang (KMT) 172 n.2. See also Guomindang (GMD)
Kyrgyz 126, 156
  tribes 32

language(s) 4, 39, 70–1, 75, 105–6, 108, 114, 125–6
  Arabic and Persian 70–1, 130
  Chinese 65, 69
  dialects 126–7
  linguistics 106, 126–7
  Mandarin 127, 139, 142, 154–5
  Tsat 127
Lanzhou 97, 132–3
Leninism 128
Liao dynasty (916–1125) 41
Lingshan cemetery 49, 57
Lipman, Jonathan N., *Familiar Strangers: A History of Muslims in Northwest China* 170 n.52
Li Shimin 13
Liu Sanjie 24
  Huihui yuanlai (The Origin of the Muslims) 23
Liu Zhi 22–3, 73, 76–7, 86, 133
  kaozheng (evidentiary studies) movement 77
  works/trilogy of 21, 77
Li Yuan (Emperor Gaozu) 13, 22
Luoyang 19, 40

Ma Anliang 91–3, 134
Ma Bufang 95–8, 100, 134
Ma Buqing 95–6
'Ma Clique' (Majia Junfa) 91, 98, 100, 133
Ma Dexin 82, 87, 101
Ma Fuxiang 85, 87–8, 92–4, 99–101
Ma Haiyan 91, 93
Ma He. See Zheng He
Ma Hongbin 94–5
Ma Hongkui 93–5, 99–100
Ma Laichi 80, 132–3. See also Khafiyya (silent); Naqshbandi Sufi order
  dhikr (silent) 80
Ma Mingxin 80, 132. See also Jahriyya (aloud); Naqshbandi Sufi order

Ma Qi 93, 95, 134
Ma Qianling 87, 91, 172 n.5
Ma Qixi 92, 133
Manchus/Manchurians 72, 74, 81, 90, 125, 137–8
Manichaeism/Manichaean 11, 31, 136, 163 n.6
al-Manṣūr 19
Maoism/Maoist 111, 128
Mao Zedong 104–5, 107, 110–11, 113
  Four Olds (Si Jiu) 111
Maritime Silk Road 10–11, 47, 151. See also Silk Roads
maritime trade 2, 10–11, 20, 34–5, 40–1, 44. See also trade/traders
marketplaces 10, 27, 30, 34
Marx, Karl/Marxist 104, 107, 128, 142
Masjid al-Ashab (Companion's Mosque(Shengyou Qingzhensi)) 41, 49
Ma Songting 98–9, 100
Ma Tai Baba 132
material culture 61, 67, 142–3
Ma Wanfu 92–3, 134
Ma Zhu 73, 75, 86
  against Qadiriyya Sufi order 76, 131
  Qingzhen zhinan (Guide to Islam) 75
Mecca 4, 8, 10, 13, 22, 63, 100, 116, 120–1, 146–7, 161. See also Ḥajj (pilgrimage)
Medina 8, 10, 13, 22, 163 n.7
  Saʻd's grave in 23–4
menhuan 80, 96, 132–6. See also Sufi/Sufism
merchants 11, 34. See also trade/traders
  Arab and Persian 11, 20, 34
  foreign 28–30, 34–6, 41, 49
  from Gulf 20, 34
  Muslim 20, 27, 29, 33, 41, 55
  Silk Road 34
Middle East 10, 14, 21, 29, 44, 66, 100–1, 115, 129, 141, 147, 154–5
migration 42, 48, 137, 145, 163 n.8. See also chain migration
military governors (*jiedushi*) 40
Emperor Mingdi 24
Ming dynasty (1368–1644) 23, 58–9, 66, 68, 71, 115, 125, 129–31, 137, 152

cultural transformation policies 60–1
Da Minglü (Great Ming Law) 61
discrimination against Muslims 66
Manchu invasion 72
privileges for Muslims 63
sub-culture 62
minorities, Muslim 1–4, 8, 16, 22, 68, 111, 114, 117, 121–2, 124, 127–8, 139, 141–3, 174 n.1. See also shaoshu minzu; unrecognized Muslim minorities
minzu 106–10, 112, 114, 117, 120, 122–7, 139, 142–5, 162, 172 n.3. See also shaoshu minzu
   Minzu Project. (see Zhonghua Minzu (Chinese Nation))
   Minzu System 124, 139, 172 n.3
   Muslim minzu 122, 124–7, 146
Minzu University of China, MUC (Zhongyang Minzue Daxue) 143
miscegenation 144
Mongolia/Mongols 19, 31, 41, 44–5, 47–50, 53–4, 57–9, 61, 64, 72, 90, 96, 125–6, 136, 138. See also Chinggis Khan; Khubilai Khan
   brutality and violence 50–1, 169 n.33
   cataclysm 58
   Muslim Bao'an 126
   and Muslims 54–5, 58–9, 68
   Pax Mongolica 50
   religious tolerance (policy) 51, 53
   slaughtering procedure 168 n.11
   Yasa law code 52–3
mosque/mosques 1, 22–4, 33, 41, 49, 60, 62–3, 65–6, 68–70, 79–80, 85, 97, 99, 111–12, 115–17, 119, 121, 129–30, 135, 146, 151, 159, 161
   Gedimu mosques 129
   mosque school 65, 70–1, 130
   mosque-based communities 68. (see also Gedimu)
   women's mosque (nüsi) 130
Muʿāwiyah ibn Abī Sufyān 164 nn.14–15
Muhuyindeni, Shaykh (Muḥyi al-Dīn) 131–2
Museum of Ethnic Cultures (Minzu Bowuguan) 143

Muslim blue (Huihuiqing) 68
myth 11, 25
   religious 24
   vs. history 8

Nanren (Southern Chinese) 53. See also Yuan dynasty
Naqshband Bukhārī, Bahāʾ al-Dīn 132
Naqshbandi Sufi order 80, 132–3. See also Jahriyya (aloud); Khafiyya (silent)
nationality/nationalities 3, 30, 90, 105–6, 108–9, 112, 114, 143
Neo-Confucian 76–7
Nestorian Christianity/Nestorianism 11, 29, 31, 33, 53. See also Christian/Christianity
'New Teaching' (Xinjiao). See Jahriyya (aloud)
Ninghai Army (Ninghaijun) 93
Ningxia 91, 93
nisba 61
Niujie (Ox Street) mosque (Niujie Qingzhensi), Beijing 79, 115, 117
non-Arab Muslims 16–17, 149, 165 n.18. See also Arab Muslims
non-Chinese 3, 30–1, 57, 61, 68, 151
non-Han Chinese 90, 104–6, 139–41
non-Hui Muslims 124–5
non-Muslim 1, 3, 8, 16, 57, 62, 64, 68–9, 75, 78, 82–3, 99, 101, 135, 146, 165 n.18
Northern Expedition (1926–8) 92–4
nüsi. See mosque/mosques; women's mosques

'Old Teaching' (Laojiao). See Gedimu; Khafiyya (silent)
'One Belt, One Road' (Yidai Yilu). See Belt and Road Initiative (BRI)
Organization of Islamic Cooperation (OIC) 149
origin of Muslims in China 8–9, 15, 23–5
overland trade routes 2, 10–11, 13, 17, 22, 29, 34, 41. See also Silk Roads

pan-Islamic revivalism 85, 117, 134–5
Panthay 172 n.27

Panthay Rebellion 81–2, 87
pan-Turanianism 138
Pax Mongolica 50
People's Liberation Army (PLA)/Jiefangjun 94, 97, 112, 139, 148
People's Republic of China (PRC) 1, 37, 95, 97–8, 104–9, 110–11, 113, 116–21, 119–22, 124–5, 135, 139–40, 142–4, 146–7, 149–53, 155–60, 162
   Constitution of 1954 108, 110
   Constitution of 1975 112
   Constitution of 1982 113–15, 121
   'The Fight Against Terrorism and Extremism and Human Rights Protection in Xinjiang' 156
Peroz III 14–15
persecution 22, 32, 47, 59, 62, 64, 128, 158
Persian Gulf 163 n.2
Persia/Persian 10–11, 14–15, 20, 29–31, 34, 40, 42, 48
pilgrimage. *See* Ḥajj (pilgrimage); Mecca; Medina
population of Muslims in China 2–3, 8, 57, 68, 146
pork taboo 69, 141–2
port cities 11, 22, 34, 36, 41, 44, 48. *See also specific cities*
Preamble to the Constitution 108–9, 112, 114
Preferential Policy (Youhui Zhengce) 114, 139
Prince Yan. *See* Yongle emperor
pro-democracy gatherings 117–18
Prophet Muhammad 4, 8, 13–14, 17, 21–5, 28, 42, 49, 77, 120, 136, 164 n.9
Prophet's Mosque (al-Masjid al-Nabawī), Medina 115
proselytization 80, 128, 132
Protestant Christianity 109. *See also* Catholicism/Christianity; Nestorian Christianity/Nestorianism
protest/protestors 36, 112, 117–20, 148
   in Beijing 117–18, 151
   on Mutallip Hajim death 148
   against Shaoguan incident 149
   Tian'anmen crackdown 117–19

   of Turkish people 150
   Ürümqi riot 149, 155
Pu Shougeng 44–5, 48, 54, 58

Qadiriyya ṭarīqa (Sufi order) 131
Qarluq 16–18
Qianlong emperor 77, 79, 137
Qing dynasty (1644–1911) 12, 23, 72–3, 77–8, 81–2, 86, 88, 104, 125, 129, 132, 136–8
Qinghai 91, 93, 95–7, 126
Qingjing Mosque. *See* Masjid al-Ashab
qingzhen (pure and true) 142
Qingzhenjiao (Pure and True Religion) 74
Quanzhou 29, 41, 44–5, 47–9, 56–7, 62–3
Qur'ān 4, 38, 101, 116, 130, 134
Qutayba ibn Muslim 15–16

realpolitik 15
Red Guards (Hong Weibing) 111
Red Turbans (Hongjin) 58–9
Reform and Opening Up (Gaige Kaifang) policies 113, 117, 128, 146
religious sites of China 24, 31, 33, 47, 131, 161–2. *See also* tourism/tourists, religious
religious tolerance 31, 50–1, 53, 55, 89
Republic of China (ROC) 88–9, 91, 97–8, 100–2, 104, 116, 125, 138, 140
Russia 52, 120

Saʿd ibn Abī Waqqāṣ 22–5, 49, 161
Salafis 116, 134–6. *See also* Chinese Salafis
Samarkand 15, 49, 51, 137–8
Sanyi (Three Unities), Wang Daiyu
   Shuyi (Unity of Multiplicity) 74–5
   Tiyi (Embodied Unity) 74–5
   Zhenyi (Unity of the Truth) 74–5
Sasanian Empire (224–651) 10, 13–15, 17, 22
Saudi Arabia 102, 116, 119, 149, 157, 161
Sayyid Safar (Su Feier) 42–3, 45
Second Dungan Revolt 81, 87, 93, 133–4. *See also* First Dungan Revolt (Donggan Bian)
Second Fitna 15–16, 164 n.15. *See also* First Fitna; Third Fitna

Second Sino-Japanese War (1937–45) 94–5, 101
secularism 128
segregation policy 31, 39, 130
Semu/Semuren (miscellaneous categories of foreigners) 53, 61, 137, 168 n.15. See also Yuan dynasty
separatism 109, 141, 156
September 11 attacks 120
Shaanxi province 32, 43, 70, 88
Shadian Incident 113, 119, 155
shaoshu minzu 106, 124, 143. See also minzu
Sharīʿa (Sacred Law of Islam) 38–9
Emperor Shenzong 42–3
Shiʿa community 16–17, 57–8, 135
  Ismāʿīlī Shiʿa/Ismailis 127, 174 n.1
Shiboshi (Overseas Trade Commissioner) of Guangzhou 37, 44
Siku quanshu (Compendium of the Four Treasuries) 77
Silk Roads 2, 9–11, 15, 20, 29, 128, 136, 162. See also overland trade routes
simultaneity 3, 73, 82, 86, 92, 101, 130
sinicization 31, 60–1, 125, 129, 142, 162
Sinophone Muslims/Sino-Muslims 4, 62, 83, 129–30. See also Hui Muslims
al-Sīrāfī, Abū Zayd, Silsilat al-Tawarikh (The Chain of Histories) 25, 40
social hierarchy 35, 42, 44, 48, 53
socialist realism 123
Song dynasty (960–1279) 40–2, 44–5, 47–9, 52, 54, 56
South China Sea 10, 35–6, 48
Strike Hard campaign (Yanli Daji) 155
Sufi/Sufism 76–7, 79–80, 97, 99, 131, 133–6
  Naqshbandi (see Naqshbandi Sufi order)
  Kubrawiyya 131–2
  Qadiriyya ṭarīqa 131
Sui dynasty (589–618) 11, 13, 21–2, 136
Sunni Islam 57–8, 96, 127, 129, 135
Sun Yat-sen 89–90, 92–3, 104
supremacy 12, 32, 58, 76, 154
Emperor Suzong 19–20
Syr Darya river, Central Asia 15, 17, 165 n.23
Syria 10, 155

Taiping Heavenly Kingdom Movement (Taiping Tianguo Yundong) 81
Emperor Taizong 13, 23
takfīr 136
Talas river, Kyrgyzstan 165 n.25
Taliban 154
Tang dynasty (618–907) 2, 11, 13–22, 25, 31, 39, 42, 125, 129, 151, 161
  ʿAbbasid Caliphate and 18–20, 28
  decline of 40
  golden age of 13
  Muslim settlers in 37
  Tang court 13–14, 17, 20, 28, 32–3, 38
  trade relations with other countries 29
  Uyghurs and 31–2
Taoism. See Daoism/Daoists
Tarim Basin of Xinjiang 126, 136–7
tawḥīd/waḥdat 74
terrorism/terrorist attacks 120, 122, 144, 147–8, 155. See also specific attacks
  campaign against 155–6
Third Fitna 16, 164 n.15. See also First Fitna; Second Fitna
Tibet/Tibetans 90, 93, 95–6, 126, 147
  Central Tibet (Bod) 165 n.21
  Tibetan Empire 17, 165 n.22
  Tibetan minzu 126
Timurid Empire (1370–1507) 137
tourism/tourists, religious 24, 161–2. See also religious sites of China
trade/traders 11, 28, 37, 50. See also commerce; merchants
  Arab and Persian traders 11, 20, 34
  foreign/international 28, 33, 35, 40, 47, 63, 67
  goods (see goods, trade)
  horse 10, 29
  illegal salt 40
  maritime 2, 10–11, 20, 29, 34–5, 40–1, 44
  overland trade routes 2, 10–11, 13, 17, 22, 29, 34, 41
  seafaring 10, 48
  tax 35–6
  welcoming reception 35–6
Transoxiana 15–17

tribe(s) 13–14, 18, 25, 31–2, 54, 82, 95, 125, 165 n.18
tributary system of foreign relations 12–14
Trump, Donald 158, 160
Turkey/Turks 29–30, 52–3, 68, 136–7, 149–50, 156–7, 165 n.22
Turkistan Islamic Party (TIP) 140, 148, 151

Umayyad Caliphate 15–17, 164 n.15, 165 n.18. *See also* ʿAbbasid Caliphate
Umma 38–9
Union of Soviet Socialist Republics (USSR) 105–6, 118, 138–9
United Nations Human Rights Council (UNHRC) 157–8
United States of America 147, 151, 154, 158, 160
unrecognized Muslim minorities 127. *See also* minorities, Muslim
Ürümqi 136, 139, 149–50, 155
ʿUthmān 14, 17, 23–4
Utsul people 127
Uyghur Human Rights Policy Act 160
Uyghur Khaganate 13, 19, 31, 53, 136, 163 n.6, 165 n.21
Uyghurs 1, 4, 12, 31, 79, 90, 96, 120, 122, 124–6, 136–41, 146–50, 154–5, 158–9
  cultural politics 140
  Islamization of 53, 136
  protest and violence 148
  violence between Han Chinese and 148–9
  in Xinjiang 155–6

Wahabbis/Wahabbism 116, 134–5
Wang Daiyu 73–4, 77, 86, 171 n.10
  ʿilm al-tawḥīd (Science of Oneness) 75
  Sanyi (Three Unities) (*see Sanyi* (Three Unities), Wang Daiyu)
  works of 74
Wang Jingzhai 85, 100–1
  'Aiguo, aijiao' (Love country, love religion) slogan 101, 121
  ḥubb al-watan min al-īmān (Love of homeland is part of faith) 100

Wan Kousi 23–4. *See also* Saʿd ibn Abī Waqqāṣ
Warlord Era (Junfa Shidai) 91
War of Resistance 95, 100
women's mosques (*nüsi*) 130
Emperor Wuzong
  on Buddhism 32–3
  religious policy of 33

xenophobia 33, 35
Xidaotang 92, 133, 136. *See also* Hall of the Western Way (Hanxue Pai)
Xi Jinping 122, 151
Xilai zongpu (Genealogy of the Arrival from the West) 24
Xing fengsu (Sexual Customs) 117
  China's *Satanic Verses* 118
Xinhai Revolution of 1911 88, 104
Xinjiang 1, 42, 79, 96, 120, 122, 125–6, 136–40, 146–7, 149–50, 152, 154, 158, 160–1
  Han Chinese to 139
  Uyghurs in 155–6
  Xinjiang Problem 140, 144, 147, 150, 162
  Xinjiang Uyghur Autonomous Region 139
Emperor Xuanzong 19, 25, 35

Yangzhou 29
Yasa law code 52–3
Yathrib. *See* Medina
Yazdegerd III 14
Yemen 10, 14
Yihewani movement 97, 99, 116, 133–6, 172 n.6
Yinchuan 161
Yiwu (Zhejiang province) 161
Yongle emperor 62–3
Yuan dynasty (1279–1368) 43, 45, 47–8, 52–5, 57, 72–3, 125, 129, 135
  four-tiered social hierarchy 53
Yuan Shikai 89–93
Yunnan 54, 62, 76, 81–2, 101, 112, 131, 152, 155

Zaytūn (City of Olives). *See* Quanzhou
Zhangmen (Zhang menhuan) 132
Zhang Qian 9, 12

Zhengde Emperor 67–8
  exotica Islamica 67
Zheng He 62–3, 170 n.61, 170 n.63
  death and burial 63
Zhenhui Laoren. *See* Wang Daiyu
Zhonghua Minzu (Chinese Nation) 90, 99, 106–8

Zhuang nationality 106
Zhu Yuanzhang. *See* Hongwu emperor
Zoroastrianism/Zoroastrians 11, 29, 31, 33, 40
Zuo Zongtang 81, 91

www.ingramcontent.com/pod-product-compliance
Ingram Content Group UK Ltd.
Pitfield, Milton Keynes, MK11 3LW, UK
UKHW021840220426
470268UK00007B/279